FOR DUMMIES
BESTSELLING BOOK SERIES

Paint Shop Pro™ 8 For Dummies®

Cheat Sheet

W9-DDO-529

WITHDRAWN

Main Tools of the Tool Palette

Button	Tool Name	What to Do with It
	Pan (Arrow)	Select image windows or drag images within windows.
	Zoom	Left-click to zoom in; right-click to zoom out.
	Deform	Click selected areas to change dimensions or rotation.
	Straighten	Drag middle and/or ends to align with vertical or horizontal edge; double-click.
	Crop	Drag a rectangle and then double-click to crop an image.
	Mover	Drag selections or vector objects.
	Selection	Drag a rectangle or other shape to select an area.
	Freehand	Select an area by tracing around it.
	Magic Wand	Select an area of similarly colored pixels.
	Dropper	Click to pick up color from the image.
	Color Replacer	Paint foreground color as you drag over background color.
	Paint Brush	Drag to paint.
	Airbrush	Applies color while you mouse down.
	Clone	Brush a copy. Right-click the source area, move, left-drag.
	Scratch Remover	Drag to remove photo scratches.
	Retouch Tools	Dodge/burn, smudge/push, sharpen/blur, emboss.
	Lighten/Darken	Left-drag to lighten; right-drag to darken.
	Saturation Up/Down	Left-drag to intensify colors; right-drag to dullen.
	Eraser	Erases (or paints background color on main layer).
	Background Eraser	Erases up to edge of color change.
	Picture Tube	Pastes multiple images as you drag.
	Flood Fill	Fills an area with solid color, patterns, or gradients.
	Text	Creates text, outlined and/or filled.
	Draw	Draw lines or shapes freehand, outlined, and/or filled.
	Preset Shapes	Draw predetermined shapes, outlined and/or filled.
	Vector Object Selection	Selects vector objects (text, shapes).

Helpful Shortcut Keys

Action	Shortcut
Open browser	Ctrl+B
Undo	Ctrl+Z
Redo	Ctrl+Alt+Z
Toggle Tool Options palette	F4
Toggle Layers palette	F8

Action	Shortcut
Select All	Ctrl+A
Remove selection	Ctrl+D
Paste as new image	Ctrl+V
Paste as selection	Ctrl+E
Paste as new layer	Ctrl+L
Paste vector object	Ctrl+G
Make image full color	Ctrl+Shift+0

For Dummies: Bestselling Book Series for Beginners

Paint Shop Pro™ 8 For Dummies®

Cheat Sheet

Working with Layers on the Layers Palette

To work with layers, open the Layers palette, as shown here. Note that any changes you make to the image apply to only the selected layer. To open the Layers palette:

Choose This Command	Or Press This Key
View⇨Palettes⇨Layers	F8

To Do This	Do This
Create layer	Click New Layer button, top left
Select a layer	Click its name
See content thumbnail	Pause cursor over name
Delete layer	Drag to trash can icon
Hide or view layer	Click eye icon

Wiley, the Wiley Publishing logo, For Dummies, the Dummies Man logo, the For Dummies Bestselling Book Series logo and all related trade dress are trademarks or registered trademarks of Wiley Publishing, Inc. All other trademarks are property of their respective owners.

For Dummies: Bestselling Book Series for Beginners

Paint Shop
Pro® 8
FOR
DUMMIES®

Paint Shop Pro® 8

FOR DUMMIES®

by David Kay and
William "The Ferrett" Steinmetz

WILEY

Wiley Publishing, Inc.

Paint Shop Pro® 8 For Dummies®

Published by
Wiley Publishing, Inc.
909 Third Avenue
New York, NY 10022
www.wiley.com

Copyright © 2003 by Wiley Publishing, Inc., Indianapolis, Indiana

Published by Wiley Publishing, Inc., Indianapolis, Indiana

Published simultaneously in Canada

For general information on our other products and services or to obtain technical support, please contact our Customer Care Department within the U.S. at 800-762-2974, outside the U.S. at 317-572-3993, or fax 317-572-4002.

Wiley also publishes its books in a variety of electronic formats. Some content that appears in print may not be available in electronic books.

Library of Congress Control Number: 2003101874

ISBN: 0-7645-2440-2

Manufactured in the United States of America

10 9 8 7 6 5 4 3 2

1O/SS/QV/QT/IN

 WILEY is a trademark of Wiley Publishing, Inc.

About the Authors

David Kay is a writer, engineer, and aspiring naturalist and artist, combining professions with the same effectiveness as his favorite business establishment, Acton Muffler, Brake, and Ice Cream (now defunct). Dave has written more than a dozen computer books, by himself or with friends. His titles include various editions of *Microsoft Works For Windows For Dummies, WordPerfect For Windows For Dummies, Graphics File Formats,* and *The Internet: Complete Reference.*

In his other life, as the Poo-bah of Brightleaf Communications, Dave writes and teaches on a variety of subjects. He and his wife, Katy, and golden retriever, Alex, live in the wilds of Massachusetts. In his spare time, Dave studies animal and human tracking and munches edible wild plants. He also has been known to make strange blobs from molten glass, sing Gilbert and Sullivan choruses in public, and hike in whatever mountains he can get to. He longs to return to New Zealand and track kiwis and hedgehogs in Wanaka. He finds writing about himself in the third person like this quite peculiar and will stop now.

William "The Ferrett" Steinmetz is a freelance webmaster and editor who helms StarCityGames.com, one of the premiere *Magic: The Gathering* collectible card game strategy sites. He has also written most of *Internet: The Complete Reference* in addition to writing computer book reviews for Amazon.com and TechSoc.com. The Ferrett lives in Cleveland and is geeky.

Dedication

To my grandparents Henry and Margie, and to Boots, who believed in me when I didn't. You should all be so lucky. — T.F.

Publisher's Acknowledgments

We're proud of this book; please send us your comments through our online registration form located at www.dummies.com/register/.

Some of the people who helped bring this book to market include the following:

Acquisitions, Editorial, and Media Development

Project Editor: Rebecca Whitney

Acquisitions Editor: Terri Varveris

Technical Editor: Lee Musick

Editorial Manager: Carol Sheehan

Media Development Manager: Laura VanWinkle

Media Development Supervisor: Richard Graves

Editorial Assistant: Amanda M. Foxworth

Cartoons: Rich Tennant www.the5thwave.com

Production

Project Coordinator: Nancee Reeves

Layout and Graphics: Seth Conley, Carrie Foster, Tiffany Muth

Proofreaders: Laura Albert, David Faust, Andy Hollandbeck, Angel Perez, Carl Pierce, Kathy Simpson, TECHBOOKS Production Services

Indexer: TECHBOOKS Production Services

Publishing and Editorial for Technology Dummies

    Richard Swadley, Vice President and Executive Group Publisher

    Andy Cummings, Vice President and Publisher

    Mary C. Corder, Editorial Director

Publishing for Consumer Dummies

    Diane Graves Steele, Vice President and Publisher

    Joyce Pepple, Acquisitions Director

Composition Services

    Gerry Fahey, Vice President of Production Services

    Debbie Stailey, Director of Composition Services

Contents at a Glance

Table of Contents

Introduction

Congratulations! Brilliant person that you are, you use Paint Shop Pro! Thousands of other brilliant people also use Paint Shop Pro, and for one intelligent reason: It does darned near anything you could want it to do, from fixing photographs to animating Web graphics, and — unlike certain more famous programs — it doesn't set you back a week's salary.

Guided by that same intelligence, you're probably asking yourself, "Is a book available that gives me what I want, quickly, without dragging me through a tutorial? One with an attractive yellow-and-black cover so that it doesn't get lost in the clutter on my desk? Preferably cheap?"

Welcome to *Paint Shop Pro 8 For Dummies,* the attractive, inexpensive, yellow-and-black book that lets you get great graphics out of Paint Shop Pro without making you feel like you're going back to school in an attractive, yellow-and-black school bus.

What Can You Do with This Book?

Books are useful, elevating things. Many people use them to elevate their PC monitors, for example. With that fate in mind, *this* book has been created to serve an even higher purpose: to enable you to do the kind of graphics stuff you really want to do. Here's a smattering of what you can do with the help of this book:

- Download photos from a digital camera.
- Fix up fuzzy, poorly exposed, or icky-colored photos.
- Print album pages or other collections of photos.
- Paint, draw, or letter-in all kinds of colors, patterns, and textures.
- Draw using lines and shapes that you can go back and change later.
- Apply cool special effects to photos and drawings.
- Change colors of objects.
- Combine photos with other images.
- Alter the content of photos and other images.
- Remove unwanted relatives from family photos.

✔ Add wanted relatives to Wanted posters.

✔ Retouch unsightly relatives on Wanted posters.

✔ Create transparent and other Web page graphics.

Is This the Book for You?

Is this the Paint Shop Pro book for you? It depends. If, like us, you tend to leave chocolate fingerprints from your bookstore *biscotti* on the books you're browsing, it's definitely yours now.

In addition, this book is for you if

✔ You find most computer books boring or useless

✔ You need solutions rather than lessons

✔ You find parts of Paint Shop Pro 8 confusing

✔ You haven't ever done much with graphics programs

✔ You have used other Windows programs

✔ You need Paint Shop Pro for business or home use

✔ You really like bulleted lists

How Is This Book Organized?

Computer software "manuals" document features because that's the easiest way to write one: "The File menu presents the following choices. . . ." If features on the File menu exactly matched what you had in mind, that would be great — but how are you to know to use the Clone Brush tool when what you're really looking for is the "Fix Uncle Dave's hair transplant scars" tool?

Some computer books are organized into lessons, teaching you how features work. They give you examples of basic tasks and then more complicated ones. Along the way — before too long, you hope — you find an example resembling what you had in mind.

This book is organized by different kinds of tasks, like working with photos or painting pictures or adding text. Wherever possible, the book tells you exactly what to do in numbered steps. Where that's not possible, it explains how things work in nontechnical language.

You don't have to read the book in any order. Just skip to the section or chapter you need. Go right to the index, if you want — or the Rich Tennant cartoons! In detail, this book is organized as described in this section.

Part I: Getting the Picture

This part puts you in the picture and puts your picture in Paint Shop Pro. Chapter 1 puts you in the picture, explaining how to get control over all the various doo-dahs floating around the Paint Shop Pro screen. The chapter also gives quick synopses of what the various tools do, which is particularly useful for anyone who needs just a few hints to get going — and it tells you how to open an image file, create a new image, or save an image as various file types. Chapter 2 tells you how to get existing images into Paint Shop Pro, whether it's from a scanner, a digital camera, or a PC screen. This chapter also gives you hints on how to do something your relatives will love: Squeeze files so that they download quickly.

Part II: Painting the Picture

Part II is for anyone who plans to paint, draw, or otherwise doodle in Paint Shop Pro. Chapter 3 addresses the new Paint Shop Pro Materials box, showing you how to not only get the color you want but also paint in the wild gradients, patterns, and textures that Paint Shop Pro 8 offers. Chapter 4 tells you how to use the basic Paint Shop Pro painting tools and also how to control the way the Paint Shop Pro paint tools work: brush size, spray patterns, brush shapes, paint density, and more. Chapter 5 shows you how to do something you have seen only in cartoons: Make images flow right off a paint brush. We explain two features that are useful for retouching: the Paint Shop Pro Picture Tubes tool (a kind of spreadable clip art) and the Clone Brush tool.

Part III: Improving Appearances

When you have an image that needs some sprucing up, Part III is the place to turn. Chapter 6 shows you how to use the Paint Shop Pro hand tools to brush away wrinkles from portraits, fix scratches, and remove red eye. Chapter 7 gives you nearly instant ways to correct overall photo problems, such as bad exposure, poor color, or blurry, speckly, and dim grayish images. In addition, we discuss the fabulous One-Step Photo Fix! Chapter 8 takes you to fun and exotic lands of artistic effects, where you can twist, make three-dimensional buttons, do cutouts, or make an image look like it was done in neon or burnished copper! Chapter 9 helps you cope with the inescapable reality that, yes, you really are using a computer, and if you want the most from Paint

Shop Pro, you need to understand just a little about how it deals with color. Chapter 10 shows you how to fine-tune the quality of an image for contrast, brightness, and color and tackle the more subtle problems of certain photos.

Part IV: Changing and Adding Content

Part IV opens the door to a brave (and fun) new world: changing the content of an image. Chapter 11 shows you how to change the size, proportion, orientation, and rotation of an image. (Straightening an image, however, is covered in Chapter 2, with the scanning information.) This chapter also shows you how to crop an image to get the composition you want or flip the image into a mirror image. Chapter 12 gives you one of the key tricks for changing content: selecting parts of an image. Because Paint Shop Pro has no idea where cousin Suzie begins and her husband ends, it's up to you to tell Paint Shop Pro "Suzie's the one in white" or to outline her by hand, when you want to abstract her into a solo portrait. Chapter 13 shows you ways to move, copy, or reshape the parts you select. Need a flock of jumping sheep when you have only a few? Clone your sheep like Dolly! Chapter 14 shows you how to divide images into layers or use layers to combine images. Layers are powerful tools that make later editing much easier and produce stunning image overlays. Chapter 15 lets you add layers of easily edited text and shapes to an image, using the Paint Shop Pro 8 expanded vector graphics tools.

Part V: Taking It to the Street

All this fooling around in Paint Shop Pro is great, but in the end you probably want an image to appear somewhere else: on a piece of paper, on the Web, or as part of an animation. Chapter 16 shows you how to best fit an image on paper. It also tells you how to print multi-image pages for photo albums, collages, or portfolios. Chapter 17 tells you how to get exactly the image file you want for the Web and gives you tips for getting the fastest-downloading images with the least sacrifice in quality. Lastly, when you have found how to do what you want in Paint Shop Pro, Chapter 18 shows you two new tricks that Paint Shop Pro 8 has put in, scripting and presets, that save you oodles of time in the long run.

Part VI: The Part of Tens

Problems often come in threes, so this book tackles them by the tens, just to be sure. Part VI has fixes for the ten most-wanted issues that people run into when they're trying to use Paint Shop Pro. Chapter 19 untangles the ten most common confusions and perplexing problems of Paint Shop Pro, and Chapter 20 gives you ten quick fixes for photography problems.

Icons Used in This Book

This icon points out important issues or tidbits of information you want to be sure to remember. Just remember to look for the Remember icon.

An all-purpose workhorse, this icon offers advice or shortcuts that can make your life a whole lot easier.

Skip over this one if you want. This icon marks geekfest stuff you don't really need to know, but might find interesting.

Tread lightly when you see this icon because something unpleasant could happen if you proceed without following this cautionary note.

Shortcuts and Conventions in this Book

This book doesn't have many conventions. It does, however, employ one basic shortcut that is a convention in all *For Dummies* books:

Rather than say "Click the word *File* on the menu bar and then click the word *Open* on the menu that drops down," this book says "Choose File➪Open." This method saves time, saves trees, and keeps you from falling asleep. (The underlined letters you see in numbered steps are the same ones you find in all Windows programs. They indicate that if the mouse breaks, you can press the Alt key on the keyboard along with the underlined letter's key to get the same result as though you had clicked the word with the mouse.)

(Oh, yes, please buy the book now. Thanks.)

If you feel inclined, drop us some e-mail. Dave's at psp8@brightleaf.com, and William's at theferrett@theferrett.com. We're just two guys with no special connections to Jasc (the company that makes Paint Shop Pro) and no helpers, so we may not be able to answer your questions — but we'll try.

Part I
Getting the Picture

In this part . . .

Need to get *in the picture* quickly? Do you need to get a picture quickly into or out of Paint Shop Pro? Start here.

The Paint Shop Pro screen has more controls, tools, and objects floating around in it than the space shuttle has. In Chapter 1, we (briefly) summarize what all this stuff does, help you bring the various floating windows under your control, and show you how to use fundamental features, like the command history and undo/redo features. If you already have some experience with graphics programs, read Chapter 1 for a fast way to discover the unique Paint Shop Pro quirks and features.

Throughout the rest of Part I, we'll show you how to get pictures into and out of Paint Shop Pro. Do you already have an image file on your PC? We give you in Chapter 1 different ways to open or create image files. For instance, Paint Shop Pro provides a helpful image browser that lets you see tiny, thumbnail images of various files before you open them. We'll also tell you how to make the various choices involved in creating a new image, such as size, resolution, and number of colors. We'll point out also the pros and cons of saving images as different types of files.

If you're downloading an image from a digital camera, scanning an image from paper, or capturing it from your PC screen, turn to Chapter 2 for help. Discover the best ways to scan printed images, the two different ways to get images from cameras, or the various ways Paint Shop Pro lets you grab the exact object you want from a computer screen. Also, Chapter 2 discusses the amazing Paint Shop Pro Straightening tool, which can help set a crooked image right.

Chapter 1

Opening, Viewing, and Saving Image Files

*I*mages, like documents, music, or any other lump of stuff you work with on a computer, are usually stored somewhere as files. After you have an image as a file on a CD, your PC, or your computer network, Paint Shop Pro can probably open it. If the image is on a camera, you may need to download it to your PC first — see Chapter 2.

Images, like children, are easy to deal with in small quantities and variety — but in large quantity and variety, they're challenging to manage. Paint Shop Pro gives you lots of tricks for keeping an eye on all your graphical progeny, from browsing and previewing them to zooming in or out or saving them as a different type of file.

Image files come in an amazing variety of different file types because various software geeks over the years have decided that they know a much better way of storing an image on a computer — a file type — than the last geek. Image files of different types have different multi-letter extensions at the end, like .jpg, .png, or .tif. People refer to them by those extensions, saying "jay-peg" or "jay pee jee" for .jpg or "a ping file" for .png. These file types sometimes behave differently in Paint Shop Pro, so see the section "Using native and foreign file types," later in this chapter, if someone gives you a file that behaves oddly. Fortunately, although you need to be aware that images come in a variety of file types, most of the time you don't have to give a hoot. Paint Shop Pro can crack open most popular types of image file.

Opening Image Files

Paint Shop Pro gives you three ways to open a file:

- **Browsing ("I'll know it when I see it"):** Choose File➪Browse or press Ctrl+B. The browser window opens, as shown in the following section, in Figure 1-1. You open folders in the left panel, and double-click tiny pictures in the right panel to open them.

- **Opening ("I know its name and where it lives"):** Choose File➪Open; or, click the Open button on the Tool Bar, or press Ctrl+O. The Open dialog box appears, as shown a couple of sections from here, in Figure 1-2.

- **Double-clicking ("There it is — open it"):** If you see a file listed and it displays a Paint Shop Pro icon (a tiny, artist's palette), double-click that puppy and Paint Shop Pro should start up and display the image.

That's all you need to know — well, at least most of the time, that's all. The following sections give you some additional tricks and tips for opening files in those three ways.

If you can see the image, but aren't sure where the image file is, see Chapter 2. Images that appear in some document (a Web page, a Microsoft Word document, an Adobe Acrobat document) may not be stored as a file on your computer. (Or, if they are, they may be very hard to find.) You may need to capture the image off your screen.

For some files, Paint Shop Pro has to translate the image file into a form it can use. Translation may especially be necessary for *vector* image files, such as DXF and WPG. To translate, Paint Shop Pro needs additional information from you: specifically, how many pixels wide and high you want the image to be. See the section "Using Vector File Types (Drawing Files)," later in this chapter for more information.

Nifty browser tricks for opening and managing files

We like the browser best for opening files because it also lets you manage them visually. Do one of the following to open the browser:

✔ Press Ctrl+B.

✔ Click the Browse icon, as shown in the margin.

✔ Choose File⇨Browse.

✔ If the Open dialog box is open already, click the Browse button.

Figure 1-1 shows the Browse window, with the sort of images you see next. (Paint Shop Pro may take a few seconds to display all the images.) To close the window when you're done, choose File⇨Close or press Ctrl+F4.

Figure 1-1:
Proving that
a picture is
better than
a thousand-
word
filename.

The left side of the Browse window looks and works like Windows Explorer. Click a folder to see its contents (thumbnail images of the graphics files in that folder). If the folder contains more folders, a + sign appears to its left. To open that folder, click the + sign; to close it, click the – sign that now appears where the + sign did.

On the right side of the window are the thumbnail images with their file-names. Here are some ways to make good use of your thumbnails:

✔ **To open an image file:** Double-click the image.

✔ **To check image type, size, and date:** Pause your cursor over any thumbnail. Paint Shop Pro displays the information near your cursor. For more detail, right-click the thumbnail and choose Information from the menu that appears.

✔ **To manually rearrange thumbnails:** Drag them where you want them.

✔ **To move an image to a different folder:** Drag the thumbnail from the right pane to your destination folder in the left pane.

✔ **To copy a file to a different folder:** Drag the thumbnail to another folder while holding the Ctrl key down.

✔ **To create a new folder:** In the left panel, click the folder in which you want to create a new folder. Choose File⇨Create New Folder, and in the Create New Folder dialog box that appears, type your new folder's name.

✔ **To delete a file:** Right-click its thumbnail and choose Delete from the menu that appears.

✔ **To rename a file:** Right-click its thumbnail, choose Rename from the drop-down menu, and enter a new name in the Rename File dialog box that appears.

✔ **To select several files for opening, moving, copying, or deleting:** Hold down the Ctrl key and click their thumbnail images. To select a series, left-click the first (or last) image; then hold down the Shift key and click the last (or first) image. Follow the instructions in the preceding bullets for opening, moving, copying, or deleting files.

To sort your thumbnails in different ways, follow these steps:

1. **Right-click the blank area to the right of the pictures and choose Sort from the context menu that appears.**

   The Thumbnail Sort dialog box appears.

2. **Choose As̲cending or D̲escending sort order from the Primary Sort tab.**

3. **Choose what to sort by in the Sort Conditions area: file attributes, such as date, or image attributes, such as dimensions (size).**

4. **To sort within a sort (such as by filename within each file date), click the Secondary Sort tab and again choose a sort order and what to sort by.**

5. **Click OK to sort.**

Helpful hints for opening files by name and location

 If you think that you know the name of your file and the disk and folder where it lives, you can choose the fastest route to opening the file. Choose the familiar old File⇨Open command (every program has one) or press Ctrl+O or click the File Open button on the toolbar (as shown in the margin of this paragraph). Paint Shop Pro adds a few special features for working with images, however. Figure 1-2 shows the Open dialog box that appears.

Double-click an image file in the Open dialog box and Paint Shop Pro tries to load it. Often, however, you find that you're poring over a big pile of files with similar names. Here are a few tricks to help you find the one you want:

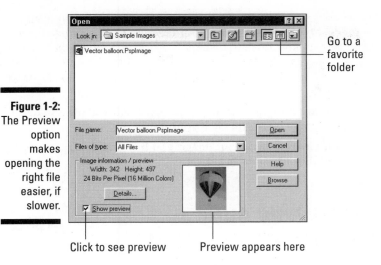

Go to a
favorite
folder

Figure 1-2:
The Preview
option
makes
opening the
right file
easier, if
slower.

Click to see preview   Preview appears here

✔ **To make sure that you're opening the right file:** Click to enable the Show Preview check box. Then click any file, and a preview appears in the Preview window, as shown in Figure 1-2. The Preview feature may slow you down. The computer takes a little extra time to display a picture, so you may want to disable the check box if you have big pictures and don't really need previews.

✔ **To switch to the browser:** Click the Browse button.

✔ **To open more than one file at a time:** Hold down the Ctrl button while clicking filenames, and then click the Open button. Or, to open a bunch of image files listed sequentially in the Open dialog box, click the first file, hold down the Shift button, click the last file, and then click the Open button.

✔ **To open a commonly used or favorite folder:** Click the Favorites button. That's the rightmost button (refer to Figure 1-2) on the dialog box toolbar. From the drop-down list that appears, choose the My Pictures folder, the My PSP8 Pictures folder (in My Documents on your hard drive), or the Paint Shop Pro 8 folder (in My Programs on your hard drive.) You can add a folder to the list. Just open that folder in the Open dialog box, click the Favorites button, and choose Add Current from the drop-down menu. To remove a folder, choose Remove and then choose the folder from the list that drops down.

✔ **To trim down the list of files to show just one type** (if you're looking for a GIF file, for example): Click the Files of Type selection box and choose that type from the many file types Paint Shop Pro can read.

If the file you want isn't listed, make sure that the wrong file type isn't chosen in the Files of Type selection box. File type choices are "sticky," in that if you previously chose to display only GIF files, the next time you use the Open dialog box it displays only GIF files. If you're looking for a JPG file now, you don't see it! Choose All Files under Files of Type to see all files again.

✔ **To see information on image width, height, and color depth:** Read the Image Information area after you click your file.

✔ **To see more information about an image you have clicked, such as date or file size:** Click the Details button.

Secrets of opening a file by double-clicking

If you see an image file listed on your computer — in a My Computer or Windows Explorer window, for example — and it displays the Paint Shop Pro palette icon, you can open it in Paint Shop Pro by double-clicking that icon. If you have several images you want to open, double-click each of them separately, and they all get a separate window in Paint Shop Pro. You don't end up with multiple copies of Paint Shop Pro running.

If you have an image file that Paint Shop Pro doesn't open when you double-click it, three things could be responsible:

✔ The file doesn't have an extension, like .jpg or .gif. This problem often happens when someone sends you a file from a Macintosh computer. Use the browsing or File⇨Open technique described in the preceding sections.

✔ Paint Shop Pro can't open the file. Paint Shop Pro can open many different types of files, but not all of them.

✔ Paint Shop Pro may not be configured to open that file type. See the nearby sidebar, "Making Paint Shop Pro open the right file types when you double-click."

Viewing and Zooming an Image

Working with images on a PC involves a great deal of *zooming* — changing the magnification of your view. Sometimes you need to work close up, taking that nasty gleam out of Uncle Charley's eye, for example (something Aunt Mabel has been trying to do for years). Other times, you really need to see the whole picture, but Uncle Charley's gleaming eye rather scarily fills the whole window.

Zooming doesn't change the size of an image (in pixels or in inches). It only changes how big Paint Shop Pro displays the image onscreen.

Zooming an image in the window

The basic way to zoom in (enlarge the view) or zoom out (see the big picture) is to use the *Zoom* tool. Click the tiny down arrow on the top button on the Tools toolbar, as shown in the margin of this paragraph. Buttons in Paint Shop Pro 8 are what we call "tool groups" from which you choose a tool.

Making Paint Shop Pro open the right file types when you double-click

Two problems can occur with double-clicking as a way of opening image files:

✔ Paint Shop Pro may open files that you would prefer to be opened by some other program. For example, if you're running AutoCAD or another AutoDesk program, you may prefer that the AutoDesk program open DXF files because they're one of AutoDesk's own file types.

✔ Paint Shop Pro may fail to open image files that you want it to open. For example, you may install new software for a new digital camera, and, suddenly, when you double-click JPG files, some program other than Paint Shop Pro opens the file.

These problems usually occur when you have more than one graphics program. The latest one installed may grab all the file types for itself. Both problems can be solved the same way. Follow these steps to determine which files are opened (or not) by Paint Shop Pro:

1. **Chose File➪Preferences➪File Format Associations.**

    The File Format Associations dialog box appears. This box directs Windows to open certain file types using Paint Shop Pro.

2. **Click the check boxes to enable or disable the file types you want opened by Paint Shop Pro.**

    To disable all check boxes, click Remove All. To enable all check boxes, click Select All. (After that, you can enable or disable check boxes manually, if you like.) To have Paint Shop Pro open only the file types that aren't opened by any other program, click Select Unused.

3. **Click OK.**

At this point, Paint Shop Pro is properly set up to open just the file types you want it to and leave the others alone. The *other* program you use, however, may still not be properly set up to open the files you want *it* to open. We can't give you much help with that, but we can tell you one place to get help: Choose Start➪Help from your Windows taskbar. In the Help window that appears, click the Index tab and then, in the text box at the top left of the window, type **File extensions**. Below that text box appears a line reading "Associating with programs." Double-click that to get help with associating file extensions with your other program.

Here, you get a choice of the Pan tool (the arrow) or the Zoom tool (the magnifying glass). Click the Zoom tool. Your cursor changes to a magnifying glass icon. Then click with it on the image in this way:

✔ **Click (left-click) to zoom in.**

✔ **Right-click to zoom out.**

To see the image at its actual size (100 percent), press Ctrl+Alt+N or choose Window➪View Full Size.

Paint Shop Pro 8 also lets you magnify a portion of the image, rather than have to enlarge the whole thing to see a detail. With either the Pan or Zoom tool selected, choose View➪Magnifier or press F11. Move your cursor over an area of the image, and a special 5x Zoom window shows you a close-up view of that area. Repeat the command or press F11 again to remove the magnifier.

Working on several images at a time

You can open several images at a time in Paint Shop Pro. Each one gets its own window. Having several images open is useful for tasks such as cutting and pasting between images. To help manage those windows, use the commands on the Paint Shop Pro Window menu. That menu contains the usual suspects of nearly all Windows programs: Cascade, Tile (Horizontally or Vertically), or Close All to close all image files.

Remember that Paint Shop Pro tools and commands apply to only the image window that's *active* (the one with the colored title bar). Click an image window's title bar to make that window active and bring it to the front.

Saving a Changed Image File

After you're done modifying an image in Paint Shop Pro, you need to save it. Saving an image in Paint Shop Pro is often just as easy as saving a Microsoft Word document, for example. Choose File➪Save or click the Save button on the standard toolbar (the diskette icon) or press Ctrl+S.

Paint Shop Pro quietly saves, in most instances, an image as the same type (format) of file (JPG, for example) that it was when you opened it. It may, however, raise a warning, depending on what changes you have made — see the following sidebar, "When Paint Shop Pro offers a merger."

If you have added text or shapes, or overlaid images on your original image, saving the modified image as a Paint Shop Pro file is a good idea; see the following section.

When Paint Shop Pro offers a merger

Paint Shop Pro lets you do some sophisticated modifications to an image, like adding fancy text, shapes, or overlaying images. To simplify this sort of image work, Paint Shop Pro keeps some stuff on separate layers. (That way, you can fool with your changes without messing up the original.)

Not all file types (like JPG) can handle layered images. So, if you start with a JPG image, put text on it, and try to save it as a JPG image file, Paint Shop Pro will have to combine all those layers into one single layer, called a merged image. Paint Shop Pro pops up the dialog box shown in this figure.

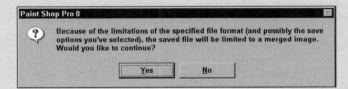

We suggest that you decline this merger: Click No. Then save your file as a Paint Shop Pro image. If you must have an image of a certain type (for example, a JPG or PNG file for a Web page), save a copy of the image in that file type instead. See "Saving a Copy of Your File As Another File Type," later in this chapter.

Saving the Image First As a Paint Shop Pro File

If you bake a pie, you can (a) save it in a nice Tupperware pie carrier if you're taking it to a community supper (b) wrap it in plastic and freeze it if you're planning ahead for a holiday or (c) mush it into a little plastic bag and put it at the bottom of your backpack if you're going hiking. In all cases, you still have tasty pie — but stored in ways that are appropriate for particular uses, and not appropriate for others.

Likewise, you can save an image as many different types of file. Some types are good for one purpose, and others for another. The choice depends on what you (or the people you give the file to) intend to do with the image. Another person, for example, may have Photoshop but not Paint Shop Pro, and so may want a Photoshop file instead. Or, you may need a JPG, GIF, or PNG file for putting on a Web page (which doesn't display many of the other image file types).

The best idea, however, is to first save the image as a Paint Shop Pro (PSP) type of file, even if it started out life as a different type. Paint Shop Pro files are a good choice because, among other things, they save layers and any current selection you may have made during the editing process. Most other file types don't save that stuff. Some file types are "lossy" (like most JPG varieties), which means that they may even lose quality. PSP files are sort of the Tupperware solution.

After you have taken the precaution of making a Paint Shop Pro file, if you (or the people to whom you're giving the file) also need a different type of file, save a *copy* as that other type of file. If you make subsequent changes to the image, always make the changes to the Paint Shop Pro file and then make copies of that file in the various file types you may need.

To save any image as a Paint Shop Pro file, first look at the filename on the title bar, in the upper-left area of the Paint Shop Pro window. (The filename appears after the words *Jasc Paint Shop Pro.*) The filename should end in a period and three letters; if not, see the following sidebar "How the FPX can I see the TIF, JPG, DXF, and other extensions?!"

If the filename has the extension .psp or .PspImage, simply choose File⇨Save or click the Save button on the toolbar. You're done! (Your image was a Paint Shop Pro file already; you just updated that file with your latest changes.)

If the filename ends in anything *other than* .psp or .PspImage, follow these steps:

1. **Choose File⇨Save As.**

   The Save As dialog box appears.

2. **Click the Save as Type box and select the Paint Shop Pro Image option.**

3. **Select a folder and type a name for the file.**

   Do this exactly as you would to save a file in any other Windows program.

   To save an image in a personal favorite folder, click the Favorites button, the rightmost button on the Save dialog box's toolbar. In the drop-down list that appears, you can choose the My Documents folder. (We don't recommend saving in the Temp, or temporary, folder.) To add your own favorite folder to the list, first open that folder in the Save dialog box. Then click the Favorite Folders button and choose Add Current from the drop-down menu. To remove a folder, choose Remove and then select the folder from the drop-down list.

4. **Click the Save button.**

The image is now safely stored as the best file type possible for a Paint Shop Pro user, with nothing lost.

Saving a Copy of Your File As Another File Type

After saving the image as a Paint Shop Pro file (see the preceding section), if you also need the image in a different file type, follow these steps:

1. **Choose File⇨Save Copy As.**

   The Save Copy As dialog box appears.

2. **Select the file type you want from the Save as Type box.**

   If you want to save the file as a Paint Shop Pro file, but in a form that earlier versions of Paint Shop Pro can read, click the Options button. The Save Options dialog box appears; choose the version you want, and then click OK.

   If you're saving the file as a non-PSP file, the Options button may be grayed-out (disabled). If not, it provides access to variations on your chosen format that can sometimes be useful, like reducing the file size or putting the file in a particular form that somebody needs. The following section provides a few examples of options.

3. **Click the Save button.**

When you save a copy in a different file type, the open file isn't affected. It remains whatever file type it was. If you have used layers (or floating selections) and save a copy as something other than a Paint Shop Pro file, Paint Shop Pro may have to merge (combine) those layers into a single image. The program displays a dialog box to warn you if it needs to merge layers into a single image. That merge *doesn't* happen to the Paint Shop Pro image you're working on, only to the file copy you're creating. Don't worry — just click Yes to proceed.

Using Native and Foreign File Types

You often have to open or create files that are not a Paint Shop Pro file, and knowing something about the file types can be helpful. The next sections describe a few of the most popular file types. Each file type is identified by the three-letter ending (extension) it uses. For example, Paint Shop Pro files end with the extension .psp or .PspImage.

Most of the time, you don't have to do anything special to open a particular file type or to save your work as that type of file — but, then again, sometimes you do. Paint Shop Pro, in most cases, simply asks you a few questions to resolve any problems when opening or saving a foreign file type.

"How the FPX can I see the TIF, JPG, DXF, and other extensions?!"

Image files are often referred to by the three-or-more letter ending *(extension)* at the end of their filenames. The file polecat.tif, for example, is a *TIF* (or TIFF) file. On many computers, Windows is set up to *hide* these extensions, which makes your life *harder* when using Paint Shop Pro. If, when you go to open a file in Paint Shop Pro, the files don't appear to end with a period and three-letter extension (such as .psp, .bmp, or .pcx), Windows is hiding valuable information from you.

To reveal the extensions, do this: Double-click the My Computer icon. In the window that appears, choose View⇨Folder Options (or in Windows XP, choose Tools⇨Folder Options) to display the Folder Options dialog box. Click the View tab there, and under Files and Folders, Hidden Files, deselect the check box labeled Hide File Extensions For Known File Types. (Then click OK.)

Paint Shop Pro files (PspImage or PSP)

PspImage is the native Paint Shop Pro 8 file type and is probably the best choice for storing your own images. (It's the metaphorical Tupperware storage solution, if you have been following our pie storage metaphor.) When you save your work as a Paint Shop Pro file, you can save everything just as it is, including any areas you have selected with the Paint Shop Pro selection tools, plus your various kinds of layers, palettes, tool settings (like current brush width), transparency, and other advanced features. You can pick up almost exactly where you left off. Paint Shop Pro files can have any color depth you choose. (See Chapter 9 to understand what we mean by color depth.). PspImage is the latest and greatest of the Paint Shop Pro native formats; earlier versions used the PSP extension.

Programs other than Paint Shop Pro or Animation Shop don't often read Paint Shop Pro files, however. You may need to save a copy of your image in a different file type for someone who uses other software. Also, earlier versions of Paint Shop Pro can't read later Paint Shop Pro files (Paint Shop Pro 7 can't read Paint Shop Pro 8 files, for example.) To create Paint Shop Pro 5.0, 6.0, or 7.0 files using Paint Shop Pro 8, see the instructions for saving a copy of your image in the section "Saving a Copy of Your File as Another File Type," earlier in this chapter.

BMP

BMP files are *Windows bitmap* files; that is, they were designed by Microsoft for storing images, and many programs under Windows can read and write them. BMP files can have color depths of 1, 4, 8, or 24 bits. (Set your color depth by using Colors⇨Decrease Color Depth or Colors⇨Increase Color Depth; see Chapter 9 for details.)

BMP files that are 24-bit can be quite large. When you save a file as BMP, you can click the Options button in the Save As, or Save Copy As, dialog box to choose higher *compression* (make smaller files). Under Encoding (in the Options dialog box that appears), select RLE and then click OK. (RLE stands for *Run-Length Encoding,* a way of making image files smaller.) Now, when you save the file, Paint Shop Pro asks your permission to switch to a 256-color (8-bit) version of the BMP file. The resulting file is much trimmer than the original, although the color quality may diminish slightly.

TIFF

TIFF (or TIF) stands for Tag Image File Format (which, of course, tells you nothing useful). Many graphics programs on the PC and Macintosh can read and write TIFF files, so it's a good choice of file type when you don't know what kinds of files the other person can read.

TIFF files can be quite large unless you compress them. To compress a TIFF file, click the Options button when using the Save As or Save Copy As dialog box. Then choose the LZW Compression option in the Compression area of the Options dialog box that appears. LZW gives you the best compression and compatibility with most other programs. (No image quality is lost by using LZW compression in TIFF files.)

For advanced users, TIFF is a good choice because it's capable of storing information not only in RGB primaries, but also CMYK (used for some high-quality printed images). It can also store advanced data for color accuracy, such as gamma.

GIF

The Web uses CompuServe GIF images all over the place. GIF is the most popular of three common file types used on the Internet. (JPG and PNG are the other two.)

Many programs read GIF files. (Older programs may read only the older GIF standard, GIF87, rather than the newer GIF89a. Paint Shop Pro lets you choose which standard to use when saving a GIF file — just click the Options button in the Save As or Save Copy As dialog box.)

GIF is the metaphorical "frozen-pie" option if you're following our pie metaphor; saving your work as GIF means that it loses something, but perhaps not enough to matter. GIF images have a maximum color depth of 256 colors, which allows fairly realistic images. That number of colors, however, isn't enough to enable Paint Shop Pro to do all operations, so it may at some point suggest that you let it increase the number of colors. (See " File Types and 'Action Required' Messages About Colors," later in this chapter.)

GIF enables you to use some special features, such as a *transparent color* (which lets the background of Web pages show through), and *interlaced display* (in which the entire image gradually forms as it is downloaded from the Web). GIF can use fewer colors than 256 if you want to save file size and, therefore, save people who view your file on the Web downloading time.

A special Paint Shop Pro tool called the *GIF Optimizer* can help you set transparency and otherwise optimize the image for Web use. See Chapter 17 for details of creating images for the Web using this tool.

Some GIF files contain a whole series of images to be displayed as an animation. You can view these images using Animation Shop; Paint Shop Pro shows you only the first image of the series.

JPEG

JPEG (or JPG) stands for Joint Photographic Experts Group, which sounds impressive. JPEG images are common on the Web for color photographs and other realistic color images because their files are small (relative to other file types) and download quickly.

The disadvantage of JPEG is that it usually uses something called *lossy compression,* which means that the image quality is reduced a bit, especially around sharp edges like text. Storing an image as a JPEG is kind of like stuffing a pie into a baggie in your backpack for a hike. The basic taste and nutrition are still there, and it doesn't take up lots of space, but because of the squeezing involved, the product may lose some of its appeal.

You can choose just how much squeezing you want in JPEG, but first storing your work in some other format (preferably PSP) is a good idea. Then follow the three steps for the Save Copy As operation at the beginning of this section. In Step 2, choose JPEG-JFIF Compliant in the Save As Type selection box.

Click the Options button; in the Save Options dialog box that appears, drag the Compression Factor slider to the left for higher quality but larger files, or to the right for lower-quality and smaller files.

The geeks at the Joint Photographics Experts Group have also come up with a new, lossless variety of JPEG format. To save your files in this maximum-quality-but-largest-file-size format, select Lossless in the Save Options dialog box.

If you're reading JPEG files, Paint Shop Pro offers an effect that removes some image distortions, called *artifacts,* that result from compression (see Chapter 7).

As with GIF, Paint Shop Pro offers a special tool, the JPEG Optimizer, for adjusting JPEG images for the Web. See Chapter 18 for details of fine-tuning JPEG images with this tool.

PNG

PNG (Progressive Network Graphics) was designed to take over for GIF on the Web, although it is catching on slowly. It does have some advantages over GIF and accomplishes the same functions as GIF, so it may yet take over. Because its main use is Web graphics, we discuss it a bit more in Chapter 18.

Using Vector File Types (Drawing Files)

Graphics images come in two main flavors: *raster* (also called *bitmap*) and *vector*. Here are the differences between them:

- ✔ **Raster (bitmap) images are made up of dots (pixels).** Most computer images are of this kind, and Paint Shop Pro is principally designed for this kind of image. It both reads and writes a wide variety of raster images.

- ✔ **Vector images are made up of lines, shapes, filled areas, and text.** You can change text, lines, and shapes more easily if they're stored as vectors than if they're stored as bitmaps. Although Paint Shop Pro is principally designed for raster images, it allows you to create vector layers that contain lines, text, and preset shapes. Images stored as .psp files retain any vector graphics you create. Paint Shop Pro can read certain vector image files other than its own .psp files, but converts them to rasters.

Vector files are typically created by popular *drawing* software (as opposed to *painting* software). AutoCAD, for example, a popular drafting application, writes DXF (Drawing eXchange Format) files. Corel Draw writes CDR files, and Corel WordPerfect uses WPG files. Many other vector file types are in use, too.

Like Paint Shop Pro files, some other file types can also contain a mix of vector and bitmap graphics. These include Windows Enhanced Metafiles (EMF, a Microsoft Windows standard), Computer Graphics Metafiles (CGM, a standard by the American National Standards Institute), PICT (a Macintosh standard), and embedded PostScript (EPS, by Adobe). Some files (like embedded PostScript) may contain in some cases both a bitmap and a vector version of the same image.

Opening vector files

Paint Shop Pro can open many kinds of vector (or mixed vector and bitmap) files. You can also copy drawings, using the Windows clipboard, from most vector programs that run under Windows, and paste the images into Paint Shop Pro.

Whether you're opening or pasting vector images, however, Paint Shop Pro converts them into bitmap images. To do the conversion, it pops up a Meta Picture Import dialog box that wants you to enter a width and height for this resulting bitmap image, in pixels. (Any dimension information in the original file doesn't survive the translation, so Paint Shop Pro needs some help from you.)

Select the Maintain Original Aspect Ratio check box if you want to keep the same proportions as the original image. Because Paint Shop Pro is translating between two different kinds of image data, it may make a few mistakes that you have to clean up afterward.

Saving vector files — not

You can't save pure vector-type image files, such as DXF, in Paint Shop Pro. You can, however, save your work as one of the file types that contains a mix of vectors and bitmaps, such as EPS or CGM.

In those instances, PSP simply stores a bitmap image and leaves the vector part blank. Because no vector data is stored, a program that handles only vector graphics may not be able to read the file.

Converting or Renaming Batches of Files

If you have lots of image files and need copies of them in a different file type or to have a series of related names like hawaii0001 through hawaii9579 for your 9,579 vacation photos, try the Paint Shop Pro batch processing.

To copy a bunch of files to a new file format, follow these steps:

1. **Choose File⇨Batch Processing⇨Convert.**

2. **In the Batch Conversion dialog box that appears, hold down the Ctrl key and click the files you want to convert, to select them.**

3. **Near the bottom of the dialog box, click the down arrow at the right end of the Type selection box and select the file type you need the files to be.**

4. **To put the newly generated files in a different folder, click the Browse button and choose a new folder.**

5. **Click the Start button.**

In a few seconds or minutes, you have copies in the new file type you need.

To give a bunch of files similar names, differing only by a number (as in hawaii01, hawaii02) take these steps:

1. **Choose File⇨Batch Processing⇨Rename.**

2. **In the Batch Rename dialog box that appears, hold down the Ctrl key and click the files you want to convert, to select them.**

3. **Click the Modify button.**

   The Modify Filename Format dialog box appears. The idea is to combine various naming and numbering elements into a sort of formula for Paint Shop Pro to follow. For example, hawaii50 is a "custom text" element of our choosing, followed by a two-digit "sequence."

4. **Click an element in the left panel to choose the first part of the new name, such as Custom Text.**

5. **Click the Add button to add that element to your formula, which gets assembled in the right panel.**

   Depending on what kind of element you choose, a one-line text box appears on the right for you to make a choice or enter some text. We stick with our simple example. If you have chosen Custom Text, type your text (**hawaii**, for example) in the Custom Text box that appears. If you have chosen Sequence, type a starting number in the Starting Sequence box that appears; use as many digits as you need for the batch (type **01** for 100 images). For today's date, choose a date format.

6. **Repeat Steps 4 and 5 to add more elements. Make sure that one of your elements is Sequence, or else you're asking the impossible: for each file to have the same name.**

   The order in which you add elements on the right is the order in which they appear in the filenames.

7. **Click OK. When the Batch Rename dialog box returns, select the files to be converted.**

The files are all renamed, and each name includes a different number.

File Types and "Action Required" Messages about Colors

When you try to use certain Paint Shop Pro features or save your work in a non-PSP format, you may get an "Action required" message from Paint Shop Pro, especially for images not originally in the Paint Shop Pro file format. For example, you may open a GIF file and want to use one of the Paint Shop Pro commands on the Adjust or Effects menu. Or, perhaps you want to add a raster layer to that GIF file. Paint Shop Pro gives you an error message like the one shown in Figure 1-3.

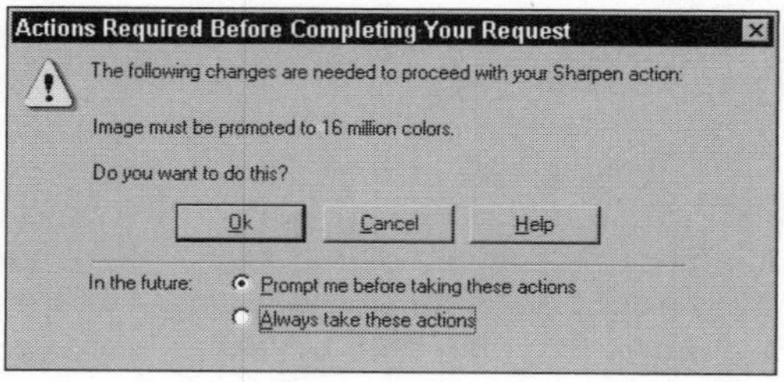

Figure 1-3:
First, Paint Shop Pro may need to improve the image quality.

Actions Required Before Completing Your Request

The following changes are needed to proceed with your Sharpen action:

Image must be promoted to 16 million colors.

Do you want to do this?

| Ok | Cancel | Help |

In the future: ⦿ Prompt me before taking these actions
                ○ Always take these actions

Don't worry — be happy; just click OK. The issue is that certain file types, like GIF, can handle only a limited number of colors (have limited "color depth") and many Paint Shop Pro features work only on images able to handle as many as 16 million colors. Paint Shop Pro is offering to create a 16-million-color image for you so that it can apply the tool you want to use.

If you get one of these messages, if you later save your work in the original, color-limited file type (GIF, for example), you also get a message requesting permission to reduce the number of colors back down to whatever that type of file can handle. Simply click OK in whatever dialog box or boxes result, and you will probably be happy with the result.

If you're a professional and are picky, you understand what's going on and can take the necessary steps to control the result. You can always change the number of colors manually by choosing Image⇨Increase Color Depth or Image⇨Decrease Color Depth. You find more about color depth in Chapter 9.

Obtaining Image Files from the Web

The Web is a grab bag of goodies for graphics gurus. Here's how to get your hands on these fabulous fruits.

One of the best ways to get graphics is to find a Web site offering them free and clear. Most of these sites provide instructions for downloading those image files. To save an image that you're viewing in your Web browser, use the following methods:

✔ Right-click the image and, on the pop-up menu that appears, look for Save Picture As or a similar choice. You're prompted for the location on your hard disk where you want the image saved.

✔ Right-click the image and, on the pop-up menu that appears, choose Copy. This choice copies the image to the Windows Clipboard; open Paint Shop Pro and press Ctrl+V to paste the image as a new image. (Choose the Edit⇨Paste command to see ways to paste the image into another open image.) Save the image by choosing File⇨Save.

A fair number of graphics images on the Web have transparent portions, especially their backgrounds. The transparent parts of these types of image have a hidden color (typically white), and that color may become visible in Paint Shop Pro. See Chapter 18 for more information about transparency in Web images.

Most Web images are one of only a few different file types: GIF, JPEG, or PNG. GIF and some PNG images are *palette images,* with a limited number of colors (typically, 256 colors). As a result of this color limitation, you may see some of the "Action Required" messages discussed in the preceding section.

Many animations on the Web are GIF files. You should open animated GIF files in Animation Shop, not Paint Shop Pro (which displays only the first frame of the animation). Some animations are, however, in a private vector format (Flash) that neither Animation Shop nor Paint Shop Pro can read.

Chapter 2

Capturing Pictures from Paper, Camera, or Screen

*W*here do your pictures come from? From your new digital camera? From a piece of paper? Or, from your PC screen?

Ironically, most people don't *paint* pictures in Paint Shop Pro. They get an image from somewhere and then mess around with it. This chapter tells you how to get that image into Paint Shop Pro.

Connecting to Your Scanner or Camera

Scanners and cameras can hook up in lots of ways to Paint Shop Pro and your computer. One way is the Microsoft Windows Image Acquisition (WIA) method. If your scanner or camera supports WIA, follow the instructions that came with the device for installing and using WIA. Some WIA devices appear like a disk drive when you open the Windows My Computer icon, and you can open or copy images much like you open or copy files on a disk drive in Windows. Otherwise, for WIA devices, use the Paint Shop Pro File⇨Import⇨Scanner or Camera command to access the device through the vendor's software. (We can't give you specific instructions for that process.)

Remarking on TWAIN

Mark Twain loved high-tech gadgets (such as typesetting machines, the computers of his day). Although he'll never meet his namesake, the TWAIN interface, we think that he would have loved the happy accident of having his pen name associated with today's high-tech scanners. (Incidentally, TWAIN, despite its capitalization, isn't an acronym, although some wags have suggested that it stands for Technology Without An Interesting Name.)

TWAIN is a go-between that links scanners, cameras, and other image sources to PC image-processing software, like Paint Shop Pro. Scanners are made by different manufacturers

and, therefore, speak different native languages. To make translation easier for your PC, most manufacturers have chosen to make their scanners comply with a standard named TWAIN. As a result, in graphics programs like Paint Shop Pro, scanning usually involves a menu choice named TWAIN.

A scanner is a sophisticated instrument that needs software to control it. When you scan, your PC launches a specialized TWAIN-speaking scanner-controlling program. Scanner manufacturers install this program on your PC during the scanner setup.

In this chapter, our instructions assume that you're using the longtime standard, the TWAIN software interface. However, the instructions also give general scanning tips for everyone, regardless of what form of connection you use.

Scanning into Paint Shop Pro

With scanners almost as cheap as a carton of paper, scanning is one of the most popular ways to get an image into a PC. Many people are surprised that scanning is a more involved process than they expect. Getting an image *from* paper isn't quite as simple as putting an image *on* paper — unless quality isn't all that important.

If your PC is equipped with more than one TWAIN-based image-acquiring device (scanners or cameras, for example), you need to tell Paint Shop Pro which one you're using before going through the following steps. Choose File➪Import➪Twain➪Select Source. The Select Source dialog box appears. Select your scanner (source) and then click Select.

In most instances, these steps scan an image from a properly installed scanner that has a TWAIN interface (although your scanning software may differ):

1. **Launch the scanning software that came with your scanner.**

    To do that, choose File➪Import➪TWAIN➪Acquire. (If your scanner uses WIA, choose File➪Import➪Scanner or Camera.)

Or, press the Scan button on your scanner, if it has one.

Some special software designed to run your scanner should appear. (If it doesn't appear, read the literature that came with your scanner and check to make sure that your scanner is properly installed.) Because that software depends on the scanner manufacturer, we can't tell you many details about it. We give you some tips, however, in the following section.

Figure 2-1 shows the software that appears if, for example, you're using a Hewlett-Packard ScanJet.

2. Find and click the Preview button.

In Figure 2-1, for example, the Preview button is in the Preview window. If you don't find a button labeled Preview, look for a similar word. The scanner starts to scan and then gives you a small preview image, as shown in the Preview window in the figure. This preview image shows the entire scanning area of the scanner (the glass area in a flatbed scanner).

3. Define the area you want to scan.

In most scanner software, you create a rectangle (the dashed line shown in Figure 2-1) in the Preview area to define the area you want to scan. (Drag from one corner of the part you want to the opposite corner.) Usually, you can then drag this rectangle to adjust its position or drag its sides or corners to adjust its size. If you don't define the scan area in this way, you may end up with an enormous image (your scanner's entire field of view) that you have to crop (trim) to the area you want.

Most scanner software allows you to enlarge (zoom in on) the preview image. Look for a magnifying glass icon, click it, and then click the image.

Figure 2-1:
One example of scanning software. Your software may be different.

4. **Adjust settings that control the resolution or number of colors or improve the appearance of the preview picture.**

   Scanner software often offers important features and controls, including whether you want color or black-and-white scanning. In the ScanWizard software shown in Figure 2-1, the controls are in the left window. We describe these and other useful controls in the following section.

5. **Find and click the Scan button.**

   If you can't find a Scan button, look for a Start or Begin button. Figure 2-1 shows a Scan button next to the Preview button. The scanner begins to scan again. (It may take longer or shorter than it did in Step 2.)

After the scanner is done, an image appears in Paint Shop Pro. You can now close the scanner software window or continue to scan more images (starting with Step 2). Each image gets its own window in Paint Shop Pro.

Getting the most from your scanning software

Whatever software your PC uses to control your scanner, it undoubtedly offers certain settings to play with. For casual scanning of images that don't have problems (such as underexposure), you can often ignore lots of those settings and do all your fiddling in Paint Shop Pro. Sometimes, however, the controls in your scanner software can improve your image in ways that Paint Shop Pro alone can't — especially with moiré problems that occur when you scan newspaper photos. (Although Paint Shop Pro has an adjustment that removes moiré patterns, it's not nearly as effective as fixing it at the source.)

Scan-ty information

What exactly goes on in a scanner? Here's a quick tour. The scanner illuminates your image while it moves a light sensor in a series of straight lines across the page. As the sensor goes along, it periodically *samples* (takes a reading of) how much light is coming from one tiny spot on the image. Usually, the scanner uses three sensors combined, one for each primary color.

These readings are converted into digital numbers, one for each primary color. During the conversion process, the scanner makes an adjustment to account for the fact that electronic sensors don't see light the way the human eye does. (This *gamma* adjustment, apart from scanning, also has to be made by software when your PC displays colors onscreen.) The scanner may also make other adjustments as directed by the scanning software.

You can usually adjust these settings *after* you do the preview. Except for resolution and color settings, the preview image reflects the changes without running your scanner again.

Choosing the number of colors

To achieve the best quality possible with color photographs (and other images that either have many colors or gradual, subtle shadings), you want the maximum number of colors the scanner can produce. Usually, this maximum is expressed as 24-bit or 32-bit color. If your PC has disk space for the large files this produces, scanning at this number of colors is best even if your final application requires fewer colors. For the sake of control, it's better to have more colors than you need to start with and use Paint Shop Pro, rather than the scanner, to reduce the colors (see Chapter 9).

If you know that your final application for the image doesn't require such high quality and you're in a rush or your disk drive is short on space, you can save yourself a bit of time in Paint Shop Pro by choosing fewer colors during scanning.

Here are some scanner settings you may find, labeled type or color depth in the scanner software, that usually work well for the following uses:

- ✔ **Business or highest-quality personal use:** Choose 16 million colors (24- or 32-bit). (You can then color-reduce these images in Paint Shop Pro for faster downloading in Web or e-mail applications.)

- ✔ **Casual family or business Web page illustrations or snapshots to be sent by e-mail:** Choose 256-color if it's available, although it's not always offered as a scanner option. Use 16 million colors if the 256-color option isn't available.

- ✔ **Black-and-white photos, pencil drawings and sketches, or line drawings with lines of varying weight:** Choose 256 shades of gray. Scanners typically scan these types of image by looking for one particular color. If your drawing is all in one color of pencil, such as green, it may not appear! Check your scanner manual for notes on scanning grayscale (black-and-white) images or line drawings, or avoid red, blue, or green pencils.

- ✔ **Clear, original printed text with good contrast or line drawings in dark ink or with thick lines:** Choose two colors (1-bit), or *line art,* if available; otherwise, choose 256 shades of gray. If you have a line drawing with uneven line darkness, you can sometimes turn it into good line art by adjusting either the Line Art Threshold or Highlight/Midtone/Shadow settings. See "Setting contrast and other adjustments," later in this chapter, for more information about the latter setting.

Choosing resolution

Resolution is the number of dots (or *samples*) per inch that your scanner reads from the paper image. Your scanning software has a control for resolution.

Higher resolution means that you get more detail — more pixels — which is generally A Good Thing. For example, if you scan a 4-inch x 6-inch snapshot at 300 dots per inch (dpi), you get an image of 4×300 (1200) pixels high and 6×300 pixels (1800) wide. (That's even more pixels than most PC screens can show at the same time.) You can always make a picture lower in resolution (reduce its size in pixels) in Paint Shop Pro, if necessary, but you can't add detail that isn't there in the first place.

Higher resolution also poses some problems. First, high resolution means bigger files! If you're just scanning a photo to e-mail to someone or to put on the Web, the people viewing your photo won't appreciate the long wait for a large photo to download — especially if it's bigger than their screen! You can reduce a photo in Paint Shop Pro, of course, but why bother if you don't need to? Besides, sometimes the shrinking process (also called *resampling*) doesn't give quite as good a result as if you had chosen the lower resolution in the first place.

To judge which resolution to use, answer these questions:

- **"How big of an image do I need?"** For most Web and e-mail work, an image 300 to 400 pixels on a side is plenty. Multiply the width or height of the region you're scanning (6 inches wide, for example) by the scanner resolution you're thinking of using (300 dpi, for example) to figure out the resulting width or height in pixels (1800 pixels wide, in this example). Select a lower resolution to get a smaller image in pixels.

- **"How big a file do I want?"** Scanning a 4-inch x 6-inch color snapshot at 300 dpi (and 24-bit color) can give you a file as large as 6 megabytes. Cutting resolution in half can reduce the file size by as much as a factor of four.

- **"How finely detailed does the image need to be?"** At 300 dpi, you can begin to see an individual human hair placed in your scanner.

You probably don't see any changes you make in resolution in your Preview image. To see the effect of resolution settings, you have to scan an image into Paint Shop Pro (click the Scan button in your scanner software).

Setting contrast and other adjustments

Some other adjustments available in your scanner software can make an enormous difference in the quality of your image. Fiddle with these after you have clicked the Preview button in your scanner software so that you have a preview image to look at as you make your adjustments. You may have to poke around to find a button or command that reveals these adjustments, or even discover that your software doesn't offer them.

Many adjustments that scanning software offers are technical. We don't have room to fully do them justice here, but you probably don't need them anyway. We describe here a few of the important ones you may find:

- **Brightness:** Brightness makes all areas darker or lighter to the same degree.

- **Contrast:** This adjustment makes dark areas darker and light areas lighter.

- **Exposure:** Increasing Exposure makes dark pixels disproportionately darker and brings out detail in the light areas.

- **Shadow/Midtone/Highlight:** The Shadow and Highlight values are also called the black-and-white points, respectively. Sometimes they're unnamed, appearing as sliding arrows under a histogram chart. These three settings are something like Contrast and Exposure, but more precise, which make an image's dark areas darker and its light areas lighter. They also bring out detail in the middle ranges of darkness and adjust a too-dark or too-light image to a more pleasing appearance. Each setting ranges from 0 to 255 (the numeric values correspond to brightness: 0 is black and 255 is white). The choices are shown in this list:

  - **Shadow:** To make the darker areas as dark as possible, adjust the Shadow value upward. All pixels *below* that value become as dark as you can make them without radically changing any colors.

  - **Highlight:** To make light areas as light as possible, adjust the Highlight value downward. All pixels *above* that value become as light as possible without radically changing their colors.

  - **Midtone:** If the rest of the image is, overall, kind of dark, adjust the Midtone value downward; if the image is light, set the value higher.

- **Descreen:** Software like Microtek Scanwizard and Umax Vistascan have special *descreen* capabilities, which means that they can minimize the moiré patterns that arise when you scan printed images. Generally, the software offers several settings that depend on whether you're scanning from a newspaper, magazine, or higher-quality printed source, like a book. (You probably have to scan to see the result of descreening — it's unlikely that you can see it in the Preview.)

- **Unsharp Mask:** Try this feature (often lurking in an area named *filter* or something similar) if your photo doesn't look quite as sharp as it should.

Without making the image sharper, this feature gives the illusion of sharpness. It raises the contrast around edges (where the pixel values change). Unsharp masking has three settings:

- **Amount:** Adjusts the degree of contrast enhancement (sharpness).

- **Radius:** Determines how far from an edge the effect extends.

- **Threshold:** Sets a limit, below which an edge isn't enhanced. A setting that's too low may make the image speckly.

(The numbers used in these settings have no intuitive meaning, so don't look for one. Just adjust them up or down.)

If you forget to use Unsharp Mask *while* scanning, you can use the Paint Shop Pro Unsharp Mask effect *after* scanning. Choose Adjust➪Sharpness➪Unsharp Mask and the Unsharp Mask dialog box appears. Make the same adjustments listed in the preceding bullet. Figure 2-2 shows the Unsharp Mask effect, as shown on a picture of one of the authors as a young Gene Simmons.

Figure 2-2: KISS and makeup — Unsharp masking refers to the effect illustrated by this before-and-after pair of images.

Before   After

Many scanner programs offer check boxes to turn on automatic features (typically auto contrast and auto color correction). These features attempt to adjust various settings for you, based on the preview scan. Sometimes they work well and sometimes they don't. Try enabling and disabling their check boxes to see the result in the Preview area.

You can find an excellent, detailed guide to using the features of scanning software — in fact, to using your scanner in general — on the Web at www.scantips.com.

Dots not nice!

Why do scans of printed images get moiré patterns? Unlike photographic prints and painted or drawn artwork, printed images are made up of ink dots of varying sizes at a certain spacing. This effect wouldn't be a problem, except that your scanner also uses dots — and they're of a different size and spacing.

Your scanner reads the image by sampling the image (looking at tiny spots on the image) at some spacing (your chosen resolution in dots per inch). The samples don't align exactly on the printed dots, except every 10 or 20 pixels, for example; the rest of the time, they align partly on the dots and partly on the white background. The usual result is a checkered or barred patterning on the image. Something similar can happen when Paint Shop Pro displays the image on your PC screen, which also uses dots.

Forever plaid: Scanning printed images

When you scan a printed image from a newspaper, magazine, or book, your image often acquires a blurry checkered plaid or barred pattern. This pattern, called a *moiré* ("mwah-RAY") pattern, is caused by conflict between the dots used to print your image and the dots that happen during scanning.

The next time you put your windows screens up or down, you can see this same effect if you look through two screens at the same time. Or, if you have a screen porch, stand outside and look through the two screens where they meet at a corner.

The moiré pattern may exist only on your PC screen in Paint Shop Pro and not in your image file, as Figure 2-3 illustrates. In this figure, the zoom of 1:3 (noted on the title bar) is responsible. Try viewing the image at full scale (press Ctrl+Alt+N), or larger. If the pattern disappears, the pattern is just the effect of using a zoom of less than 1:1. Don't worry about it. When the image is printed at a high printer resolution or used on the Web at full size, that pattern probably won't appear. If the pattern is still visible at a 1:1 zoom, it's permanent and you need to do something about it.

Permanent moiré pattern problems? Try these solutions:

- ✔ **Higher resolution:** The pattern may fade if you set the resolution of your scanner's software (the dots-per-inch value) higher.

- ✔ **Descreening:** If your scanner software provides descreening, use this option. See "Setting contrast and other adjustments," earlier in this chapter, for more information.

- ✔ **Special filter:** Choose Adjust⇨Add/Remove Noise⇨Moiré Pattern Removal (see Chapter 7).

Figure 2-3:
A moiré
pattern
appears on
this roof, but
isn't an
image flaw.

Printed images pose more problems than just moiré patterns. Although the images appear to have a wide variety of tones, printed images are composed of alternating dots of primary colors (black-and-white photos have only two colors, for example). When these images are scanned (particularly at high resolution), they retain that spotty, dotty character. Zoom in to see them.

As a result, Paint Shop Pro features that use color selection and replacement don't work as your eye would lead you to expect. An area that looks uniformly green, for example, may be made up of blue and yellow dots. You can't select that green area of your scanned-in logo, for example, because it's not really green! This problem gets worse at higher resolutions.

To partially solve this problem, you can apply the Paint Shop Pro blur adjustment (see Chapter 7) to make the dots blur together. If you have problems selecting a colored area with the Magic Wand tool (see Chapter 12), try increasing the Tolerance setting in the Tool Options dialog box.

Straightening crooked scans

Lining up your photos neatly across the bottom of most scanners is a pain — and even then you normally don't get it quite right, leading to a tilted picture of your sweet snookielumps. Fortunately, Paint Shop Pro has a useful tool that straightens your pictures for you.

Here's how to get your pictures to straighten up and fly right:

   1. **Select the Straighten tool from the Deformation toolset, as shown in Figure 2-4.**

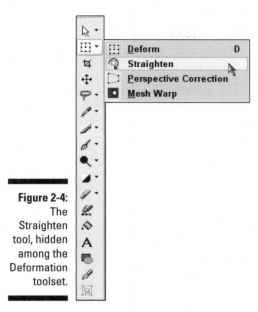

Figure 2-4:
The
Straighten
tool, hidden
among the
Deformation
toolset.

2. **Find a horizontal line in your crooked picture that should be level, but isn't.**

   In Figure 2-5, which we show you momentarily, that line is the top edge of the photo. In other images that don't have easily accessible photo edges to work with, try looking for flat horizons (oceans disappearing against the sky are usually a good bet), pictures, benches, kitchen counters, or windows.

   This tilted straight line is your way of telling the Straighten tool, "If you rotate the image until *this line* is perfectly level, the image will be fixed." So choose it carefully!

   If your image has no horizontal lines that you can use but it does have vertical ones, you can use the Straighten tool on a vertical line as well. Paint Shop Pro notices that your baseline is vertical, not horizontal, and instead rotates your image so that the baseline is perfectly north-to-south.

3. **Position the Straighten line so that it's next to your baseline.**

   A straightening line, complete with a handle on each end, appears in your picture. Move your mouse over it until the cursor becomes a four-headed arrow with a line over it, as shown in Figure 2-5.

   Click and drag the Straighten line to the tilted line you have chosen to use as a baseline.

4. Click and drag the handles on each end of the Straighten line until both of them are on the tilted line you have chosen.

When you're finished, the Straighten tool should be lying along the edge of your baseline.

If you want to have your image automatically cropped to snip out the blank spaces around the edge of the picture after it has been straightened, check the Crop Image box on the Tool Options palette (press F4 if you don't see the palette).

Double-click your image to straighten it (and crop it, if you have chosen to).

Figure 2-5:
The Straighten line, and a truly twisted image.

5. Make sure that it's straight!

For the picture shown in Figure 2-5, we chose to use the top edge of the photo as a baseline for straightening . . . and we were wrong. As you can see in Figure 2-6, we have adjusted the image so that the photo is level, but the photo itself was taken at an angle (as though it weren't embarrassing *enough*)! On the right side of the figure, William is on the level — a feat he would not manage to duplicate until years later.

Press Ctrl+Z to undo any changes. Note that when we went back and straightened the image again using the top line of the television set as a baseline, it came out much better.

Figure 2-6:
The image on the left has been adjusted so that the photo is straight, but the photo itself is crooked.

Getting Images from a Digital Camera

Paint Shop Pro can be a great tool for digital photography. First, however, you have to get your camera and your PC talking to each other. They have to connect (*interface* in geek-speak) physically and in software:

- ✔ **Physical interface:** Digital cameras physically connect to PCs in all kinds of ways. Your physical connection may be a serial port (a connector on the back of most PCs, if a modem or something else isn't already using it), a parallel (printer) port, a USB port, a FireWire port, a memory card that plugs into your computer, a floppy disk, an infrared beam, X-rays, semaphore flags, or magical auras — who knows what the camera people will come up with next? See your camera manual for details. You also probably have to set a switch on your camera to prepare it for sending images to the PC.

- ✔ **Software interface:** You also need a software interface, unless your camera stores photos on some disk or other device your PC can read. (In that circumstance, pop the floppy disk, memory stick, or whatever in the proper place in your PC, copy the files to a folder on your hard disk, and open the files in Paint Shop Pro.)

  Cameras come with the interface software they need, and to read photos from your camera, you need to install it. If the installation gives you a way to install either a Windows Image Acquisition (WIA) interface or a TWAIN interface, you're in business. If the installation program lets you, avoid installing any freebie image software (like a cheap Paint Shop Pro) that comes with the camera. If you do, the installation process may assign certain image file types to that program rather than to Paint Shop Pro. If that happens, refer to the sidebar in Chapter 1 about making Paint Shop Pro open the right file types when you double-click.

Many cameras have TWAIN-compliant software because TWAIN is a long-standing PC standard that allows every program on your computer to talk to image-acquisition devices, like cameras and scanners.

If your digital camera uses WIA, you need to follow the instructions that came with the camera. In Paint Shop Pro, choose File⇨Import⇨From Scanner or Camera to open camera files using the WIA method.

Downloading and Opening Photos

If you have on your computer more than one TWAIN device (a scanner and your camera, for example), first choose File⇨Import⇨TWAIN⇨Select Source. In the Select Source dialog box that appears, click the camera and then click Select.

To begin the downloading process, choose File⇨Import⇨TWAIN⇨Acquire. Some form of dialog box, similar to the one shown in Figure 2-7, arrives on the scene.

Figure 2-7:
Transferring one or more photos to your PC with a TWAIN-compliant camera — in this case, an Olympus D-340R.

If you have more than one TWAIN source set up (like a scanner and a camera on the same computer), choosing From Camera or Scanner starts up the scanner rather than the camera. Yes, it's irritating if you use your camera more than your scanner.

If that's the case, choose File⇨Import⇨TWAIN⇨Select Source to access your camera; a small dialog box, showing all your TWAIN-compliant devices, is displayed. Click the one that has a name something like your camera model (ours was Olympus Digital Vision 3.0 33-32) and click OK. Then choose File⇨Import⇨TWAIN⇨Acquire to start your camera's download.

As in the scanner section, we can't tell you exactly how this process happens because the interface that downloads the pictures is unique to each camera. Fortunately, most of them are similar; they present a selection of thumbnails or preview images you can flip through in some manner.

If you don't see a set of thumbnail images, you may need to hunt for a Get Previews button or menu option.

You see buttons or menu options that allow you to accomplish these common camera tasks:

- ✔ **Download photos — the whole enchilada:** Look for a Download All, Save All, or perhaps (as in the Olympus example) Select All command before you can click the Download button. *Downloading* means that your photos go directly to your PC's disk drive, as files. You don't see them in Paint Shop Pro. You then can open them in Paint Shop Pro by choosing File⇨Open, as you can any other image file (refer to Chapter 1).

- ✔ **Download selected images — the ones where your child isn't sticking out his tongue:** Browse through the thumbnails (which are sometimes also called *previews*), which you can generally do by clicking the left and right arrows under the thumbnail image, or scrolling up and down. The exposure number, date, and time appear next to the image in some cameras, and others may have an Information or Details button to display details.

  When you come to a tongue-free or otherwise desirable photo you want to download to your PC, click the image you like and then look for a Save to Disk or Download button or something similar. (You can select multiple images by holding down Ctrl while you click.) You then can open them in Paint Shop Pro by choosing File⇨Open.

- ✔ **Erase the images where your child *is* sticking out his tongue:** Browse through the thumbnails and find the offending images. Click that image and first try pressing Delete, and then look for a Delete, Erase, or Trash button. Clicking this button removes the image from your camera.

✔ **Open a particular image in Paint Shop Pro:** Browse through the thumbnails (as the preceding bullets describe) to that image. Click the image and then look for an Open button. You can also open *all* images in Paint Shop Pro if you select them all and then press Open. That choice may use so much memory, however, that Paint Shop Pro becomes sluggish. To save an open image to disk, refer to the instructions for saving a file in Chapter 1.

For most makes of digital cameras, downloading images doesn't delete them from the camera. Erasing images, however, generally does wipe them from the camera, which you want to do to clear out space for future photos.

Making E-Mail-Ready Photos

William's family *means* well. About twice a month, they send him pictures of his niece Amanda. Unfortunately, these pictures are the size of billboards and take about an hour-and-a-half to download, preventing him from doing anything else while he waits for the new picture to arrive.

He loves Amanda, but it's not worth waiting 90 minutes just to see a picture of her.

Chances are, your friends feel the same about your pictures: They want to see your little bubbeleh, but they want to see her quickly. Unfortunately, scanners and digital photos, left to their own devices, give you the biggest, the most detailed, and above all the *largest* files they can possibly produce. On the Internet, large files mean large download times — and long waits.

Shrinking Photo Download Times

Your friends never tell you that they hate waiting four hours for a picture of your newborn; they just force a smile and say "Those humongous photos were *lovely*." Be proactive and take these steps to condense your photos — and save your friendship!

1. **Crop the photo so that it shows only the important parts.**

   If Amanda is on the right side of the picture, there's no sense in showing everyone the wallpaper in the left half of the room. Cropping is ridiculously easy, and we show you how to do it in Chapter 11.

2. **Reduce the physical size of the photo.**

   Most digital cameras produce photos roughly the size of this page; the smaller the photo, the quicker it downloads. Again, this information is in Chapter 11.

3. **Reduce the quality of the image.**

   It sounds horrible — our darling Amanda, in a *low-grade image?* — but the fact is that most images can have their quality reduced by 10 or 20 percent without anyone noticing a thing — and it saves *lots* of download time. We show you how to compress photos in Chapter 17.

Capturing Images from Your PC Screen

There it is, onscreen: the exact image you need. But it's in some other program, not Paint Shop Pro. You figure that there must be some way to get it into Paint Shop Pro — after all, it's already in your computer.

You're right. Paint Shop Pro has several different ways to capture that image.

When an image appears in a window on your PC, it comes with all kinds of other stuff that is part of the program displaying the image: toolbars, status bars, a title bar, and a sushi bar, for example. Maybe you want that stuff, and maybe you don't. Paint Shop Pro helps you capture only the part of the window you really want: It's most likely an image, but if (like us) you're illustrating software, you may want to see just a toolbar from the program window or where a mouse cursor is pointing. For all these captures, use the Paint Shop Pro capture features, on the Capture menu.

Preparing to capture

To set your snare, follow these steps:

1. **Choose File⇨Import⇨Screen Capture⇨Setup from the menu bar.**

   The Capture Setup dialog box, as shown in Figure 2-8, comes to your aid.

Figure 2-8: Setting your snare for elusive Windows wildlife.

From left to right in the figure, you can see that you have three kinds of choices: what you want to capture, how you want to *trigger* (activate) the snare, and a couple of options (Include Cursor or Multiple Captures).

2. **Choose what to capture.**

Paint Shop Pro can capture five different species of Windows wildebeest. In the Capture Setup dialog box, choose one of the possibilities listed in Column 1 of Table 2-1.

Table 2-1	Using Different Types of Capture
Type of Capture	*What It Does*
Area	Captures a rectangular area you define anywhere onscreen.
Full screen	Captures the whole nine yards, the entire enchilada, the full Monty — everything onscreen.
Client area	Captures everything in a window except the title bar.
Window	Captures the application window you specify (don't use for a document window; use Object for that).
Object	Captures an application window, a document window, or any individual feature in a window, like a toolbar — a useful catchall category that works for toolbars, menu bars, scroll bars, palettes, and sometimes portions of those objects.

3. **Choose your trigger.**

You must choose a *trigger,* which is an action (such as pressing a particular key) that you take, after setup finishes, to tell Paint Shop Pro to start capturing images. Without a trigger, the capture would start immediately. All you would ever capture is Paint Shop Pro itself! In the Capture Setup dialog box (refer to Figure 2-8), you can see that you have three choices for triggering the capture. Select one of these options:

- **Right mouse click:** A right mouse click begins the capture.

- **Hot key:** From the Hot Key selection box, choose a key to serve as a trigger. You can choose any of the function keys, F1 through F12, alone or in combination with Shift, Alt, or Ctrl. F11 is initially chosen for you.

- **Delay timer:** Select this option and then enter a delay time (in seconds) in the Delay Timer box.

4. **Choose options.**

Paint Shop Pro gives you two options:

- **Capture multiple images:** If you plan to capture a series of onscreen images, select the Multiple Captures check box in the Capture Setup dialog box (refer to Figure 2-8). You then can simply snap a series of images without returning to Paint Shop Pro each time. If you're creating a tutorial for using some software, for example, you can set up Paint Shop Pro and then easily capture a screen for each step.

- **Include mouse cursor in capture:** You may want to show the mouse cursor in your screen captures to point out some feature. If so, select the Include Cursor check box in the Capture Setup dialog box (refer to Figure 2-8).

Using the Include Cursor option may not work if you're only capturing an object. You need to use your cursor to select the object, placing the cursor somewhere other than where you want it in the picture. If you're capturing a client area or window, you have to be sure that your cursor is within the captured area.

Making the capture

After you're set up to capture from the PC screen in Paint Shop Pro, you're ready to make the capture. To capture an image, follow these steps:

1. **Click the Capture Now button in the Capture Setup dialog box.**

The Capture Now command starts the capture process. (Or you can press Shift+P.) Paint Shop Pro discreetly shrinks to a button on the taskbar to get out of your way.

2. **Make any last-minute changes to the thing you want to capture.**

You have a final opportunity to adjust the appearance of the screen area that contains the image — before you trigger the capture. If you have chosen the option of capturing the mouse cursor, position the cursor now.

3. **Trigger the capture (or wait for the timer to trigger it).**

Depending on the kind of trigger you chose (refer to Step 3 in the preceding section), either right-click with your mouse, press the hot key (F11, for example), or wait for the time interval to elapse.

If you're capturing a full screen, Paint Shop Pro restores itself to full window size now. You're done and can skip the next steps. Otherwise, Paint Shop Pro waits for you to choose your capture area.

4. Choose the capture area (unless you're capturing the full screen).

How you choose the capture area depends on what kind of capture you have chosen, as shown in Table 2-2.

After you choose the capture area, the capture occurs instantly. Paint Shop Pro immediately restores itself to its original window size (unless you have chosen the multiple capture option) and displays the capture as a new image.

5. Repeat Steps 3 and 4 if you have chosen the multiple capture option.

Paint Shop Pro acquires each capture as a separate image. You don't see them because Paint Shop Pro remains minimized as a button on the taskbar. To restore Paint Shop Pro, click its button on the Windows taskbar.

Table 2-2	Pointing Out Your Quarry to Paint Shop Pro
Type of Capture	*What to Do after Triggering the Capture*
Area	Left-click once where you want one corner of the area. Then, with your mouse button released (don't drag), move your cursor diagonally to where you want the opposite corner and click again.
Full screen	Do nothing; after you trigger, Paint Shop Pro immediately restores itself to full window size.
Client area	Left-click the window you want.
Window	Left-click the window you want.
Object	A black rectangle encloses whatever object is directly under the mouse cursor. You don't have to keep that object. Move your cursor around and, when the black rectangle encloses the object you want, left-click.

For better and easier captures, read and heed these tips:

✔ Set up your screen the way you want it to look before you enable the trigger (before you press the Capture Now button or press Shift+P). If you try to make adjustments after you set the trigger, you may accidentally trigger the capture.

✔ To enhance colors — for those captured colors that come out fairly accurate, but faded, murky, or otherwise less than satisfactory — see Chapters 7 or 10.

✔ If you're capturing an image from your Web browser, use Save As or Copy rather than the Paint Shop Pro screen capture. To save an image as a file in Internet Explorer, for example, right-click the image and choose Save Picture As.

Part II
Painting the Picture

The 5th Wave   By Rich Tennant

In this part . . .

If you need to paint, spray, fill, erase, or otherwise get creative with brushes and paint, start here. Begin with paint in Chapter 3. The wild new Paint Shop Pro Materials palette goes beyond basic paint and lets you flow gradients (shadings), patterns, and textures right off your brush. Choose paint that simulates the texture of scribbling on surfaces like asphalt, brick, or wood, or apply a real wood-grain pattern. Simulate three-dimensional shading with gradient fills, or paint in patterns of neon colors.

In Chapter 4, we show you the magic of the Paint Shop Pro basic brushes and other hand tools. Discover how to get exactly the stroke and effect you want. Paint Shop Pro lets you easily control brush attributes, such as shape, softness, paint transparency or thickness, spray patterns, and evenness of flow. Even erasing can be an art in Paint Shop Pro — and erasing has never been easier, with the Paint Shop Pro 8 new Background Eraser tool, which can remove the ugly wallpaper behind Aunt Tillie without removing Aunt Tillie!

For real magic, we show you in Chapter 5 how to make images flow right off a paint brush. We introduce you to the magic of the Clone Brush tool, which is useful for seamlessly retouching photographs by brushing a duplicate of patterns, backgrounds, or other areas that already exist in a photo. We also discuss the Paint Shop Pro Picture Tubes tool, which applies a sort of spreadable clip art. Need a cloud of butterflies? Wave the Picture Tube tool.

Chapter 3

Choosing Colors, Styles, and Textures

*B*efore you go flinging your paintbrush around with wild abandon, choosing a color to fling is a good idea (unless, of course, you're one of those devil-may-care creative types). Here's where to get the inside story on the fastest and best ways to choose a color under various circumstances.

In Paint Shop Pro, however, you don't just paint with color. How boring and pedestrian! No, you paint with materials! Material, in this case, is the Paint Shop Pro way of referring to anything from plain old solid colors to textured colors, gradients (shaded areas with transitions from one color to another), or even multihued geometric patterns. Your work can look like you're rubbing chalk on concrete or spray-painting an elephant's ear or doing something else *far* more interesting than just smearing paint smoothly on paper. Any of these effects can be smeared across the page at your whim. Think of the Paint Shop Pro drawing tools as multicolored felt-tip markers with an adjustable tip. You can even save your carefully designed materials as *swatches* for future use.

In Paint Shop Pro, *material* is a catchall term that includes color, any textures you have applied to that color, and any patterns or gradients. This concept is slightly confusing because most users work with plain colors and ignore all this patterning and texturing jazz. If you're confused, whenever you see the word *material,* think *color.* It won't hurt.

All this excitement springs from the Material palette, which in Paint Shop Pro 8 hides more secrets than a black dog hides ticks. Figure 3-1 shows the palette and some of its more important features.

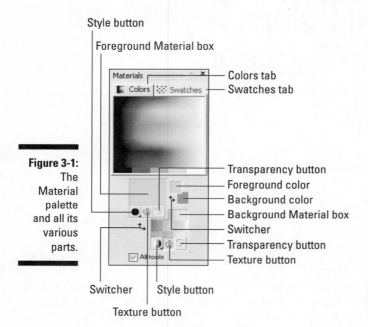

Style button
Foreground Material box
Colors tab
Swatches tab
Transparency button
Foreground color
Background color
Background Material box
Switcher
Transparency button
Texture button
Switcher
Style button
Texture button

Figure 3-1: The Material palette and all its various parts.

"Help! I just want plain, solid paint!"

Are you getting weird, patterned, or thin paint — perhaps not even in the color you chose — when you just want plain, unpatterned color? Are you getting no paint at all? The problem is that you have somehow chosen a fancier style than plain paint, chosen a texture, or requested a transparent material.

Here's how to return to the ordinary, using controls on the Materials palette:

Click the Style button (the leftmost one) just under the Foreground Material box (refer to Figure 3-1 to find these buttons) and then click the solid black dot in the drop-down panel that appears. If the Material box has a checkerboard pattern in it, click the Texture button once (the middle one under the Foreground Material box). The checkerboard pattern (indicating texture) disappears. If the Material box is grayed out with the international No slash through it, transparency is enabled; click the Transparency button (the rightmost button under the Material box) to turn transparency off. To do the same thing for your background color, repeat these steps for the Background Material box.

Ignoring the color boxes

In past versions of Paint Shop Pro, the Colors box was pretty much all that most people knew about; adding snazzy textures or patterns was handled via a dialog box that was conveniently buried underneath about 15 menus. Realizing that confusing people is a strategy that works only for Microsoft, Paint Shop Pro has moved away from the Colors box and moved toward the Material box, an all-in-one stop that allows you to change your colors, textures, and patterns in just a few clicks.

However, because too little confusion is never enough, Jasc has left the Colors box on the Material palette for those rare occasions when you would want to switch colors, but not any textures or patterns you have applied. Most people never do this, so our advice is to simply ignore these two little remnants and do all your work in the Material box — with one exception, which we get to later in this chapter.

If the Material palette isn't on your screen, press F6 or choose View⇨ Palettes⇨Materials. *Palettes* are lumps of useful tools and settings in Paint Shop Pro; the Materials palette is one of them. You can drag them around to different places in your Paint Shop Pro window; they stick *(dock)* to various edges. Here's a summary of what the various parts shown in Figure 3-1 do:

- **Colors tab:** Click with either of the mouse buttons on this area to pick up a color conveniently from the spectrum of available colors and put it in a Material box, where you can paint with it. Left-click and the color becomes the foreground (principal) color. Right-click and it becomes the background (secondary) color. As you scroll the pointer across the color panel, you see a preview of the color and three numbers (the primary colors) that define exactly what color your cursor is pointing at. These colors can be in either the RGB system, the HSL system, or HTML hexadecimal format; see Chapter 10 to understand these numbers better.

  If you see fewer colors than Figure 3-1 shows, your image has 256 colors or fewer. See "Working with 256 Colors or Fewer," later in this chapter.

- **Swatches tab:** If you create a cool material that you don't want to forget — an ochre-and-purple gradient, for example, with a torn-paper texture that would be a pain to re-create (and a pain to look at, but hey, we're not here to judge), you can save it as a swatch for future use. It works the same way as the Colors tab: Left-click a swatch and it's loaded into the Foreground Material box, which takes on all aspects of the swatch, including color, pattern, texture, and opacity. Right-click and it becomes your background material. When you first install Paint Shop Pro, it has 16 sample swatches for you to try, but you can save many more than that.

- **Foreground Material box:** This setting is the best single indicator of what you're going to paint, and it's what you look at most often. It has three buttons: Style (which controls whether your material is a plain color, gradient, or pattern), Texture, and Transparency. If none of those three buttons accomplishes what you're looking for, you can click the Material box to bring up a rather comprehensive dialog box of options. Paint Shop Pro also refers to foreground material as the *stroke* material because you use it for the line or stroke that defines shape outlines.

✔ **Background Material box:** This box works exactly like the Foreground Material box. Background materials are simply a second painting color used for either two-color operations or as a convenient second color that gets applied by tools whenever you use the right mouse button. Paint Shop Pro also refers to this material as the *fill* material because you use it to fill shape outlines.

✔ **Style button:** Choosing a color is all fine and well, but sometimes you want more than an ordinary paintbrush. You can select one of three options from this drop-down menu. Most people opt to stay with plain paint, but you can also apply a multihued pattern called a *gradient* or add a pattern called, well, a pattern (a geometric or photograph-like image). Paint Shop Pro assigns rather boring gradients and patterns to the style buttons when you first install it, but we show you how to change them later on in this chapter.

✔ **Texture button:** Clicking this button applies a kind of roughness that appears wherever you paint foreground color or style. If it's selected, as it is in this image, the Material box has a checkered pattern to it.

✔ **Transparency button:** Clicking this button instantly transforms the material so that it has no color, texture, or pattern. This button is useful sometimes when you're working with text or vector objects — but not regular paintbrushes or fills, so it's unavailable when you're working with those tools.

✔ **Switchers:** As you may have gathered from their name, switchers switch foreground and background settings. Two switchers are available: The smaller one swaps colors but keeps all patterns and textures where they were, and the larger one swaps everything. Click the switcher's two-headed arrow icon to switch.

✔ **All Tools check box:** Quite often, you just want to retouch a color in one spot, but don't want to change the materials you have already assigned to your paintbrush. Clearing this check box restricts any changes you make to the tool you're working with — change the Paint Brush tool all you like, and it doesn't affect the Fill tool in the least.

✔ **Foreground Color:** Unless you have chosen a fancier *style* than plain paint, this box shows you what you paint when you apply a tool to the canvas with the left mouse button pressed. (Paint Shop Pro also refers to this color as the *stroke* color.) This box is something of a dinosaur, and we advise you to simply ignore it; see the preceding sidebar, "Ignoring the color boxes."

✔ **Background Color:** This box shows you what color you paint when you apply a tool to the canvas with the right mouse button pressed. (Paint Shop Pro also refers to this color as the *fill* color.)

Choosing Paint

How do you choose what color to paint with? To choose any color, from screaming chartreuse to insipid indigo, just click the Paint Shop Pro palette of colors.

Or, in full and gory detail, it goes like this:

1. **Move your cursor over the Available Colors panel on the Material palette.**

   Figure 3-1 points out that area: the multi-hued box that (unless you have moved the Material palette) lives in the upper-right corner of the Paint Shop Pro window. (If you don't see the Material palette, display it by pressing the F6 key on your keyboard.) The cursor is a Dropper icon while it's over this area, to indicate that you pick up a color if you click. (If you see a bunch of tiny, colored boxes rather than a large, rainbowish blur, click the Colors tab along the upper-left side of the palette.)

   As you move the cursor, you see an enlarged sample of the color your cursor is over. The primary color values give you the exact numerical color you're using.

2. **Left-click to choose your main painting color, called the *foreground* (or *stroke*) color.**

   That color appears in both the Foreground Material box and the foreground color sample (refer to Figure 3-1).

   This color is what we sometimes call the left-mouse-button color — it's the one that appears when you use the Paint Brush, Airbrush, or Fill tool by pressing the left mouse button. It doesn't have much to do with foreground. It's just one of two colors.

3. **Right-click anywhere on the available colors area to choose a secondary color, the *background* (or *fill*) color.**

   See the following sidebar "Do you need a background color?" to figure out whether you need or want a secondary color; if the answer is No, you can skip this step. If you do choose a background color, it appears in the Background Material box, as shown in Figure 3-1. The term *Background color*, like Foreground color, is kind of a misnomer because it doesn't have much to do with the background of your image. It just defines a second, or alternative, color you can work with.

Do you need a background color?

How do you know whether you need or want a secondary color? It depends on the tool you're using and how you intend to use it:

✔ If you want to be able to switch quickly between painting with one color and another, you can paint foreground color with the left mouse button on many tools and background color with the right mouse button.

✔ The Shapes tools require a background color if you want solid shapes. If you plan to draw filled-in squares (as opposed to just the outline of a square), you need to choose a background color to fill the shape in with.

✔ If you're using the Eraser tool, you can choose what the eraser leaves behind: a transparent streak (useful if you're using layers) or the background color.

✔ If you're using a tool that involves two colors — for example, the Color Replacer tool to replace one color with another — you need a second color, and the background color is that second color. Background color also provides the fill of filled shapes and text.

Check to make sure that the Foreground Material box (or Background Material box, if that's what you chose) displays the color you chose. If not, the palette is set up to paint patterns, which have their own colors. Click the Style button under the Foreground (or Background) Material box and then click the solid dot (for solid paint) or the striped dot (for gradient paint). See the upcoming section "Working with Style: Beyond Plain Paint" for more information about gradients and patterns and transparency. Or, for plain paint, see the earlier sidebar "Help! I just want plain, solid paint!"

Here are a couple of tips for choosing and using colors:

✔ **To swap the background and foreground colors, click the Material Switcher (the larger double-headed arrow), as shown in Figure 3-1.** The background color becomes the foreground color and vice versa. Just to make things confusing, you can choose to click the smaller button, which swaps colors but not any textures or gradients. Our advice: Unless you have a good reason to do otherwise, *always click the big arrow.*

✔ **To get pure black, white, red, yellow, or other "just plain" colors, use the Color Picker. (We describe this tool in the following section.)** You can also find pure black and white along the bottom of the Colors panel; pure black is on the left, and pure white is on the right.

Choosing a basic color or a recently used pattern

You may want to use your everyday, smiley-face yellow — but locating exactly that same color in the Available Colors area is often next to impos-sible: Your eyes and fingers can't be that precise. Likewise, you may have developed a cool gradient that slid from cool blue to a sea green, but do you think that you can do that again?

Fortunately, Paint Shop Pro gives you another way to choose a recently used material: the Recent Materials dialog box. The Recent Materials dialog box also gives you basic black, totally white, and a variety of other basic colors you can return to again and again.

Here's how to get this helpful box of recently used materials and basic colors:

1. ***Right*-click the Foreground Material or Background Material box, whichever one you want to set.**

   The Recent Materials dialog box appears, as Figure 3-2 shows. The ten most recent materials you have used appear along the top two rows; ten standard colors appear along the bottom rows (including black, white, and two shades of gray). If the colors have circles with slashes, you're using a palette image, and those colors aren't available. See Chapter 10 for a discussion of increasing the number of colors.

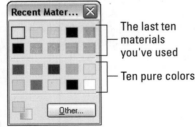

The last ten materials you've used

Ten pure colors

Figure 3-2:
The Recent Materials box.

Colors in the bottom two basic-color rows are *pure* colors — except for the grays — that is, they are the reddest red, bluest blue, magenta-est magenta, and so on.

Technically speaking, the top row contains the pure red, green, and blue primary colors of radiant light. The second row contains the pure cyan, magenta, and yellow primary colors of printed ink.

2. **Click any color or material to choose it (or press the Esc key if you see nothing you like).**

   The Recent Materials dialog box disappears immediately. The color you clicked is now chosen and appears in the color sample on the Materials palette.

   You may think that right-clicking in the Recent Materials dialog box would choose the background color, as it does on the Materials palette. You would be wrong. Right-clicking does nothing here.

To get shades of color other than the ones you see in the Recent Materials dialog box, click the Other button. This button takes you to the Material dialog box. See the upcoming section "Choosing a Color More Precisely" for details.

Choosing a recently used color

Choosing that same fantastic shade of fluorescent orange you may have already used involves the same problems as selecting a pure color. We tell you earlier in this chapter that most of the time you should ignore the Color boxes except for one instance — and here it is:

1. *Right*-click the Foreground or Background Color box — whichever one you want to set.

   The Recent Colors dialog box appears, as Figure 3-3 shows. The ten most recent colors you have used are in the top two rows of the dialog box, and the ten pure colors — exactly the same colors from the Recent Material box — are in the bottom two rows. If the colors have circles with slashes, you're using a palette image, and those colors aren't available. See Chapter 10 for a discussion of increasing the number of colors.

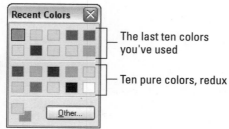

Figure 3-3:
The Recent
Colors box.

The last ten colors you've used

Ten pure colors, redux

2. **Click any color to choose it (or press the Esc key if you see nothing you like).**

   The Recent Colors dialog box disappears immediately. The color you clicked is now chosen and appears in the color sample in both the Color and Material boxes. Again, right-clicking does nothing here.

Choosing paint for each tool separately or all tools together

In real life, if you paint with your brush dipped in red paint and then switch to spray-painting with a can of green paint, your brush remains red. It doesn't switch to green. Of course, in real life you can't insert your dog into a picture of Elvis and then spray-paint him purple, so you have to assume that Paint Shop Pro is a little stranger than the world outside your door.

Unless you tell it otherwise, Paint Shop Pro applies the same style and texture to all the tools you're using; if you use the Spray Paint tool with red paint and a rough texture and then switch to the Paint Brush tool, the paintbrush is red with a rough texture. You can, however, choose to change this rather odd behavior by unchecking the All Tools box on the Material palette. Checking All Tools applies your current paint choice to all tools; deselecting All Tools means that you choose paint individually for each tool.

Choosing a color from your picture

Sometimes, the easiest way to choose a color is to pick up that color from your picture. You have two ways to pick up color. Choose the one that makes your life easier:

✔ When using any tool that applies paint (for example, the Paint Brush tool), hold down the Ctrl button and the cursor turns into a Dropper icon. Left-click to pick up foreground color, and right-click for background color.

✔ On the Tools toolbar, click the Dropper tool icon, as shown in the margin. (If you see no Dropper icon, you may have been using the Color Replacer tool — click the Color Replacer tool and select the Dropper icon from the drop-down menu.) The cursor turns into a Dropper icon. Left-click to pick up foreground color, and right-click for background color.

If you have deselected the All Tools check box, colors you select for one tool don't apply to other tools.

Choosing a Color More Precisely

Choosing a color from the Material palette's Available Colors area is all well and good, but if you're working with higher-quality color images, it's not a precise way to go. The area is tiny, and as many as 16.7 million colors may be squished together in that area. (If your image has 256 or fewer colors, you can discern individual color boxes in the Available Colors area.)

Creating shadows and highlights

For brushing highlights or shadows onto an object, you often want a color that's the same hue as an existing one — just a little lighter or darker. Pick up the existing color from your picture, making it the foreground color by clicking it with the Dropper tool.

Click the Foreground Material swatch to bring up the Material dialog box and then click the Color tab, if it isn't already selected. In the Saturation/Lightness box, drag the tiny circle up to make a shadow color, or down to make a highlight color.

To choose a color more precisely, *left*-click the Material box (foreground or background, whichever one you want to set). (If the Style button is in Gradient or Pattern mode, their respective dialog boxes are displayed. Don't worry — a row of tabs is at the top. In that case, click the Color tab.)

The amazingly colorful Material dialog box, as shown in Figure 3-4, appears. (What's that? You say that it looks funny and has rows of tiny boxes where the color wheel and Saturation/Lightness box should be? In that event, you're working with an image that has fewer than 32,000 colors. See the upcoming section "Working with 256 Colors or Fewer.")

Precise color using the color wheel

The callouts shown in Figure 3-4 give you the simplest way to be more precise. You need to follow only three steps:

1. **Drag the little circle on the color wheel to the basic hue you want.**

   Hue has a technical meaning, but forget about that for now. Hue means basic color, apart from that color's exact shade.

   The square in the middle of the circle turns to your chosen hue, showing you all kinds of variations in shade — or, more precisely, in color intensity (called *saturation*) and lightness. The square is the Saturation/Lightness box.

2. **Drag the little circle on the square to the precise shade you want.**

   The Current swatch in the lower-right corner of the dialog box shows exactly what color you're choosing, overlaid with any textures you have selected. (The Previous swatch shows the foreground or background color.)

Drag this circle up to make your color darker or down to make it lighter. Drag the circle left to make your color grayer, or right to make it more intense (saturated).

3. Click OK.

Your foreground or background color has been changed.

Additional shades of basic colors

The Color tab in the Material dialog box (as shown in Figure 3-4) is also home to 48 basic colors. These colors are shades of 6 primary colors (red, yellow, green, cyan, blue, and magenta) plus 6 shades of gray (including white and black).

Open the Color dialog box as usual by clicking either the Foreground Material box or the Background Material box and selecting the Color tab.

Forty-eight basic colors

Saturation/Lightness box
Color wheel

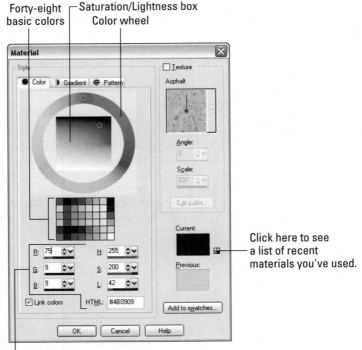

Figure 3-4:
It's time to play Wheel . . . of . . . Colors, starring the color wheel and the Saturation/ Lightness box. Vanna White, eat your heart out.

Click here to see a list of recent materials you've used.

RGB, HSL, and HTML values

Choose a basic color by clicking it in the Basic Colors area, in the middle-left corner of the dialog box. Click OK and your foreground or background color is changed to your chosen color.

Precise color adjustments — by the numbers

Just as saying "1 foot, 3 inches" is much more precise than saying "a little bigger than my shoe," choosing a color by using numbers is much more precise than clicking it on a palette or color wheel. But, how can you do color by the numbers?

As it turns out, you can specify any color by using just three values. Adjusting these values independently gives you more control. For example, you can change just the *lightness* of a color and be certain that you haven't changed the *hue*.

Chapter 10 gives you more detail about how these values relate to colors. For now, knowing that you can set these three values in the Material dialog box can help you make more precise adjustments, if you need them.

Just as with specifying distance, where you can use either the English (feet, inches) or metric (meters) systems, you can use one of three alternative systems to specify colors: Hue/Saturation/Lightness (HSL to its friends) or Red/Green/Blue (known as RGB), or HTML.

The Color tab in the Material dialog box, as shown in Figure 3-4, shows the three values that describe your chosen color in all three systems (RGB, HSL, and HTML). The area displays values for Red, Green, and Blue (on the left) and Hue, Saturation, and Lightness (on the right). When you choose a new color using any control in this dialog box, those numbers change. In value, the numbers range from 0 to 255. An optional visual control appears when you click and hold the down arrow at the far right end of a value box (see Figure 3-5).

Figure 3-5:
Numerically
precise.

To adjust a color precisely, you can edit the numbers in either the RGB or HSL value boxes (your choice). For example, do you want more red? Use the RGB controls and increase the value in the Red box. More yellow? To use the RGB controls, you would have to know that red and green make yellow in the RGB system (perhaps having read Chapter 10) and then increase the values in Red and Green (perhaps decreasing the value in Blue).

The HTML value is a numerical representation of the three RGB values, rendered into one hexadecimal code that Web browsers like Internet Explorer can understand. You should never try to adjust a color using the HTML value. If you're designing for the Web, though, the only way to tell a browser that a sidebar should be precisely *this* shade of red is to use hexadecimals. If you're a Web designer, you know that you can use the HTML value within the color attributes of HTML; if you're not, you can safely ignore this section and go in peace.

Using the HSL values is sometimes a more intuitive alternative to using the RGB values. HSL values are connected to the controls on the color wheel and the Saturation/Lightness box. Here's how they work:

- **Hue:** The Hue value connects to your chosen position on the Color wheel, beginning at zero at the top (red) and increasing as you go around the circle counterclockwise. As you increase the number, the hue passes through red, yellow, green, cyan, blue, violet, and magenta.

- **Saturation:** The Saturation value connects to horizontal motion in the Saturation/Lightness box: left (for a lower value) or right (for a higher value). Use a higher value for a more intense (saturated) color.

- **Lightness:** The Lightness value connects to vertical motion in the Saturation/Lightness box: up (for a lower value) or down (for a higher value). Use a higher value for a lighter color.

As with any value box in a Windows program, you can change the values by either typing new numbers or clicking the tiny up and down arrows to gradually increase or decrease the value.

A more visual way to fiddle with the RGB or HSL values is to click the down arrow at the far right end of any of the RGB or HSL value boxes. As Figure 3-5 shows, a multicolored bar appears, showing the range of colors you can achieve by dragging left or right. Holding the mouse button down, drag left or right to choose a color. Release the button when you're done.

Working with 256 Colors or Fewer

Images that have 256 colors or fewer are *palette* images: They use only a specific set of colors — the image's palette of available colors. You can change any of those colors individually, but you can't have any more colors than the palette size (color depth) allows. (See Chapter 10 for ways to change color depth.)

When you work with a palette image, the Available Colors area of the Color palette shows you the palette. You can choose any of those colors by clicking the color. The squares are tiny, however, and colors aren't always in a useful order.

To choose colors from larger squares or see them in a more useful order, click one of the Material boxes and select the Color tab from the Material dialog box. You see a somewhat larger view of the palette. To reorder the colors, click the Sort Order drop-down list box, choosing either Palette Order (an arbitrary, numbered order), By Luminance (ordered from light to dark), or By Hue (ordered by color). To choose a color, click it; then click OK.

To change any color on the image's palette, choose Image⇨Palette⇨ Edit Palette. The Edit Palette dialog box that appears is identical to the Select Color from Palette dialog box, with one exception: If you double-click any color on the palette, the Color tab in the Material dialog box is displayed. See the section "Choosing a Color More Precisely," earlier in this chapter, for instructions on choosing a color in this dialog box.

Working with Style: Beyond Plain Paint

In Paint Shop Pro 8, painting in a single, flat color is just the simplest of three painting modes called *styles*. (Whether or not you can use the other two kinds of styles depends on which tool you're using.) Those styles, controlled by the Style button on the Materials palette, deliver these effects:

- ✔ **Solid color:** Plain old color
- ✔ **Gradient:** A cool multihued shading
- ✔ **Pattern:** A seamless photographic-quality surface, like wood grain or gravel, or repeated images of your own design

After you choose a style and it's displayed in the Material box, you can choose from a cool variety of shades and patterns by simply clicking the swatch. The details are in the following sections.

Choosing a style

To choose a style, click the Style button (underneath the appropriate Foreground or Background Material box). Figure 3-6 shows the result.

A tiny menu flies out, displaying icons for the three styles (color, gradient, and pattern, in order). Any icons that are grayed out aren't available in your chosen tool. To choose a style of painting, click the appropriate icon as described in these bullets:

- ✓ **Color style (solid circle icon):** The Material box displays just a solid color: your chosen foreground or background color.

- ✓ **Gradient style (Shaded icon):** The Material box displays the chosen gradient. To choose a different gradient, click the Material box to access a gallery of gradients; see the following section for details.

- ✓ **Pattern style (Waffle icon):** The Material box displays the chosen pattern. To choose a pattern, click the Material box to access a gallery of patterns; see "Choosing and making patterns," later in this chapter, for details.

Figure 3-6:
Clicking
the Style
button gives
you three
choices:
plain paint,
gradient
paint, or a
pattern.
Click one
to choose
that style.

Pattern

Gradient paint

Plain paint

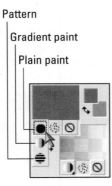

Choosing gradients

After your chosen (foreground or background) Material box shows a gradient style (refer to the list in the preceding section for instructions), click the Material box to choose a different gradient. The Gradient tab in the Material dialog box appears, as shown in Figure 3-7.

Here's what to do:

1. **Choose a gradient style by clicking one of the buttons in the Style area that appears on the left side of the Gradient dialog box (See Figure 3-7).**

   Each button depicts a different kind of gradient: from side to side, from center to edges in a rectangular or circular fashion, or proceeding radially around in a circle. The Preview box on the left then displays a gradient in your chosen style.

2. **Click the down-arrow button to the right of the Preview box and choose from the ultrafabulous gallery of gradients that appears.**

   The colors of all choices are prechosen, except for those that use the terms foreground and background. Those choices make use of whatever foreground or background colors are current at the time you paint with this gradient.

3. **Customize the angle or center of the gradient by dragging the control in the Preview window.**

   Gradients in the linear style (linear is the leftmost button in the Style column) have an angle setting. In the Preview window, drag the gadget that looks like the hand on a clock to set the angle.

   Gradients in other styles have a center point. In the Preview window, drag the crosshairs to set the center point.

4. **Make the gradient pattern repeat several times if you want.**

   Increase the number in the Repeats value box.

5. **Click OK.**

   Your chosen gradient appears in the Material box of your choosing (Foreground or Background).

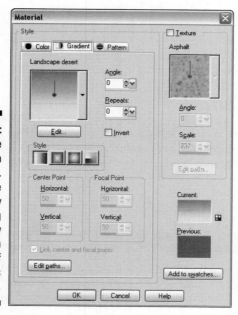

Figure 3-7:
Making the grade with gradients. Click the down arrow adjoining the Preview box to open a gallery of gradients you can use.

Creating gradients in your choice of colors is easy, although not many patterns are available for that purpose. Choose a foreground or background color or both as the one or two colors for your gradient. In the gradient gallery, choose any gradient you like that uses the term foreground or background.

Creating your own gradient patterns is possible, as is altering the existing ones, but — wow! It's definitely not a *For Dummies* kind of project. If you want to fool around with the controls, click the Edit button on the Gradient tab in the Material dialog box to access the Gradient Editor dialog box. Whoa! Have fun; try dragging the little pointers around, and good luck.

Painting with gradients

Gradients fill a painted area with a series of colors. When you paint with a gradient using the Text, Draw, or Preset Shapes tools, or fill with a selection using the Flood Fill tool, Paint Shop Pro scales the gradient to fit within the object you have created or area you have selected. For example, to apply a sunset-like gradient from blue to orange to the sky in your photo, select the sky and use the Flood Fill tool. Paint Shop Pro ensures that the full range of colors (blue to orange) fills the sky area. Or, if you create text and use a gradient style, the text displays the full range of colors.

If you paint with the Paint Brush or Air Brush tool, however, the gradient is scaled to the *entire image*. If you paint with a sunset-like blue-to-orange gradient, anything painted near the top of the image is blue and anything near the bottom is orange.

Choosing and making patterns

Patterns are interesting surface images, like brick or wood, or other more exotic or creative patterns not found in nature. Their colors are fixed, like those in a photograph, and are unaffected by your choice of foreground or background color. The patterns that come with Paint Shop Pro are *seamless,* which means that they can maintain an unbroken pattern, filling any area without appearing like tiles (with distinct edges). The process of choosing a pattern is much like choosing a gradient.

With your chosen material (foreground or background), click the box and select the Pattern tab in the dialog box that appears. The Pattern tab slightly resembles the Gradient tab shown in Figure 3-7, but it's not as complicated.

1. **Click the down-arrow button to the right of the Preview box and choose from the boffo gallery of patterns that appears.**

   The preview window shows your choice.

2. **Customize the angle of the pattern by dragging the clock-hand Angle control to point in any direction.**

3. **Click OK.**

   Your chosen pattern appears in the Material box.

To apply a pattern to an existing image, try the Sculpture effect, setting its Depth control to 1. We describe artistic effects and how to use them in Chapter 8.

Applying a Texture

Textures give a result like rubbing chalk on concrete, or like rubbing a pencil on paper that is placed over a coin or another raised surface. Paint Shop Pro supplies a variety of textures, such as concrete, construction paper, and bricks. When you use one, anything you do with the Paint Brush, Erase, Airbrush, Fill, Text, Draw, or Preset Shapes tools displays that texture. Textures don't change your choice of color. Textures do work with solid color, gradients, or patterns — that is, with any material.

You can apply texture to either the foreground material, the background material, or both; you can turn textures on or off by either clicking the texture button on the Material palette or using the Material dialog box that pops up whenever you click the Material box. Texture is normally turned off (disabled). To use a texture, follow these steps:

1. **On the Material palette, click the Foreground Material box or Background Material box.**

   Figure 3-8 shows the dialog box that appears — and regardless of whether the Material dialog box is asking for color, gradient, or pattern, the texture information is always on the right side.

2. **If the Texture check box isn't checked, check it.**

   Or, alternatively, if you don't want texture right now, uncheck it.

3. **Click the down-arrow button to the right of the texture sample.**

   A gallery of textures appears, as Figure 3-9 shows. Scroll down the gallery to find a texture you like.

Figure 3-8:
The Texture
controls,
shown here,
are always
on the right
side of the
Material
dialog box.

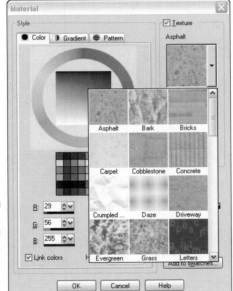

Figure 3-9:
A gallery of
textures to
choose
from.

4. **Click the texture you want in the gallery.**

   The gallery disappears and the sample area of the Texture dialog box shows your chosen texture.

5. **Customize the angle or scale of the texture by dragging the controls in the Preview window.**

   Textures have an angle setting that allows you to spin the setting around to point in any direction you want the textures to face. In the Preview window, drag the gadget that looks like the hand on a clock to set the angle.

You can also make the texture larger or smaller by typing different percentages in the Scale box; you can shrink the texture to a tiny 10 percent of its normal size or swell it to a massive 250 percent.

6. **Click OK in the Material dialog box.**

   The Material box you originally clicked displays your chosen texture, laid over the top of any colors, gradients, or patterns you have selected.

Now, anything you create or erase appears textured.

Paint Shop Pro remembers the last texture you used — so even if you stop using a texture, all you have to do click the appropriate Material box to bring up this dialog box again, and then click the check box to reenable it.

To apply a texture to an existing image, use the Texture effect we describe in Chapter 8.

Storing Custom Materials to Use Again

After you have done all this texturing and gradienting and coloring, sometimes you don't want to have to re-create it all again the next day. The Swatches tab in the Material dialog box also provides a place to store swatches of material to save the colors and patterns you want to use repeatedly.

A *material* is a combination of a color and any effects, like textures or patterns, that you have applied to them. It's still a material even if you *haven't* applied any textures or patterns to the color.

To save a material, follow these steps:

1. **Click the Material box of the material you want to save.**

2. **Click the Add to Swatches button in the Material dialog box.**

   This step displays a dialog box in which you're asked to name your colorful creation. Name it as you like, and then click OK.

   Your material is now stored on the Swatches tab, ready to be accessed whenever you want. Click OK if you're done using the Material dialog box.

Using a Stored Material

This task is so easy that you can do it in two clicks. Of course, if you have a number of swatches, sorting through them all can be cumbersome.

1. **Select the Swatches tab on the Materials palette, as shown in Figure 3-10.**

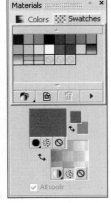

Figure 3-10: Swatch this space for further details! The Swatches tab.

2. **If you need to narrow the number of available swatches in order to find one, left-click the View button of the Swatches tab and hold the button down.**

   A drop-down menu appears, where you can choose one of four options: all swatches, colors only, gradients only, or patterns only. Choosing one hides all others until you change the view.

   To find out more about each swatch, hover the cursor over the swatch; a small, informational pop-up message appears, giving you the name of the swatch in question, the RGB numbers, the types of textures in the swatch, and the names of the gradients and patterns used.

3. **Click the swatch you want to use.**

   Left-click it if you want it to be in the Foreground Material box, right-click if you want it to be in the Background Material box. Whatever tool you use next is now loaded up with that swatch's material.

Deleting a Stored Material

Deleting a swatch is *so* easy that it's scandalous we're getting paid to tell you how to do it (don't worry — writing the rest of this chapter was darned hard work):

1. **Select the swatch you want to delete.**

   Remember that you can sort through the swatches if you need to hunt one down, as discussed in the preceding section.

2. **Click the Delete button on the Swatches tab.**

Texture thins your paint

When you use texture, paint goes on thin (with low opacity) with each click or stroke. Make repeated strokes or scribble with your paint tool to build up the thickness.

Likewise for the eraser: Only a thin layer of paint comes off with each pass. Disable Texture and, on the Tool Options palette, set Opacity to 100 to erase fully in a single stroke.

When you use texture with the Fill tool, make repeated clicks if you need to increase the opacity.

Chapter 4

Painting, Spraying, and Filling

* * *

* * *

Whether you paint like Rembrandt or like Phil (the guy who paints Dave's house), Paint Shop Pro can help you do your thing. You can use a brush, a sprayer, or an eraser or simply pour the paint on. Use different sizes and shapes of brush. Use paint, chalk, markers, or even different kinds of paper. Paint Shop Pro can do nearly anything you can do with real artist's media. (Okay, body painting loses something in the translation.)

We talk about fundamentals of painting, spraying, and filling in this chapter, including basic tool options, such as brush size, that apply to many other tools. Paint Shop Pro has other features we cover in other chapters of this book. For example, Paint Shop Pro draws as well as paints. Its drawing features mimic tasks you can do with a pen or pencil, using a straightedge or template of basic shapes. We discuss those tools in Chapter 15.

Paint Shop Pro also has fancy painting tools for a job that only a computer (or perhaps a character in a cartoon) can do, such as paint with pictures that flow right off your brush or paint a copy of one part of the image onto another part. We discuss these special tools in Chapter 5.

As with most jobs you do in Paint Shop Pro, painting affects only the active layer and only the selected area. If it appears that a painting or retouching tool isn't working, make sure that you're on the right layer and working within a selected area (or clear the selection by pressing Ctrl+D). If you don't use more than one layer or don't have any current selection, don't worry about those restrictions. Also, remember that by pressing Ctrl+Z, you can undo any painting or erasing.

Choosing the Tool for the Job

Figure 4-1 shows the Paint Shop Pro Tools toolbar. The toolbar is normally on the left side of your Paint Shop Pro window, but you can drag it elsewhere — to the top, the right side, the bottom, or even a free-floating toolbar hanging about in the middle of the screen! Left-click the small horizontal row of slashes just above the Pan icon and hold down the mouse button; the toolbar is suddenly surrounded by a large, thick line to indicate that it's ready to go. Drag it to wherever you want and then let go. You can double-click the title bar to put it back in place, anchoring it to the side.

Figure 4-1:
The Tools
toolbar.

Choose your tool (the Paint Brush tool, for example), by clicking the small down arrow next to the toolset and then selecting its icon from its toolset menu. Your cursor then *becomes* that tool (it displays that tool's icon) whenever the cursor is over your image.

Throughout the rest of this chapter, we give you the details, but here are the jobs you can do with each tool and the simplest description of how each one works:

The Brush toolset

Take a look at the Brush toolset in Figure 4-2, which you rapidly become familiar with:

- **Paint Brush:** Click the Paint Brush tool, click a color on the Material box, and then click or drag your image to paint.
- **Airbrush:** Click the Airbrush tool, click a color on the Material box, and then click or drag the image to mimic the effect of a spray can or airbrush.
- **Warp Brush:** Click the Warp Brush tool and then drag it across your image to smear it like a finger painting or stretch it like it's taffy.

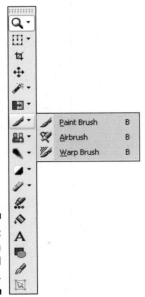

Figure 4-2:
The Brush
toolset, in all
its glory.

Don't forget textures, gradients, and patterns

In Paint Shop Pro, if you can paint it with a color, you can apply a texture to it. Textures apply your chosen color as though you were rubbing on a surface of some kind, such as asphalt pavement. To texturize a color, click the Material box (the one with the color in it) to display the Material dialog box, and then check the Texture box in the upper-right corner and select a texture from the drop-down menu. To remove a texture from a color, click the texture button underneath the box — it's the middle button, the sort of grainy one. Visit Chapter 3 for help.

You can also apply gradients and patterns with any tool that applies paint. These special shadings and images are determined by the Style button underneath the Material box. Again, refer to Chapter 3 for instructions.

The Eraser toolset

The Eraser toolset, as shown in Figure 4-3, conveniently eradicates all the ugly portions of your image:

- ✔ **Eraser tool:** Click the Eraser tool and drag across the image to erase.

- ✔ **Background Eraser:** Click the Eraser tool on the background of the image you want to see gone, hold the tool down for two seconds, and then drag it slowly across the image to erase.

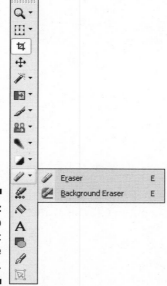

Figure 4-3: How not to be seen: The Erase toolset.

The Flood Fill tool

 To fill an area with a solid color or a fade, click the Flood Fill tool, click a color on the Material box, and then click within a selection area or an area of a particular color to fill that area.

The Color Selection toolset

Oh, we show you the Color Selection toolset in Figure 4-4, but the only thing you care about in this chapter is the Color Replacer tool.

To replace a color, click the Color Replacer tool, choose the color to replace and the replacement color, and then drag or double-click the image.

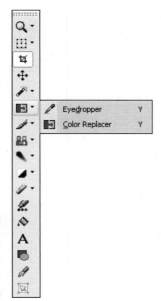

Figure 4-4:
The Color
Selection
toolset.

Using Basic Artist's Tools: Paint Brush, Airbrush, and Eraser

Using the Paint Brush, Airbrush, and Eraser tools is much like using real paint, paper, and erasers. Okay, okay — you would never use an eraser on *paint* in real life, but you get the idea.

Painting a straight line

Can't draw a straight line? Paint Shop Pro comes to your rescue. The starting point of the line is the last place you clicked, or wherever your last brush stroke ended.

To create a straight line from that point, hold down the Shift key and click where you want the line to end. This trick works with all the tools from the Brush toolset (Paint Brush, Airbrush, Warp Brush) and with the Eraser tool.

In Paint Shop Pro, however, you don't simply paint a color — you paint a material. A *material* is the combination of a color and any patterns, gradients, or textures that you have added onto it. As we advise in Chapter 3, whenever you see the word *material,* you can think *color* — but if you want more detail, Chapter 3 tells you how to put exactly what you want in the Material box.

Like most Paint Shop Pro tools and commands, the Paint Brush, Airbrush, and Eraser tools do their thing on the active layer of your image. If they don't seem to be working correctly or are grayed out, you may be on the wrong layer. See Chapter 14 for more information about layers.

Painting with the Paint Brush or Airbrush tool

The Paint Brush tool, like a real paintbrush, paints a spot of paint when you click it on your image or a line when you drag it. The Airbrush works similarly, but like a can of spray paint, it puts down a speckly spot or line that gets denser as you hold the button down.

The Airbrush tool paints speckly and the Paint Brush tool paints solid for a reason: Jasc initially gives the two tools different density settings on the Tool Options palette. You could easily change their density settings and make the Paint Brush tool paint speckly or the Airbrush tool paint solid. The real difference between the tools is that if you pause the Airbrush tool or move it slowly while keeping the mouse button pressed, paint continues to fill in the speckles. As a result, you increase the paint density just as you can with real spray paint. Not so with the Paint Brush tool: You would have to click repeatedly to get that effect.

Otherwise, the two tools work similarly. Here's how to paint with the Paint Brush or Airbrush (spray can) tools:

1. **Select the Paint Brush or Airbrush tool from the Brush toolset.**

2. **Inspect the Foreground Material box to make sure that it shows the colors you want to paint with.**

   If you want a pattern, gradient, or texture applied to that color, make sure that the appropriate Style and Texture buttons are selected.

   See Chapter 3 for more information about choosing colors, styles, and textures.

   If you can't paint with anything and a small international No sign with a slash cuts through the box, you may have accidentally set your color to Transparent. To undo this setting, click the small button directly underneath the Material box — the one that has the small No slash on it.

3. **Change the options for your brush on the Tool Options palette, if you want.**

   If the industry standard Paint Shop Pro brush doesn't tickle your fancy, here's where you get to change the kind of brush you paint with; you can make it a tiny, crisp square or a ghostly, rocket ship-shaped brush or a watercolorish schmearer. We go over this technique in the next section, but feel free to experiment. It's fun! (If you don't see a Tool Options palette along the top of your image, press F4 on your keyboard.)

4. **Drag on your image (or click to make just a single spot).**

   As you drag or click with the left mouse button, you apply whatever material you have selected in the Foreground Material box. (To apply the background material, click or drag with the *right* mouse button.)

   If you're using the Airbrush tool, you can keep the cursor in one place and hold down the mouse button. The paint density gradually builds up.

If the spot or stroke doesn't look right, press Ctrl+Z (or click the Undo button on the toolbar) to undo it; you may need to use the Tool Options palette to change the brush features. See the upcoming section, "Controlling Strokes, Sizes, Shapes, and Spatters: Tool Options," for details on changing appearances.

Erasing with the Eraser tool

Erasing works a bit differently on different layers of your image:

✔ If you erase on the background layer, you *apply* whatever material is in the Background Material box! (If your image began its life with a transparent background, which isn't usual, the erased area becomes transparent instead.)

> ✔ If you erase on any layer other than the background layer, the erased area becomes transparent. If the background texture box shows a texture, you get textured transparency! Style settings don't matter.

Here's how to erase:

1. **Click the Eraser tool, as shown in the margin.**

2. **Check the Background Material box to make sure that its style, color, and texture (if any) are what you want to leave behind as you erase.**

   If the current selections in those boxes aren't what you want to leave behind, see Chapter 3 to find out how to change them. For unpatterned, untextured erasing, set the Background style to a solid color (using the Paintbrush icon) and deselect the Background texture button.

3. **Drag on your image to erase, or click to erase a single spot.**

   Drag with the *right* mouse button pressed if you want to leave behind *Foreground* style and texture.

If the size, shape, and density (speckliness) of your eraser aren't what you want, press Ctrl+Z (or click the Undo button on the toolbar) to undo; see the section "Controlling Strokes, Sizes, Shapes, and Spatters: Tool Options," a little later in this chapter.

Erasing backdrops with the Background Eraser tool

A common problem in any Paint Shop Pro project is erasing specific areas; for example, you want to erase an ugly wallpaper print — but not Cousin Charlie, who's standing in front of it. You *could* carefully erase that ghastly wallpaper, pixel by pixel. Not only is that method incredibly time-consuming, though, but also one slip of the wrist and you have accidentally removed his left elbow.

The incredibly handy Paint Shop Pro Background Eraser tool makes this process easy by doing some complex calculations to determine what is Charlie and what is the background *behind* Charlie and then automatically erasing that background. (You can also select *around* Charlie to make normal erasing easier; we get into this topic in Chapter 12.)

For example, in Figure 4-5, erasing the jagged edge between the rocks and the Alaskan sea would have been a huge deal in previous versions of Paint Shop Pro. Thanks to the miraculous Background Eraser, though, it was all done in one clean sweep!

Figure 4-5:
If the
mountain
will not
come to
Mohammed,
erase that
sucker!

Just to confuse you, Paint Shop Pro calls this tool the Background Eraser, even though it has nothing to do with the Background Material box, as shown in Chapter 3. Whereas *background* in every other aspect of Paint Shop Pro means "The secondary color that's used to fill the middle of a shape," here it means what most people think it does: the stuff behind the interesting things in a picture. Why they didn't call it something like the Erase to Edge tool in order to keep their terminology consistent is beyond us.

Here's how to do it:

1. **Click the Background Eraser tool, as shown in the margin.**

2. **Change settings on the Tool Options palette if you need to fine-tune the way the eraser erases (press F4 if you don't see the palette).**

   Mostly, the options that Paint Shop Pro picks work pretty darned well, but sometimes you may need to tweak them. Paint Shop Pro has the usual array of Brush options — which we get to in a bit — but it also has several options specific to the Background Eraser. Just in case, here they are:

   Sampling

   Continuous: The Background Eraser continually checks the image to discern a difference between the foreground and the background. This setting generally provides the best results.

   Once: The image is checked only once, where you first clicked. Generally, this setting does very little erasing.

   Foreswatch and *Backswatch:* The Background Eraser attempts to erase colors that are similar to what is in the Foreground or Background Material box, respectively. Use this setting if what you want to erase is one color and the Continuous setting isn't getting it right.

   Limits

   Contiguous: Paint Shop Pro erases only areas that are within what it considers to be the background, removing up to the edge of Cousin Charlie.

Discontiguous: The tool erases everywhere, so if a little bit of the wallpaper's color is on Charlie's shirt, it may well erase that too.

Find Edge: The tool removes the border between what it considers the background and the foreground, erasing a thin line between Charlie and the wallpaper.

Sharpness

Low values produce a fuzzy line between the background and Cousin Charlie; high values create a crisp, sharp line. (Low values in the 40s look more natural.)

Auto Tolerance

If you're familiar with the Magic Wand tool, the Background Eraser works much the same way. You can clear this check box to set your tolerance manually; see Chapter 12 for details.

3. **Click a section of the area you want erased, and hold the mouse button down for one second.**

   In our example, you would want to click that ugly wallpaper. Holding the button down for a second or two gives Paint Shop Pro time to do the calculations to figure out what wallpaper looks like so that it can erase it.

4. **Drag on your image slowly across the edge in question.**

   Dragging quickly may go too fast for Paint Shop Pro to keep up, and as a result it may start erasing bits you want to keep. Drag at a slow, sure pace across the edge.

Using the Background Eraser is great for removing the bits around edges, but it's very slow (and not very efficient) at removing large areas. If you're trying to erase everything except Cousin Charlie, we suggest that you use the Background Eraser to clear a "moat" of transparent space around Charlie and then switch to the regular Eraser tool to mop up the rest of the image.

Controlling Strokes, Sizes, Shapes, and Spatters: Tool Options

The Painting and Eraser tools can do much more than just create a plain, boring spot or line. The Tool Options palette in Figure 4-6 is your key to variety, artistic success, and fame and fortune. The palette works the same — or nearly the same — for all painting and erasing tools, except for the Warp Brush.

Figure 4-6:
The Tool
Options
palette, key
to making
your paint
tool work
the way you
want.

One key role of your Tool Options palette is to show you what your brush looks like. As Figure 4-6 shows, a preview area in the upper-left corner shows you the size, fuzziness (hardness), and speckliness (density) of the spot you make if you clicked your image. The Tool Options palette is so incredibly useful that it should almost always be open so that you can check your brush before you paint.

The Tool Options palette (or its title bar, labeled Tool Options) is probably already floating around somewhere on your PC screen. If you can't find the Tool Options palette, follow these steps:

1. **Press the F4 key on your keyboard a few times.**

   The palette appears and disappears. Leave it visible.

2. **If Tool Options appears as a floating window and you don't want it hovering over your painting, double-click the title bar to dock it.**

3. **If the Tool Options palette isn't where you want it (we prefer along the top), click the vertical double-row of small indented dots shown in Figure 4-7 and drag it to wherever you want.**

Figure 4-7:
Click the
double-row
of dots to
move the
Tool Options
palette — or
any other
palette —
about.

Click and drag either of these to open and close panels within the Tool Options palette.

Click and drag here to move the Tool Options palette around.

4. **If you don't see all the options on the Tool Options palette, you may need to slide the palette open to see everything.**

   There are three sections of the Tool Options palette; the brush shape section, the opacity/blend section, and the shape/size/hardness section. Slide the small, single row of vertical dots and drag them left and right and up and down, until you can see all of them clearly, as shown in Figure 4-7.

   (Of course, if you can see everything you intend to change, you don't *have* to open everything. Think of the three sections of the Tool Options palette as a chest of drawers; you can open them all at one time or close the ones you're not working on and keep open the ones you need.)

You don't need to put away the Tool Options palette before working on your image. Leave it up so that you can make adjustments as you go. Drag it out of the way, if necessary, like we just showed you.

Not all tools offer all the adjustments we discuss in the next few sections.

Using convenient controls on the Tool Options palette

You can make adjustments on the Tool Options palette by using the dialog box gadgets you're familiar with from other programs. You can click the Size and other boxes and edit or type a new value or click either of the *spin dial* buttons (the pair of up and down arrows) to increase or decrease a value.

Besides the usual ways of adjusting values, Paint Shop Pro has a nifty adjustment feature, as shown in Figure 4-8. Click the tiny down arrow at the far right edge of the box for any numerical value, such as the Size box. Hold your mouse button down, and a tiny ruler-like bar appears, with a pointer. Keeping your mouse button down, drag the pointer left or right to adjust the value down or up, respectively.

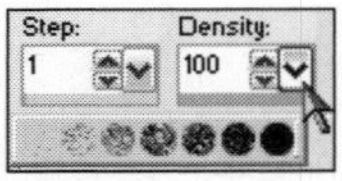

Figure 4-8:
The preview
adjustment
slider.

Figure 4-8 shows the Paint Brush tool window, although all or most of these same controls exist for the other painting tools. Clicking the far right down arrow for a given widget opens the adjustment slider that gives you a rough preview of what your tool will look like.

If you repeatedly use the same tool with the same tool options, you can save that tool's settings as a preset. *Presets* allow you to load a bunch of tool options in one click as opposed to entering them over and over again. See Chapter 18 for more details on this timesaver.

Making lines wider or narrower: Size

You most frequently adjust *size*. One size of tool definitely does not fit all. Even Phil, Dave's house painter, uses different sizes of brushes. (What an *artiste!*) On the Tool Options palette, adjust the Size value to any value from 1 through 255 (from 1 to 255 pixels).

You can see just how big your tool is at any time by moving your cursor over the image. Big brushes may need smaller step values (the number in the box labeled Step) to avoid painting dotted lines.

Shaping clicks, lines, and line ends: Shape

Shape changes the way the painted (or erased) line looks when it ends or bends. It also lets you stamp a shape by clicking the image, as though you had a rubber stamp or were spraying paint through a template.

On the Tool Options palette, you have two options: You can go with a generic round or square brush, some brushes that simulate chalk or watercolor, or you can even select a variety of strange and unearthly brushes (like cherries, comets, or fuzzy circles) to paint with, as shown in Figure 4-9.

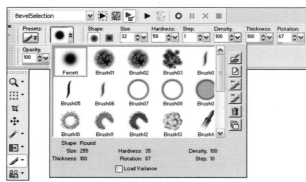

Figure 4-9: The round and square brushes and a gallery of brushes that don't exist in nature!

Selecting a round or square brush couldn't be simpler: Click the round or square box. If you want something a little more esoteric, however, you can select a brush tip from the brush tip drop-down menu next to the Presets menu. You're presented with a gallery of brushes you can scroll through; double-click a brush tip to load it.

Some brush tips emulate other brush styles; chalk, for example, or watercolor. Experiment to see which is closest to your media.

Using the various brush tips, you can make your lines look as though you have drawn them with a calligraphic pen. Figure 4-10 shows, from top to bottom, the square, round, chalky, and calligraphic brush shapes.

Figure 4-10:
Choose your
brush
shape!

As you make strokes, you see repeated stampings of this shape. The Step control (which we discuss in the section "Making lines more or less dotty: Step," later in this chapter) helps you change the separation between stampings.

Painting with a softer or harder edge: Hardness

Hardness determines how sharp the edges of your tool are. Maximum hardness (100) gives your tool a sharp edge; lower hardness applies a gradual fade to the edge. Zero hardness gradually fades the edge all the way to the center of the brush shape. At low hardness, you may need to decrease the step to avoid creating a dotted line. Figure 4-11 shows the effect of changing hardness.

Reduce hardness to minimize jaggies (a staircase effect also called *aliasing*) where your line bends.

Making paint thinner or thicker: Opacity

Opacity is how thick (opaque or solid) your paint is. A value of 100 means that your paint is completely opaque. Reduce opacity to make a more transparent paint. A value of 50, for example, means that an individual spot of paint (caused by clicking once with your mouse) is 50 percent transparent. Overlapping spots cause each stroke, or click of the mouse, to add paint and make the area more opaque. Figure 4-12 shows single spots with decreasing opacity.

Figure 4-11: A single spot showing hardness of 100, 80, 60, 40, and 20 (from left to right).

A brush stroke (*dragging* with your mouse) is more opaque than a single spot (*clicking* with your mouse) because strokes are simply repeated, overlapping spots. If you increase the values of the step variable (which controls spacing of those spots), you make the stroke more transparent.

For the Eraser tool, opacity refers to how completely you erase. If you use maximum opacity (100), you erase the line entirely. Use repeated strokes or clicks with values under 100 to shave the paint thickness and reduce opacity.

Figure 4-12: Out, damned spot! Spots with opacity of 100, 80, 60, 40, and 20 (from left to right).

Getting speckles of spray: Density

The word *density* doesn't accurately describe this adjustment. The words speckly-ness or speckle-osity are more accurate, but still confusing. Density works like this: When density is at its maximum (100), you get nice, solid paint coverage (or *eraserage,* if you're using the eraser). At lower settings of density, you get random speckles, as though you were spattering or spraying. Figure 4-13 shows the effect of different density settings.

Figure 4-13:
A single
spot, at
densities of
100, 80, 60,
40, and 20
(from left
to right).

For the Airbrush tool to do its job (which is spraying paint), you must set the density to less than 100. Yet, you can set density less than 100 for the Paint Brush or Eraser tools too, and they also give a speckly result, similar to the results you would get with the Airbrush tool.

Making lines more or less dotty: Step

It's time you knew the truth: The Paint Shop Pro paint tools don't apply paint continuously as you drag. (Gasp!) No, they apply repeated stampings of the brush's shape. (Imagine a jackhammer tipped with a rubber stamp.) The *Step control* determines the distance between those stampings.

If you set the Step value at its maximum (100, meaning 100 percent), the shapes don't overlap; the step is 100 percent of the tool size, so you get a dotted line. At 50, the shapes overlap halfway, and at 25 they overlap three-quarters (25 is often a good choice). Figure 4-14 shows increasing step values.

Figure 4-14:
Step values
of 20, 40, 60,
and 100
(from top to
bottom). The
larger the
step values,
the more
dotted the
line.

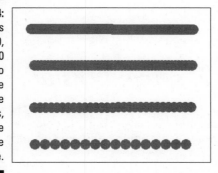

Very low Step values use up lots of processor power because the computer has to draw a new stamp every time the mouse moves. If you're drawing and the computer hesitates a moment before it renders the line on the screen, you may consider raising the Step value 10 or 20 percent.

Each brush tip is simply a particular set of values on the Tool Options palette, values predetermined by Paint Shop Pro. In other words, each medium specifies particular settings for density, opacity, step, and hardness. Choosing the Chalk brush tip, for example, simply sets Hardness to 90, Opacity to 80, Step to 25, and Density to 33 for whatever tool (the Paint Brush tool, for example) you're using. Choosing the Marker produces different settings.

Coloring within the Lines by Using Selection

When you're using painting tools in Paint Shop Pro and have selected an area, those painting tools work only within that selection. This feature is great for keeping you "within the lines" as you paint.

First, select the area you want to paint. (See Chapter 12 to find out how to make selections.) If you have chosen to use multiple layers in your image, make sure that you're on the layer that contains the object you want to paint. (See Chapter 14 or the Cheat Sheet for help with layers.) Then, choose a painting tool and paint! Feel free to scribble or spray paint over the edges; the paint falls only within the selection.

Feathered selections work, too, for blending the edges of your painting efforts into the rest of the image. Paint Shop Pro applies less paint in the feathered zone. Feathering expands the marquee to include feathered pixels outside the selection, however. If the selection has Swiss-cheese-like holes in it (as the Magic Wand tool selections often do), those holes may now be invisible because the feathered expansion covers them. As you paint, because the holes are feathered areas, they reappear as fuzzy spots that resist being painted. If you don't want that effect, eliminate the holes in your selection before you apply feathering. See Chapter 12 for help.

Replacing Colors

Here's your chance to make that purple cow — the one that people always prefer to see, rather than be. The Color Replacer tool is your companion in creative cow coloring.

Color replacement, like most Paint Shop Pro actions, works on only the active layer and within any selection you may have made. If you have chosen to use layers in your image, make sure that you're working on the correct layer during the following steps, or else replacement may not work.

Here's how to put new hue in your moo:

1. **Click the Color Replacer from the Color Selection toolset.**

   Your cursor becomes a brush shape. As with the Paint Brush and other painting tools, the brush size, shape, and other properties are controlled by the Tool Options palette. See "Controlling Strokes, Sizes, Shapes, and Spatters: Tool Options," earlier in this chapter.

2. **Hold down the Ctrl key and *right*-click in your image on the color you want to *replace*.**

   The Background Material box takes on this color.

3. **Again, hold down the Ctrl key and *left*-click your new, replacement color, either in the image or in the Available Colors of the Color palette.**

   The Foreground Material box takes on this color. Alternatively, you can use any technique we describe in Chapter 3 to set a new foreground material, complete with textures and gradients and whatnot.

4. **To replace the color in specific areas, drag across those areas. Double-click anywhere to replace the color everywhere.**

   Like most tools, the Color Replacer tool's action is constrained by layers and selections. If you have used layers in your image, color is replaced only throughout the active layer. If you have a current selection, replacement happens only within that selection.

The Color Replacer tool replaces a range of colors that are close to the one you picked to be replaced. Adjust the Tolerance setting on the Tool Options palette to control closeness. (Press F4 if you don't see the Tool Options palette.) The larger the Tolerance setting, the broader the range of colors the Color Replacer tool replaces. If you're replacing a single, uniform color, set the tolerance to zero. If you're purpling a cow in a photograph, you need to replace a range of browns (or blacks, or whites, depending on the cow). Set the tolerance higher in that event; try 25 or so, to start. In short, do this:

✔ If the Color Replacer tool replaces more than you want, decrease the tolerance. Press Ctrl+Z to undo the overenthusiastic replacement, and then drag or double-click again.

✔ If the Color Replacer tool doesn't replace enough, increase tolerance and then drag or double-click again.

Filling Areas

For flooding an area with nice, even color, nothing beats the Flood Fill tool, except possibly spilling a glass of red wine on a white sweater. (Fortunately, unlike the wine spill, you can undo the Flood Fill tool's actions by pressing Ctrl+Z.)

 Using the Flood Fill tool (not to be confused with Phil, Dave's painter), as shown in the margin, you can fill an area with whatever is in the Material box — although a material can be a simple color, it can also be complex gradients or patterns, allowing you to fill an area with a multicolored gradient or a tiger-skin rug pattern. Moreover, by adding a texture to your material, you can give a virtual surface roughness to any area you fill. Chapter 3 describes how to choose a solid color, gradient, or pattern using the Material box.

Filling a selected area with solid color

The most basic kind of fill you can perform is filling a selected area with a uniform color (the sort of work that Phil, Dave's house painter, does). For example, the sky in your photograph may be gray — perhaps with clouds and power lines running through it — and you want to make it solid, cloudless blue with no power lines.

1. **Select the area you want to fill, using any of the selection tools.**

   For example, click the sky in your picture with the Magic Wand tool. See Chapter 12 for help with getting exactly the selection you want. The selection marquee indicates your selected area.

   If you have chosen to use layers in your image, you must also select the layer that contains the portion of the image you want to fill. See Chapter 14 for more help with layers. If you don't use layers in your image, just make your selection and move on to Step 2.

2. **Click the Flood Fill tool on the Tools toolbar.**

   Your cursor icon changes to the paint can, the Fill tool icon.

3. **Choose a Foreground Material to fill with.**

   Make sure that the Foreground Material box is set to a solid color. (Chapter 3 shows you how to undo it if it's anything else.)

4. **Open the Tool Options palette.**

   If the Tool Options palette isn't visible on your screen, press the F4 key on your keyboard to display the palette.

5. **Make the following choices from the drop-down lists there:**

> **Blend mode:** Normal
>
> **Match mode:** None
>
> **Opacity:** 100 percent for a fill that nothing shows through, or lower for a more transparent fill

6. **Click your selection in the image.**

> The color completely fills the selected area (in your chosen layer, if you use layers). If you choose an opacity lower than 100, the color just tints the selected area and increases in thickness if you click again.

Figure 4-15 shows the effect of a solid fill in a selection of the sky, using deep blue to fill the sky uniformly. (The edge of the selection is feathered a bit, causing the white band to appear along the skyline.)

Figure 4-15:
A solid fill of the sky. In this image, a solid fill doesn't look natural.

If you're modifying a drawing, a solid color may be exactly what you want. In our photo, however, a solid color doesn't look natural as sky. Sky is never a uniform color in real life; it changes in color gradually as it approaches the horizon. For a more natural look, you need a gradient, or shaded, fill.

Filling with a gradient, pattern, or texture

In real life, you rarely see a uniform color (even if you think you do). Changes in lighting or the angles at which light strikes an object cause a gradual change across the object from one color to another, lighter color. The surface of your desk, for example, is probably a lighter color nearer your source of light.

If you need a realistic shading like that, or if for any other reason you want colors in an area to make a smooth transition from one color to another, try a shaded, or *gradient* fill. Figure 4-16 shows the effect of a gradient fill on the sky area of the photograph.

Figure 4-16: Gradient fills make filled areas (the sky, in this photo) more realistic.

For some fills, like filling a rectangle to look like a brick wall or a tree trunk, use a pattern rather than a solid color. To use gradients or patterns, you must first set your Foreground Material to be a gradient or pattern; see Chapter 3 for instructions on choosing the gradient or pattern you need.

Or, you may want to apply color with a textured appearance. Just like the other painting tools, if the Material box has a texture, such as canvas or asphalt, the Fill tool applies it. Again, refer to Chapter 3 for more details.

Blend modes

Sometimes, you don't want to overpaint the underlying image; you want to just tint or infuse the image with a color or increase or decrease color saturation or apply some other quality. The Fill tool has some fancy features, called *blend modes,* that combine attributes of your chosen fill, such as hue and saturation, with the underlying image in complex and subtle ways. In general, these blend modes are too obscure to be useful for any except the most dedicated graphics professional. For the rest of us, two of the modes, Color and Hue, can be occasionally useful because they can infuse an area with color, although the Colorize command, which we describe in Chapter 9, does that job quite nicely.

To experiment with blend modes, click the Blend Mode drop-down list on the Fill tool's Tool Options palette and choose a mode. Then try filling a selected area of your image.

What about tolerance?

Technical types may be wondering what the Tolerance control, on the Fill tool's Tool Options palette, is good for. In this chapter, we bypass the need to use that control by instructing you to select the area you want to fill and then use a Match mode of None. We think that's the easiest way to fill a specific area.

An alternative to selecting an area beforehand with a selection tool is to use the Fill tool itself to determine which pixels are to be filled, according to their color or other qualities. Choose a Match mode other than None, and then set tolerance. The Fill tool determines what pixels to fill based on those settings, exactly as the Magic Wand tool does to determine what pixels to select.

Alex, the Saintly Dog

As an example of all this brushing and filling hoo-hah, we have decided that Dave's dog Alex is the best-behaved dog in the world. We're attempting to convince the *Weekly World News* tabloid that Alex is *such* a good dog that he has a halo. (The *Weekly World News* may be naïve, but it pays well.) Two problems show up in the current picture of Alex, shown in Figure 4-17, though.

Figure 4-17: Alex, unedited dog about town.

One, he has no halo — but we draw that. Two, the *Weekly World News* uses only black-and-white photos, and that light slatted background behind Alex isn't dark enough to make the halo stand out. We rectify that in eight easy steps!

If you're reading ahead in this chapter, you may notice that the doorbell directly above Alex's head, as shown in all the other pictures of Alex in this book, isn't present here. We got rid of that using the Clone Brush; see Chapter 5 to find out how to remove unsightly doorbells from your pictures.

1. **Select the slatted background behind Alex.**

   As we discuss earlier in this chapter, in "Coloring within the Lines by Using Selection," you want to select the background to make sure that you don't accidentally draw over Alex's head while you're changing the slats. See Chapter 12 for help with getting exactly the selection you want.

   (For the record, we used the Magic Wand toolset to a Match mode of Color, a tolerance of 17, a feather of 1, and a large amount of judicious Shift+clicking to clean up the small patches of unselected areas.)

2. **Select the Paint Brush tool from the Brush toolset.**

3. **Change the Material (as we discuss in Chapter 3), and then do a test paint along the edges to make sure that the edges look good.**

   We selected a dark red material for our paint, but we set the opacity for our Paint Brush to 50 (half-transparent) so that the slatting still appears through the paint. As you can see in Figure 4-18, our brush strokes have stopped at the marquee edge of the selection, right above Alex's Buddha-like gaze.

   If you don't see the Tool Options palette, press F4.

Figure 4-18:
Alex, close to the edge.

4. **Paint the entire selected area.**

   You could also use the Fill tool with a Match set to none. The Fill tool is at its best, though, on fairly even areas that are mostly the same color, like the sky in the Fill example earlier in this chapter — not areas with dark vertical streaks through it, like this one. Besides, you're already using the Paint Brush tool, so why switch? The final results are just as good, as shown in Figure 4-19.

5. **Deselect the area.**

   Alex's halo needs to be big and impressive. *So* big and impressive, in fact, that it sticks out of the current selection — and as long as we have the background selected, we can't paint outside the lines. If you don't feel like skipping to Chapter 12, where we tell you how to deselect, you can either press Ctrl+D or choose Selections⇨Select None.

Figure 4-19:
Alex,
against a
darker
background.

6. **Select the Airbrush tool from the Brush toolset.**

   A halo is supposed to be fuzzy, so we airbrushed it in.

7. **Set the Airbrush options on the Tool Options palette and the Material box.**

   A halo is supposed to be fuzzy and bright white, so we picked a pure white color in the Material box — see Chapter 3 for details on that. We wanted a reasonably small line for our halo, so a size of 11 seemed about right — and a halo is supposed to be bright, so we cranked up the Opacity to 100 so that the background didn't bleed through.

   This still doesn't address the "fuzziness" issue — but the Hardness and Step settings do. We reduced the Hardness to 0 to provide maximum fuzziness, and we set the Step to 35 to produce a slightly spottier line.

8. **Draw a halo.**

   Keep a steady hand! Alex's reputation is at stake (see Figure 4-20).

Figure 4-20:
Beatific
Alex.

What's that, you say? It looks *fake*? Have you ever *seen* the *Weekly World News?*

You may be asking, "Isn't Alex's halo a little shaky there? Doesn't Paint Shop Pro have a tool for drawing perfect shapes, like circles, squares, and elliptic halos?" Of course, it does — and we show you how to draw better halos in Chapter 15.

Warping Your Picture

After you have your image the way you like it, you may feel the urge to smoosh parts of it up, or maybe to create a tiny, black hole that sucks part of the image into the middle, or to create a swirly whirlpool in the middle of it. The Warp brush allows you to apply all sorts of kooky 1960s psychedelia to your pictures.

(The authors want you to note how painstakingly we're avoiding the urge to make "Warp Brush Ten, Scotty!" jokes. Thank you.)

The Warp Brush tool uses up *lots* of computer horsepower. If you find that warping takes too long as your computer struggles to render every skew and twist, you can lower the Draft mode quality from the Tool Options palette to Low or Coarse and set the Final Apply Mode setting to Same as draft. The tradeoff, naturally, is that your warping looks a little jagged.

To "pinwheel" your image chaotically, follow these steps:

1. **Select the Warp Brush tool from the Brush toolset.**

2. **Select one of the following warp modes from the Tool Options palette.**

   With the exception of Push mode, each of the warp modes works like the Airbrush tool: If you keep the brush in one place or move it around slowly while you hold the mouse button down, the image continues to distort until you finally decide to let up.

   - **Push:** If you have ever finger painted, you understand instinctively how this tool works; as you move the brush around, everything else in the image gets dragged around behind it.

   - **Expand:** As the brush moves, the image swells, as though it's being tugged up closer to the screen.

   - **Contract:** As the brush moves, the image shrinks, as though it's being pulled away from the screen and into a black hole.

   - **Right Twirl or Left Twirl:** These settings create a slow whirlpool within the image, swirling the image in the direction you have selected.

   - **Noise:** This setting applies various tools at random, twisting your image in different directions to create a truly crazed effect.

   - **Iron:** If you have been going a little loony with the other modes, you can undo them a little at a time with Iron mode. Rub over the image in Iron mode before you click the Apply button and the twists slowly unkink.

   - **Unwarp:** Like Iron mode, this mode also undoes the images, but you have slightly better control. Still, they're similar.

3. Change your options.

The Warp Brush tool has many of the same settings as the Paint and Airbrush tools — Size, Hardness, and Step — and it has two new ones:

- A higher *Strength* setting means that the slightest sweep of the Warp brush deforms the area like it was Michael Jackson's face; a low Strength settings means that the brush barely affects the picture.

- *Noise* is available only for the Noise tool. The higher the setting, the more it sprinkles the image with random dots, taken from colors within the brush areas itself, creating a sort of static that accelerates the warping.

4. Draw.

Hold down the left mouse button and *drag*, baby! (The right mouse button does nothing here.)

5. Decide whether you want to keep the image.

If you like the results, click the green Apply check mark in the upper-left corner of the Tool Options palette and the warping changes are applied — a part of your image forevermore. (Or, if you switch to another tool that needs the changes to be applied before it can work, the program asks whether you want to save the changes.) If you think that it looks like a Jackson Pollock painting in a blender and want to get rid of it, click the cancel (X) button.

Nothing is *really* forevermore as long as you have the Undo function; as with the rest of Paint Shop Pro, you can always undo your last action by pressing Ctrl+Z or clicking the Undo Last Command button on the top row.

Chapter 5

Painting with Pictures

· ·

In This Chapter

▶ Duplicating with the Clone Brush tool

▶ Choosing cloning over selecting

▶ Using the Picture Tube tool

▶ Creating your own picture tube pictures

· ·

*R*emember those cartoons where an image would flow, full-blown, off the tip of a brush? In just a few brush strokes, Daffy Duck would paint an image of a door on the wall, open the door, and run through it.

With Paint Shop Pro, you can have images flow off the tip of your brush, just like Daffy does. (You have to figure out on your own how to run through walls.) Paint Shop Pro offers two ways to paint with pictures that you would be daffy *not* to use:

✔ **Clone Brush:** The Clone Brush tool simultaneously picks up an image from one area of an open image while you brush a copy of that image somewhere else — either within the same image or within another open image. (It's a bit like a newfangled version of the pantograph, for all you antique machinery mavens.)

✔ **Picture Tubes:** The Picture Tube tool lays down a series of images, fully formed. As you stroke, the images are drawn from a collection of images you choose, such as variously numbered billiard balls, different types of flowers, or an abstract shape in various orientations.

Why paint with pictures? The Clone Brush tool simplifies lots of jobs. Using the Clone Brush tool, you can retouch a photo by copying a texture (like grass) or a background image (like sky) over some offending portion of the image. No need to worry about tedious color matching or finicky copying and pasting; the cloned image blends right in. Or, you can simply clone Alex from this cold, snowy winter and put him in the photo of the beach at Club Med. (We would have brought him to Club Med with us, but Alex hates flying.)

The Picture Tube tool does a fast job of creating backgrounds of swarm images — a lawnful of grass, a pile of candies, or a heaping mound of coffee beans. A few individual images clicked off the Picture Tube can quickly brighten up a poster, logo, or banner. You can also use the Picture Tube to create banners and edges — items such as filmstrip edges, a huge Slinky, or a large snakeskin.

Cloning Alex the Dog

The *Clone Brush tool* gives you results similar to copying and pasting, but allows you precise control over exactly what gets copied. This tool is frequently used in photograph retouching to "erase" areas in a picture, replacing them with a neutral background. In certain circumstances, clone brushing is also easier than copying and pasting.

Suppose that you have determined in the picture of Alex that the green carpet he's sitting on just *has* to go (see Figure 5-1). You had better cover it up with some snow!

Figure 5-1:
The original image, complete with green blanket.

1. **Click the Clone Brush tool (as shown in Figure 5-2) on the Tools toolbar.**

   If you don't see the Clone Brush tool, you may have selected the Scratch Remover tool earlier. If that's the case, click the arrow next to the Scratch Remover tool and select the Clone Brush tool from the drop-down menu.

2. **If necessary, adjust the size and hardness of the Clone Brush tool on the Tool Options palette (see Figure 5-3).**

Sometimes you want to have a very large Clone selection to replace huge areas of a picture — or you want a small selection to make sure that you can get right in between Alex's paws. You can adjust the size on the Size control on the Tool Options palette; large numbers mean that you copy a large sample of the picture, and smaller numbers mean tiny samples. You want a teeny selection, so choose 20.

The *hardness* is a percentage that determines how crisp the edge of a cloned copy is; 100 percent is a razor-sharp edge, whereas 0 percent is a fuzzy selection that looks almost blurred and blends easily into the background (see Figure 5-4). We keep ours at 50 percent.

If you don't see the Tool Options palette, press F4 on the keyboard.

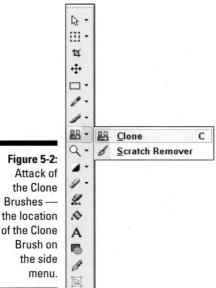

Figure 5-2:
Attack of the Clone Brushes — the location of the Clone Brush on the side menu.

Figure 5-3:
The Tool Options palette, Clone Brush-style.

3. *Right*-click the source area (the area you want to copy).

Clicking an edge or corner of the object you want helps you with the next step. In this case, because you want to cover up the green blanket with a fluffy coating of snow, right-click the snow in the lower-right corner, as shown in Figure 5-5.

Figure 5-4: Values of 100 percent, 50 percent, and 0 percent hardness.

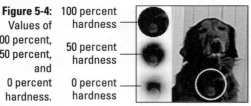

100 percent hardness

50 percent hardness

0 percent hardness

Figure 5-5: A small section of the blanket has been replaced with a copy of the snow from the lower-right corner.

4. Brush (*left*-click or drag) on the destination area (the area you want to paint).

As you brush, keep an eye on the source area too. An X marks the spot on the source image where the Clone Brush tool is picking up (copying) pixels. As you move your brush, the X on the source image tracks your movement. Move so that the X sweeps across the object you want to copy, as shown in Figure 5-6.

If you ever want to choose another area to clone, all you have to do is right-click a new section.

If, in Step 3, you right-clicked the upper-left corner of the area you're copying, begin painting where you want the upper-left corner of the clone to appear in Step 4. Stroke down and to the right so that the X traverses the original object.

Figure 5-6: Thanks to the magic of the Clone Brush, the blanket has vanished, replaced completely with cloned snow!

Other Clone Brush options

As you have already seen, the size of the area and the hardness can be set on the Tool Options palette. In fact, using the Tool Options palette, you can set *all* the usual variations available to Paint Shop Pro brushes: shape, opacity (transparency), step, and density (speckliness). You can find more information on these settings in Chapter 4.

Cloning versus selection

When you copy individual people or objects, you can either use the Clone Brush tool or copy and paste. Which to choose? The Clone Brush tool isn't really the best tool for copying objects because constraining the tool to just the object you're copying is difficult — but sometimes it's the fastest tool to use.

Here are three tips to tell you when the Clone Brush is the way to go:

✔ **Use the Clone Brush when you have a large enough background to clone.** If you left-click very near where you originally right-clicked, you may soon start cloning your clones. (Your X may traverse areas you just painted.) You don't lose quality, but a pattern becomes apparent more quickly. If you look carefully at Figure 5-7, where we have begun to clone over Alex, you can discern a pattern in the slats we have cloned.

Figure 5-7: Bad patterning, Indy.

✔ **Use the Clone Brush to put an object behind something.** For example, you may want Alex to appear behind a palm tree at Club Med. With the Clone Brush tool, you can paint his image on either side of the palm tree. Paint Shop Pro has ways of doing this job that give cleaner results, but the Clone Brush tool is often simpler.

✔ **Use the Clone Brush only when backgrounds are similar.** Copying an object without picking up a few border pixels is difficult using the Clone Brush tool, so it works best when backgrounds match.

Painting with Picture Tubes

Imagine a paint tube that, rather than containing paint, is crammed with images that pour out as you squeeze the tube. You now have a good mental image of the Paint Shop Pro *Picture Tube tool.* Paint Shop Pro comes with a gallery of tubes to use.

Each tube contains a set of images on a particular theme. For example, you can squeeze out a set of airplanes, butterflies, billiard balls, or coins. Each individual image in a tube is different. Figure 5-8 shows an illustration that uses two tubes: various blades of grass and many raindrops.

Picture tubes have several purposes. They can serve as

✔ A source of clip art on various themes

✔ Brushes for interesting textures and shapes, such as grass, fire, or three-dimensional tubes

✔ Creative painting tools that are sensitive to your brush strokes

Cloning between images or layers

The Clone Brush tool copies just as well from one image window to another window as it does within one image. It also copies between layers, if you want.

To clone between images, open both images. They appear in separate windows in Paint Shop Pro. Just right-click the source image where you want to copy, and then left-click or drag where you want to paint on the destination image.

To clone between layers, select your source layer on the Layer palette. Then, right-click the image you want copied. Select the destination layer on the Layer palette, and then left-click or drag on the image.

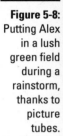

Figure 5-8:
Putting Alex
in a lush
green field
during a
rainstorm,
thanks to
picture
tubes.

Basic tubing

Picture tubing is fundamentally easy. You choose what kind of pictures you want and click or drag the picture tube across the image. Here are the details:

1. **Click the Picture Tube tool (as shown in the margin) on the toolbar.**

   You may have to wait when you first choose this tool because Paint Shop Pro loads its cache with pictures. A Cache Status box may briefly appear.

2. **Choose which picture set you want from the Tool Options palette.**

   A sample image from the selected picture tube appears next to the Presets menu. Click the down arrow to the right of that sample to reveal a gallery of picture tubes of different types. Some picture tube pictures aren't much to look at individually, like the 3-D items, but they create cool effects when you drag your brush. Scroll through those images to review them, and then click the one you want.

3. **Click in the image window to deposit one picture at a time or drag to paint a line of pictures.**

   As you click or drag, various pictures similar to the sample you chose appear at intervals on the image. (If the image isn't much bigger than an individual picture, few pictures may appear. See "Adjusting basic tube behavior," just a bit later in this chapter, for instructions on reducing the picture size.)

The basic way to use picture tubes is as a sort of randomly chosen clip art to ornament an illustration. Choose a tube and then click the illustration in various places to drop in some art. However, other tubes are meant to be dragged to create a banner, like Filmstrip, Rope, and Neon Pink.

Cloning neatly within the lines

You can paint neatly within a precisely defined area by selecting that area in the destination image. (We describe selection in Chapter 12.) Paint Shop Pro paints only within the selection marquee.

To paint Alex behind a palm tree, for example, you can select the palm tree's trunk and then invert the selection to select everything *except* the palm tree. Then your brush stroke can slop right over the tree without leaving paint on it.

Creating a selection around the *source* area doesn't help you copy *from* a precise area, however. A selection works on only the *destination* area.

Adjusting basic tube behavior

If the Picture Tube tool doesn't deliver images in quite the way you want, you can change its behavior. Behaviors you can modify include

- ✔ **Picture size:** Reduce the number in the Scale value box if the pictures are too large. Scale is initially set to 100 (percent), the largest setting.

- ✔ **Spacing between pictures:** Pictures initially flow off the brush at a certain preset spacing. Increase the step value on the Tool Options palette to separate pictures. To jam them together, decrease the value.

- ✔ **Regular or random spacing:** The Picture Tube tool is initially set to randomly vary the spacing between pictures as you drag. To make it deliver an evenly spaced stream of pictures, choose Continuous from the Placement Mode drop-down menu on the Tool Options palette.

- ✔ **Picture sequence:** The tool is initially set to choose pictures randomly from its set of images. To have it select images in sequence, choose Incremental from the Selection Mode drop-down menu on the Tool Options palette.

The artist who created the tube determined the sequence. For each stroke you make, the sequence picks up where you last left off. The tube doesn't repeat the initial picture until it has delivered the last picture.

Part III
Improving Appearances

The 5th Wave   By Rich Tennant

"Hey- let's put scanned photos of ourselves through a ripple filter and see if we can make ourselves look weird."

In this part . . .

*T*his part is the place to turn when you have an image that needs work. If your image has individual defects, Chapter 6 is the place for you. We show you which Paint Shop Pro hand tools can help. You can brush away freckles or paint speckles, repair scratches, or remove that evil red glow from the eyes of people or animals caught in a too-direct flash.

For overall appearance problems in photographs, check out Chapter 7. Over- or underexposed photos? Green people? Blurry or speckly images? Dull colors? No problem. Paint Shop Pro 8 offers several effects specifically designed to fix common photo problems — including the amazing One Step Photo Fix, which can clarify all your photos with a click.

If your image needs to go beyond not bad and into the world of *wow,* Chapter 8 is the place to go. Paint Shop Pro provides all kinds of stunning and clever special effects. You can bend, twist, chisel, cut out, or translate an image into exotic media, like neon or metal. In Chapter 8, we give you examples to work from.

To get the most from your art, you need to understand your medium. With Paint Shop Pro, your medium is software. When you need to get precise about color, turn to Chapter 9, where we show you how to talk clearly to Paint Shop Pro about exactly what you need, whether it's more saturation or a color that's a bit more yellow.

When automatic solutions, like the Paint Shop Pro effects, don't quite solve overall image problems, your image may need fine-tuning with the Paint Shop Pro color commands. We show you how to clean up subtle problems of contrast, brightness, and color in Chapter 10.

Chapter 6

Retouching Touchy Spots

· ·

In This Chapter

▶ Softening

▶ Smudging

▶ Lightening

▶ Darkening

▶ Removing a scratch

▶ Removing red-eye

· ·

Can Paint Shop Pro remove worrisome wrinkles, unwanted warts, or malevolent moles? Would Uncle Andrew look any less evil without red eyes? Can you do anything about the scratches and creases in that family heirloom photo?

The Paint Shop Pro answer to these questions is an emphatic "yes!" (For trickier tasks, like looking a bit skinnier or restoring lost hair, the Paint Shop Pro answer is an emphatic "Um . . . well, sort of." Believe us, we've tried.)

In this chapter, we focus on the Paint Shop Pro tools you can direct toward problem areas. They don't help you shed pounds or grow hair, but they do help you improve specific spots on your photograph or illustration:

✔ Retouch toolset

✔ Scratch Remover tool

✔ Red-eye Removal adjustment

If your image has a color depth of fewer than 16.7 million colors, Paint Shop Pro needs to increase the number of colors in your image before you can use any of these tools and adjustments; if you're tired of it always asking you whether it's okay to increase the colors, see Chapter 19.

Paint Shop Pro has other, automatic *adjustments* that can enhance the entire image or selected areas of it. See Chapter 7 for more information about those.

Adjusting Your Retouch and Hue Strokes

To use any of the retouching or hue tools, open the Tool Options palette; if it isn't already open, press F4 on your keyboard.

You want to adjust the size and other stroke attributes of the Retouch and Hue tools you have chosen to match your task. The specific controls vary from tool to tool, but they're pretty much the same as the Paint Shop Pro brushes. Because we're running short on space, we refer you to Chapter 4 for the skinny on brush controls.

Using layers? The Retouch and Hue tools, like most of the Paint Shop Pro tools, normally work on only the selected layer. (If you have selected an area, it works only within that area, too.) To have the Retouch tool modify all layers at one time, enable the Sample Merged check box if it's available. If the tool doesn't seem to be working, check to make sure that you have the correct layer selected (see Chapter 14) and that you don't have a selection encompassing some other area (press Ctrl+D to deselect everything).

The Friendly Finger of the Retouch Toolset

The retoucher's best friend in Paint Shop Pro is the friendly finger of the Retouch toolset, as shown in Figure 6-1. The Retouch toolset, which lurks on the toolbar, is a kind of virtual fingertip with which you can rub away many defects, like Mom rubbing a bit of soot off your nose.

The Retouch toolset offers many tools to choose from. For many of these tools, using them well requires a pretty technical insight into computer graphics. In this chapter, we cover other effects you're likely to use most.

Softening

One of the most useful Paint Shop Pro effects is great for retouching portraits: the Soften tool. The Soften tool, well, softens sharp edges — wrinkles, for instance. Just brush the tool across those edges or click them.

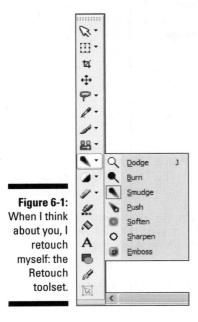

Figure 6-1:
When I think about you, I retouch myself: the Retouch toolset.

Figure 6-2 shows a frighteningly close shot of the left eye of wrinkled, old Uncle Dave, a friendly author. On the left is an unretouched copy; on the right is the Soften tool softening his wrinkles.

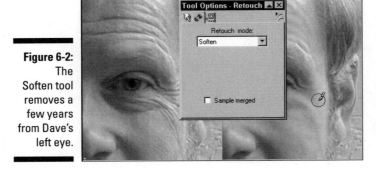

Figure 6-2:
The Soften tool removes a few years from Dave's left eye.

You could get the same result by selecting the wrinkled area and applying the Blur or Blur More Effect, but that's more work. (See Chapter 7 for help with adjustments.) If you want a nice, soft angelic glow to your entire image, the Soft Focus Adjustment (also in Chapter 7) makes everything radiant.

To work more gradually and do less softening in each stroke, set Opacity to a lower value on the Tool Options palette.

Smudging

The Smudge tool picks up paint from the place where you set it down and smears that paint as you drag to other areas, making it the closest thing Paint Shop Pro has to finger painting. As it smears, it loses paint just as your finger would. You can use smudging to soften edges, rub out pimples, or even blend in a dot of rouge (in the form of low-opacity red paint) you have added to the cheek of your CEO's portrait.

To minimize moles, pimples, and similar imperfections, start not *on* the discolored area, but rather off to one side. Smudge across the discolored area and release the mouse button after you're through the area. Repeat in the opposite direction, again starting on clear skin.

Figure 6-3 shows the smudge effect as the Retouch tool is dragged from left to right, starting with white and passing through the center of three differently colored squares in a single stroke. Notice how the paint fades as the tool moves from left to right. The tops of the three squares have also been smudged, but with repeated, circular strokes.

Figure 6-3:
The Retouch tool in Smudge mode. A single stroke through the middle creates a "bullet through an apple" look, and a circular motion smudges the tops.

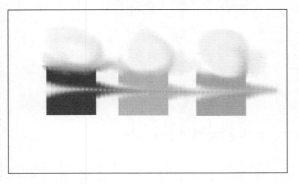

As in the center of Figure 6-3, a single stroke may reveal the inherent dottiness of computer stroking, which you can minimize by reducing the Step value on the Tool Options palette. Repeated strokes, as along the tops of the squares in Figure 6-3, tend to smear out those dots.

Other Retouch tools

Not all the Retouch tools are useful; some are obscure, and others are more creative than restorative. Still, they may be worth a try. The following are brief synopses of what they do:

- **Sharpen:** Amplifies edges, wrinkles, and other sudden transitions (the opposite of Soften).
- **Emboss:** Creates a grayscale image that appears to be embossed, like George Washington's face on a U.S. quarter.
- **Push:** Picks up the image area where you begin dragging and pushes it along, leaving a trail of finely overlapping copies of that area. (Overlap is controlled by the Step value on the Tool Options palette.)
- **Dodge:** A term taken from photographic darkroom work that means to lighten areas that are already somewhat light. It lightens the image and enhances contrast at the same time.
- **Burn:** The opposite of Dodge; darkens pixels that are already somewhat dark. It darkens the image while enhancing contrast.

The Color Madness of the Hue Toolset

Although Paint Shop Pro offers a dizzying variety of ways to change colors and intensities, the Hue toolset, as shown in Figure 6-4, is the easiest. You can lighten or darken areas of your image, swap colors in a target area, intensify the colors, or leach them to a dull gray.

Lightening and darkening

You can lighten or darken in lots of different ways in Paint Shop Pro — but the most basic is the Lighten/Darken tool in the Hue toolset. You're given two options here: RGB and Lightness. In most cases, RGB works just fine. Hold down the left mouse button and drag to lighten an image; hold the right button and drag to sink it into the shadows.

"Lightness" adjusts the lightness portion — the *L* in HSL — and RGB adjusts the red, green, and blue portions. If you really want to know what the difference is, check out Chapter 10.

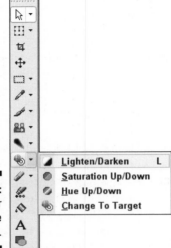

Figure 6-4:
Hue's your
daddy? The
Hue toolset.

◢	**Lighten/Darken** L
⬤	**Saturation Up/Down**
◖	**Hue Up/Down**
☝	**Change To Target**

The left side of Figure 6-5 shows an image of Dave's trusty golden retriever, Alex, that was taken a bit too close to the camera's flash. On the copy on the right side, we have right-clicked with the Lighten/Darken tool in RGB mode in order to tone down the gleam on his nose and reduce the flash's reflection in his eyes.

Figure 6-5:
Lightening
strikes
as the
Lighten/
Darken tool
takes the
shine off
Alex's nose
and the
glare off
his right
eyeball.

To darken more gradually and gain more control over the results, set the opacity to a lower value on the Tool Options palette.

The rest of the Hue toolset

Other tools are in the Hue toolset, but they're not used much:

- **Saturation Up/Down:** Holding down the left mouse button and dragging while you have the Saturation tool selected amplifies the inherent colors in your image; holding down the right button leaches the colors out, rendering it a lifeless gray. (For more information on what Saturation is, see Chapter 10.)

- **Change to Target:** You can use the Change to Target tool to transform all the colors under your brush into shades of the color in the Foreground Material box. If you're really feeling comfortable with the whole HSL thing (as shown in Chapter 10), you can replace the hue, saturation, or lightness instead.

- **Hue Up/Down:** This pushes colors counterclockwise (red, yellow, green, cyan, blue, violet, and magenta) or clockwise on the Paint Shop Pro color wheel. We don't know when you would use it, but hey — it came with the program, right?

The Scratch Remover Tool

Having photos come back from the developer with a scratch is heartbreaking. Usually, it means that a scratch is on the negative, so making a new print can't help. Equally traumatic is having a valued print creased, torn, or scratched when you don't have a negative and can't replace the print. Paint Shop Pro has an answer for all your folds, creases, and scratches. After you scan the picture into Paint Shop Pro (refer to Chapter 2), here's what to do:

1. **Zoom in on your scratched area so that it fills the screen.**

   Select the magnifying-glass icon from the Pan and Zoom toolset and zoom in; refer to Chapter 1 for details.

2. **Click the Scratch Remover tool from the Clone toolset, as shown in Figure 6-6.**

   This tool is the trowel-looking icon shown in the margin.

3. **Position your mouse cursor at one end of the scratch and drag along the scratch.**

   As you drag, a frame area stretches to follow your mouse cursor and extends across the width of the scratch, as shown in Figure 6-7.

Figure 6-6:
The Scratch
Remover
tool, and
where to
find it.

4. **Release your mouse button at the end of the scratch.**

   If you're following a curved or irregular scratch, release your mouse button at the point where the curve can no longer fit within the frame. (Later, you can go back and remove remaining segments of scratch.)

   When you release the mouse button, the Scratch Remover tool picks up paint from either side of the scratch and pushes it into the scratch. If you had to stop short of the end of the scratch, drag a second time to cover the remaining portion.

Figure 6-7:
Having
a dog
requires
familiarity
with
scratching.
Here, Alex
looks
pleased as
we remove
a scratch.

That's it! You now have a slightly fuzzy band where the scratch was, but it's probably much better than a scratch.

If your photo has lots of small scratches from improper handling, try the Automatic Small Scratch Removal adjustment we describe in Chapter 7.

If the scratch wasn't completely filled in, you may need to repeat your action for another segment of scratch or adjust some tool options and try again. For irregular scratches, remove the scratch in sections. To adjust options, first undo any failed attempt (press Ctrl+Z). Next, open the Tool Options palette (press F4 to toggle the window on or off). Follow one of these methods:

✔ **If the scratch didn't fill in because the scratch was wider than the tool's frame:** A value box on the Tool Options palette allows you to adjust the Scratch Remover's width in pixels. Increase the value in that box and again try to remove the scratch. With tool settings larger than 20, the frame exhibits an inner and outer zone as you drag. As you drag, make sure that the scratch fits in the inner zone and that the outer zone is completely filled with the bordering colors you want to use for filling in.

✔ **If you end up with an unacceptably wide, fuzzy band where the scratch was:** The tool's width was set too high. Lower the width value on the Tool Options palette.

✔ **If the end points of the scratch didn't properly fill in:** An outline option gives you an alternative shape to drag, one that has pointed ends rather than square ones. That shape is good for clicking in tight spaces or corners. Click that alternative shape button and then try scratch removal again.

If the scratch runs along an edge in the image, use the smallest width possible to avoid blurring that edge. For instance, in Figure 6-7, the scratch grazes Dave's shoulder, where his shirt ends and the trees begin. The Scratch Remover blurs that edge. Rather than remove the entire irregular scratch in one broad attempt, he may do better to remove that shoulder-grazing portion of the scratch separately, with the width value set very low. If all else fails, use the Clone tool, as shown in Chapter 5.

The Red-Eye Remover

In our youth, we longed for something to remove the telltale morning red-eye that bespoke a long, hard night out. Regrettably, Paint Shop Pro doesn't remove *that* kind of red-eye, where the blood vessels in the whites of your eyes throb reproachingly.

The Paint Shop Pro red-eye remover *does,* however, fix the evil red glow that sometimes appears in photographs, emanating from the pupils of the eye as the result of a camera's flash. In animals, that glow may not be red, but, rather, yellow or other colors.

The red-eye remover in Paint Shop Pro is a red-eye *replacer.* Rather than attempt to restore the original pupil of the eye, Paint Shop Pro says "The heck with it" and paints a whole new pupil, complete with the glint of the flashbulb. In fact, the red-eye remover can even construct a new iris (the colored portion of your eye) if the camera's flash has obliterated it!

Reconstructing the pupil

Usually, red-eye affects only the pupil. If it has affected the iris in your photo, see the section "Replacing pupil and iris," later in this chapter. Here's how to get rid of red-eye if the flash hasn't affected the iris area:

1. **Choose Adjust⇨Red-eye Removal.**

   The amazingly complex-looking Red-eye Removal dialog box appears. Figure 6-8 gives you the picture.

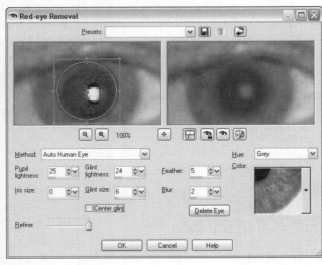

Figure 6-8: If this figure were in color, the left eye's pupil would be a scary red. Figure C-1b in the color insert of this book shows the actual color.

2. **Zoom in close on one of the red eyes, in the preview windows.**

   To zoom in, click the button displaying a magnifying glass with a + sign, located between the two preview windows. Repeat until the eye practically fills the windows.

TIP

To move the photo around behind the window, drag in the *right* (not left) window. Your cursor displays a hand icon when it's over the right window.

If you mistakenly drag or click in the left window, click the Delete Eye button to remove the replacement iris you have accidentally created.

3. **Choose Auto Human Eye (if you're working on a human) from the Method selection box.**

   If you're working on an animal, choose Auto Animal Eye.

4. **Set Iris Size to zero.**

   Or, if you have changed your mind and decided that the red really does afflict the iris, see the section "Replacing pupil and iris," later in this chapter.

5. **Click once on the dead center of the (red) pupil of the eye in the left window.**

   A circle appears, with a dot in the center and a square frame surrounding the circle. The circle has handles on it (tiny squares you can drag). Figure 6-8 shows this tool.

   You want the circle to just cover the red pupil and be centered over it.

6. **Adjust the circle's position or size if the circle doesn't cover the red pupil.**

   You can drag the circle by the dot in its center. To resize the circle, drag one of the handles on the box surrounding the circle.

7. **Looking at the right window, adjust the Refine control left and right until the red is just covered by a dark spot (the new pupil).**

   The Refine control determines to what extent the new pupil covers the red. When you're done, little or no red should be showing. For precise control of Refine, click the slider and press the left- and right-arrow keys on your keyboard to decrement or increment the slider. The new pupil should be no larger than the original and shouldn't cover the eyelid. If you can't achieve a result you like, return to Step 5 and resize the circle.

8. **Adjust the Pupil lightness value box to set the lightness of your new pupil to your liking.**

   Decrease the value for a darker pupil. For a normal appearance, the pupil should be darker than the iris.

9. **Check the new, white glint in the right window against the original in the left window.**

   If the new glint isn't roughly the same size as the original, adjust the Glint size control up or down until they match. Feel free, however, to make the new glint any size you like, including removing it altogether by setting the glint size to zero. If you prefer the glint in the center of the eye, click to enable the Center Glint check box. Otherwise, the glint tracks the original one. Adjust the Glint Lightness control up or down to match the brightness of the original glint. If the new glint has a noticeably sharper edge than the old, adjust the Blur control upward.

10. **Increase the Feather control to get a softer edge or to mute any remaining red spots around the edge.**

   Alternatively, if the original photo is a bit blurry, try adjusting the Blur control upward instead. Fool around with these two controls until the edges look properly blended into the rest of the eye.

11. **Click the Proof button (with the eye icon) to check your results in the main image window.**

   (Drag the Red-eye Removal dialog box out of the way, if necessary; don't close it yet.)

   Return to any earlier steps that seem necessary to adjust size, darkness, coverage, glint, and so forth.

   If you decide that you need to give up and start again, click the Delete Eye button. If you want to return all the settings to their original positions, click the Reset button in the upper-right corner.

   If you can't get acceptable coverage of the pupil, click the Cancel button and see the following section.

12. **Click OK.**

When you're done with one eye, repeat those steps for the other eye. When you proof your work in Step 11, make sure that the eyes match!

Outlining problem pupils

As you undoubtedly remember from school, some pupils are troublemakers. They don't cooperate if you try to doctor their red-eye. In that case, change from using automatic red-eye removal to *manual outlining*.

Open the Red-eye Removal dialog box and zoom in as directed in Steps 1 and 2 in the preceding section. Rather than choose Auto Human (or Auto Animal) Eye in Step 3, which tells Paint Shop Pro to automatically outline the red area, choose one of these two manual outlining options:

✔ **Freehand Pupil Outline:** Choose this option if you prefer to drag a continuous line around the red area to outline it. (This technique requires a steady hand, but can give a more rounded outline.) When you release the mouse button, Paint Shop Pro connects the line's end with its beginning.

✔ **Point-to-Point Pupil Outline:** Choose this option if you prefer to click a series of points around the red area. Paint Shop Pro draws a straight line between the points. When you're ready to complete the circle, don't click the starting point again. Instead, double-click somewhere short of that point. Paint Shop Pro completes the circle for you.

Drag or click an outline, according to your choice of options. After you outline the pupil, resume with Step 7 in the steps in the preceding section to refine the red-eye correction.

Replacing pupil and iris

If the flash has affected the colored iris of the eye, first follow Steps 1 through 4 in the steps under "Reconstructing the pupil," earlier in this chapter. (In those steps, you open the Red-eye Removal dialog box, zoom in on an eye, and click in its center.)

Then, after Step 3, follow these steps:

1. **Enlarge the circle in the left window to cover an area equal to the *iris* (not just the pupil) you need.**

   Drag any corner handle of the square frame surrounding the circle to enlarge the circle. Often, the circle needs to overlap the top eyelid and possibly a bit of the bottom.

2. **Adjust the value in the Iris Size value box up or down, a little at a time, until the iris and pupil size either matches the other eye or simply looks correct.**

   Click the tiny up arrow or down arrow adjoining the Iris Size value box to change the value by one.

3. **Click the Hue selection box and choose an iris color from the list.**

   Choose from Aqua, Blue, Brown, Gray, Green, or Violet.

4. **Click the down arrow to the right of the Color sample box and choose a precise shade of color from the gallery that appears.**

5. **Adjust the Refine control left or right to set the shape and extent of the iris.**

   The optimal setting of the Refine control occurs when the iris doesn't significantly overlap an eyelid and is reasonably round elsewhere. A black spot with a white glint should cover the pupil of the eye.

Resume with Step 8 in the "Reconstructing the pupil." From here, you adjust the darkness of the pupil, set any feathering or blurring you need, and adjust the glint size, if necessary.

Chapter 7

Finessing Photos with Adjustments

- -

In This Chapter

▶ Correcting color balance

▶ Boosting or bucking contrast and brightness

▶ Intensifying colors

▶ Removing patterns and scratches

▶ Clarifying

▶ Getting specific colors right

▶ Sharpening and blurring

▶ Despeckling

- -

*W*ith today's point-and-shoot cameras, you may wonder whether any-thing could really go wrong with your photos. They autofocus, auto-expose, autoadvance, autoflash, and, therefore, autobedarnednearperfect. But despite all this automation, we all still make seriously flawed photographs from time to time — or have to scan in scratched photos from the dark days when people still used flash cubes. Maybe we autogiveup?

Fear not, fellow photo flubbers! If your photos get an F for Faulty, you can find a flock of effects for finessing your photos to a fare-thee-well. Even for people whose pictures are practically perfect, Paint Shop Pro is replete with photo-polishing possibilities. Now, if only they had an answer for authors' unlicensed alliteration.

 A common problem with scanned photos is that they're a little off-kilter, like a picture hung wrong. Paint Shop Pro offers a handy straightening feature to put your photos back on the level — but because that's usually a scanning problem, we cover that in Chapter 2.

Adjustments in Paint Shop Pro are used to enhance photographs and images of all kinds. (The program also has effects, described in Chapter 8, which apply all sorts of artsy effects to your image.)

Like most other features of Paint Shop Pro, effects work only on whatever layer of an image is active, and within a current selection. If your image has multiple layers, you need to choose the layer you want before applying an effect. See Chapter 14 for help with layers.

If your image has a color depth of less than 16.7 million colors, Paint Shop Pro asks whether you want to increase the number of colors in your image first. Considering that these adjustments don't work unless you answer Yes, this question is sort of silly. If you get tired of continually clicking OK to no-brainer questions like this, see Chapter 19.

The One Step Photo Fix

Paint Shop Pro offers a special selection that allows you to run all the most commonly used photo enhancements in a single click! Much like baking store-bought chocolate chip cookie dough, the One Step Photo Fix isn't *quite* as good as doing it by hand — it tends to err on the light side, giving slightly washed-out photos — but if you're pressed for time, it can be a lifesaver.

In the Photo toolbar up top, you see a drop-down menu that says Enhance Photo; select it and choose One Step Photo Fix. (If for some reason you don't see it, choose View➪Toolbars➪Photo.) Paint Shop Pro then adjusts the color, sharpens the sucker, fixes the contrast, and washes your windows and tops off your gas tank while it's at it. (You still need to correct any red-eye and remove any scratches by hand.)

If you don't like the results of the Photo Fix, read on! Sometimes you just have to roll up your sleeves and get a little dirty to create the vibrant picture that your friends deserve to see.

Using the Adjustment Dialog Boxes

Many adjustment dialog boxes on the Paint Shop Pro Effects (and Colors) menu have similar adjustment, preview, and proofing features. The Automatic Color Balance dialog box provides an example in Figure 7-1.

Adjustments are made using three types of control:

- ✔ **Sliders:** You make many adjustments by dragging sliders. Dragging varies an associated value (number) that appears in a text box near each slider.

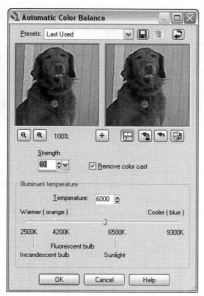

Figure 7-1:
The
Automatic
Color
Balance
dialog box
illustrates
controls
common
to all the
adjustment
dialog boxes
on the
Effects
menu.

✔ **Slider values:** Rather than drag the slider, you may click in its associated text box and type a value. This action gives you more precise control than dragging the slider.

✔ **Value boxes:** Value boxes in Paint Shop Pro (like the Strength box shown in Figure 7-1) are just like value boxes anywhere, but with an additional feature. You can type a value, or increment or decrement the value by clicking the up and down arrows that appear in a pair to the right of the box. You can also adjust the value by clicking and holding the down arrow to the right of the increment buttons and then dragging left or right the slider that appears.

All the dialog boxes let you see the effect of your adjustments (preview them or proof them) before you commit to them. Here's how to preview or proof your changes by using the row of buttons underneath the images:

✔ **Zoom:** To zoom in or out in the preview windows, click the Zoom In button (a magnifier with a +) or Zoom Out button (with a –); refer to Figure 7-1.

✔ **Drag:** To move an image behind the preview windows, drag the image within a preview window. In almost all dialog boxes, you can drag in either window, although some of them use the left window for defining areas of interest. Get in the habit of dragging in the right window.

✔ **Navigate:** To move quickly to a new area of the image, click the Navigate button shown in Figure 7-1 and hold the mouse button down for a moment. A small version of the entire image is displayed, with a rectangle representing your preview area. Drag the rectangle to the area you want to preview and then release the mouse button.

✔ **Proof:** To see the effect of your adjustments in the main image window, known as *proofing,* click the Proof button. (The changes you see aren't permanent until you click the OK button.) Click the Proof button again to remove the change.

✔ **Auto Proof:** If you would prefer to always proof your adjustments rather than just see them in the preview windows, click the Auto Proof button. Paint Shop Pro now shows the effect of your changes in the main image window every time you make a change. For large images or older computers, however, you may find this proofing method slow. Turn off auto proofing by clicking the button again.

✔ **Randomize Parameters:** If you're feeling lucky, click the die; Paint Shop Pro chooses settings at random for you.

After you make an adjustment, click OK to apply it to your image.

Changes are rarely final in Paint Shop Pro because you can undo them by clicking the Undo button on the toolbar, pressing Ctrl+Z, or choosing the Edit⇨Command History command (refer to Chapter 1).

If you use a certain adjustment often, you can save its settings as *presets;* see Chapter 18 for more details on this timesaver.

If you're not sure which photographic adjustment will make your picture look the way you want, the Effect Browser gives you a gallery of different versions of your photo, showing you how it looks under the effect of each of the various adjustments. See the section in Chapter 8 about trying on browsing effects for more details.

Correcting Lighting Color

Despite automatic flashes, lighting is still one of the prime photographic problems. Your flash fails to go off, the room is lit by incandescent or fluorescent light, the sunset casts an orange light, the forest reflects green, or the swimming pool reflects blue. Many of these problems go away almost magically with the Paint Shop Pro Automatic Color Balance effect.

Choose Adjust⇨Color Balance⇨Automatic Color Balance. The Automatic Color Balance dialog box makes the scene (refer to Figure 7-1).

Adjust the slider left or right in the grandiosely named Illuminant Temperature area, or edit the value in the Temperature text box. Dragging the slider left (lower Temperature value) makes the color of your photo visually warmer, or more orange. (Yes, lower Temperature makes color warmer.) Dragging right makes the color visually cooler, or bluer. Notice that the Temperature scale is labeled with various light sources, such as Sunlight; position the slider at a given label to simulate that light source.

Adjust the Strength value higher for greater effect — generally, a brighter picture. Adjust it down for the opposite effect.

You want to check the Remove color cast box when a picture is predominantly one color — for example, Dave's wife is mostly blue. Paint Shop Pro then analyzes the image to try to find what the dominant color is and then attempts to mute that color to bring out the other hues.

See the color section of this book for a color version of Figure 7-1, in which the Automatic Color Balance adjustment salvages a rather blue picture of Dave's wife. That photo was accidentally taken indoors without a flash.

The Temperature thing is about the illumination term *color temperature,* referring to the temperature of an incandescent light source. A lower-temperature light source generally gives a warmer (more orange) light. You can see the effect in a fireplace or barbecue; as the fire dies down, it gives off a more orange glow.

Correcting Contrast and Brightness

Paint Shop Pro offers several ways to adjust contrast (see Chapter 10 for additional ways), but for photos the Automatic Contrast Enhancement effect is a great place to start. It simultaneously fiddles with brightness and contrast — two interlinked attributes — to optimize your photo's appearance. Whether your photo has too little contrast or too much, this tool can help.

Choose Adjust⇨Brightness and Contrast⇨Automatic Contrast Enhancement and the Automatic Contrast Enhancement control of Figure 7-2 rushes to your aid. It has three control areas: *Bias* (or lightness), *Strength* (amount of effect), and *Appearance* (amount of contrast).

In the figure, a photo we took of a cardinal (through a window) suffers from poor contrast — a dark fate for such a bright bird. The Automatic Contrast Enhancement effect restores his outstanding appearance. Use the controls of this effect in the following ways:

✔ If your photo needs contrast adjustment, use the Appearance controls. If your photo needs more contrast, click Bold; for less contrast, click Flat; and, if it's just right, click Natural.

✔ If your photo needs lightening or darkening, use the Bias controls. If it's overall too dark, click Lighter; if it's too light, click Darker; if it's just right, click Neutral.

✔ For a greater effect on contrast and brightness, click Normal in the Strength area. Otherwise, choose Mild.

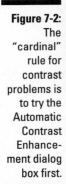

Figure 7-2:
The "cardinal" rule for contrast problems is to try the Automatic Contrast Enhancement dialog box first.

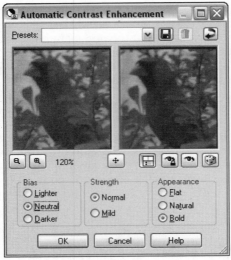

Intensifying (or Dulling) Colors

The more common problem with photos is dull colors that need more intensity. However, if you're shooting Ronald McDonald, for example, at a sunny tulip festival, we can imagine that you may need duller colors, too. Either way, the Automatic Saturation Enhancement effect fills the bill.

Choose Adjust➪Hue and Saturation➪Automatic Saturation Enhancement to enter the land of more intense (or dimmer) colors. The Automatic Saturation Enhancement dialog box glimmers onto your screen.

Figure 7-3 shows the dialog box in action. Showing you intensified colors in a black-and-white illustration is a bit too much of a challenge, however, so please turn to the color section of this book to see what kind of results you can achieve.

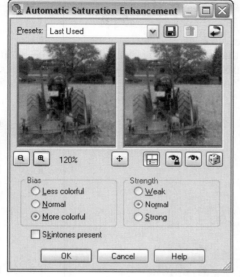

Figure 7-3:
Brightening
up a dull
day at the
farm with
Automatic
Saturation
Enhance-
ment.

Controls in the Bias area determine whether you intensify or dull your colors. Choose Less Colorful to dull your colors or More Colorful to intensify colors. Normal may intensify or dull your colors, depending on how intense they are now.

Controls in the Strength area determine to what degree you dull or intensify colors (according to your choice in the Bias area). Choose Weak to barely affect colors, Normal to moderately affect them, or Strong to have the most effect.

If you have people in your image, the Automatic Saturation Enhancement may brighten their faces by mistake, amplifying a healthy pink into a drunkard's blush. Or, it may dampen a vibrant brown into a sallow gray. If you have people in your picture, check the Skintones present check box to warn Paint Shop Pro to leave those pinks and browns alone!

Removing JPEG, Moiré, and Other Patterns

Unwanted patterns, or other disturbances, are common in images created or stored in certain ways. Paint Shop Pro offers several effects to help you rid your images of these imperfections.

Unearthing JPEG artifacts

When photos are stored in JPEG format, as they often are, the result is nice, small files. But JPEGs that have been compressed to save space often exhibit strange patterns and checkerboard patterns around text and other objects with sharp edges. Figure 7-4 shows those patterns, also called *artifacts*.

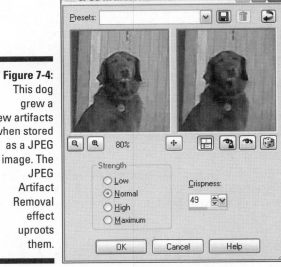

Figure 7-4: This dog grew a few artifacts when stored as a JPEG image. The JPEG Artifact Removal effect uproots them.

To clean up JPEG images, choose the Adjust➪Add/Remove Noise➪ JPEG Artifact Removal option. The JPEG Artifact Removal expert appears on your doorstep in the form of the dialog box shown in the figure.

Checking your image by either looking in the right preview window or proofing your choice, choose the strength (Low, Normal, High, or Maximum) needed to clean up your artifacts. Another casualty in JPEG files is a certain amount of detail, which you can restore by increasing the value in the Crispness value box.

Don't want no moiré

Scanned-in photos from print media (books, magazines, newsletters, PC-printed images) often have moiré patterns. (Refer to Chapter 2 for more information about moiré and ways to avoid it in the first place.)

You can fix moiré patterns by choosing Adjust⇔Noise⇔ Moiré Pattern Removal. The rather simple Moire Pattern Removal dialog box arrives to do your bidding.

The Moire Pattern Removal dialog box offers two controls: Fine Details and Remove Bands. Adjusting Fine Details upward (sliding it to the right) blurs your image, removing fine, grainy moiré patterning. Adjusting Remove Bands upward counters the distracting bands that often are part of moiré patterning.

Unlacing your interlacing

Images captured from videocameras are often *interlaced*. The image is made up of horizontal lines created in two passes: The first pass fills in the odd-numbered lines, and the second fills in the even-numbered lines. Because the two passes occur at slightly different times, the result is often a motion-induced blur. The Paint Shop Pro answer to interlacing problems is the straightforward Deinterlace effect.

Choose Adjust⇔Add/Remove Noise⇔Deinterlace. The Deinterlace dialog box appears. It has one control named Scanlines To Retain. Choose which set of lines you like by clicking either Odd or Even. Paint Shop Pro fills in the eliminated lines by averaging between the lines you retain.

Rubbing Out Scratchiness

Some photos or their negatives can get pretty seriously abused, picking up tiny scratches, pits, or other imperfections while being handled, while living in suitcases or sandy beach bags, or while being badly processed. Hey, who wouldn't get a little abraded under those circumstances? To fix individual scratches, creases, or folds, see the Scratch Remover tool in Chapter 6. To get rid of lots of scratches at one time, try the Automatic Small Scratch Removal effect.

Choose Adjust⇔Add/Remove Noise⇔Automatic Small Scratch Removal. The Automatic Small Scratch Removal dialog box scratches its way onto your screen.

First, determine whether your scratches are light or dark or both. Next, select Remove Light Scratches, Remove Dark Scratches, or both. If the preview image on the right side isn't already adequately cleaned up, change the Strength setting from Normal to Aggressive. If the effect is removing things that aren't scratches or making your photo too fuzzy, try changing Strength to Mild. (A necessary side effect of cleaning up scratches with this effect is a bit of added fuzziness, so you can't be too picky.) If the effect is removing too many tiny features, try adjusting the Local Contrast Limits. To restore low-contrast features, drag the pointer at the left end of the line to the right. To restore high-contrast features, drag the pointer at the right end of the line to the left.

If the result is still too fuzzy, check out "Removing Noise (Speckles)," later in this chapter, for alternative methods like the Salt-and-Pepper filter.

Bringing into Soft Focus

Directors learned long ago that smearing the lens with Vaseline produced a soft, gentle look that gives everything a faint glow and makes the leading lady look angelic. (Not coincidentally, it also hid wrinkles on aging marquee stars like Doris Day.) If you want to put the romance back in your photos, you too can simulate this effect!

Choose Adjust⇨Softness⇨Soft Focus to bring up the Soft Focus controls, as shown in Figure 7-5, which allow you to smear all the virtual Vaseline you want:

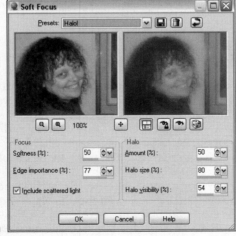

Figure 7-5:
William's wife, Gini, seen through the eyes of love.

✔ **Softness:** This option controls how blurry you want your image, much like defocusing a camera. Slide it to the right to give it that total I-forgot-my-glasses look.

✔ **Edge Importance:** Blurring the image may cause faces to turn into peachlike, fuzzy mushes; sliding this control to the right attempts to keep the edges (and eyes) distinct. It also helps to produce halos that surround objects, as opposed to a more general haze.

✔ **Halo Amount:** You can produce halos that lend an angelic look to the items in your image. Slide this control to the right for halo effects that surround just about everything, or yank it all the way to the left to turn off haloing altogether.

✔ **Halo Size:** Sliding this control to the right creates large, wide bands of halos, and moving it left produces tighter, "borderlike" halos.

✔ **Halo Visibility:** To create halos of pure white light, drag this control to 100 percent; for softer, more background-colored halos, pull it leftward.

Correcting for a Specific Color

Sometimes you don't know exactly what's wrong with the color of a photo. You may, however, know that the color of a specific object in the photo is wrong. For instance, skin color may be too blue in those underwater shots, or your cat is simply not that shade of brown. Would you recognize the correct color of that skin or cat if you saw it? If so, you have an easy way to correct the color of your photo: the Paint Shop Pro Manual Color Correction effect.

Note that Manual Color Correction adjusts the color of the *entire* image so that your selected object (skin or fur, for example) is then the correct color. It presumes that every object in your photograph was shot in the same, bad light. If it gets your selected portion of the image correct, the entire image is then correct. You *can* use it to correct just the object itself, but you must first select that object using the Paint Shop Pro selection tools.

Ready? Choose Adjust➪Color Balance➪Manual Color Correction to give this targeted tool its instructions. The Manual Color Correction dialog box appears, as shown in Figure 7-6. (Refer to the color section of this book to see the difference in colors.)

1. **Click the Preset Colors radio button and choose a likely-sounding category from the menu that matches some portion of your object, like Skintones or Hair.**

2. **Click and drag in the left preview window to select a small swatch in your image that matches the menu selection.**

   In this case, we have selected Skintones and have selected a tiny box of skin on Katy's cheek. We could also have selected Hair and selected her bangs, if we had wanted.

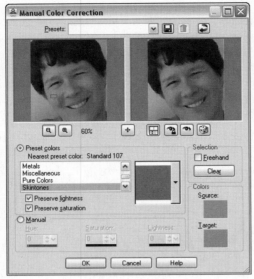

Figure 7-6:
Correcting
the entire
photo so
that Katy's
skin tone is
correct.

Drag diagonally to define a rectangular area. For instance, drag across the forehead of your subject, creating a rectangle that surrounds a fairly uniform skin color, if you intend to match the person's skin tone to a color. Choose an area that isn't strongly affected by highlights or shadows. Drag again if you want to change your selection.

If the area you want to define is irregular in shape, enable the Freehand Selection check box. Then, drag (draw) the irregular shape you want to use on the left window.

Use the zoom, drag, and locating features of the dialog box (see "Using the Adjustment Dialog Boxes," earlier in this chapter) to get to the right place in the left preview window, if need be.

3. **Click the down arrow to the right of the Preset Colors box.**

   A gallery of color appears.

4. **Choose a color from the gallery that is what that swatch *should* look like.**

   If you can't find the color you want, click the Manual button and then click in the Target box to choose a color from the Paint Shop Pro Color dialog box. Refer to Chapter 3 for the details of using this dialog box.

Paint Shop Pro then alters the image in the right preview window, matching the hue of your selected area to the hue of the color you chose in Step 4.

"But," you may say, "the color doesn't match exactly." Don't panic. Unless you have previously fiddled with the check boxes in the Options section of the Manual Color Correction dialog box, the color *shouldn't* match exactly — yet. The Preserve Lightness and Preserve Saturation check boxes, which are initially selected, cause your photo's color to be corrected only to the *hue* (a kind of fundamental color) of the color you have selected, and not to its saturation or lightness. (See Chapter 9 for more information about hue, saturation, and lightness.) If you want to make the color match your chosen sample exactly, you must clear both check boxes. However, you may find that you get good results more easily by leaving both check boxes selected and choosing different colors.

Sharpening, Edge Enhancing, or Blurring

Many photos need sharpening — well, many of ours do, anyway. Not many *need* blurring. Blurring is more of an artistic effect (like those we cover in Chapter 8) than it is a photo-enhancing effect but, because it's conceptually the opposite of sharpening, we discuss it here.

You can apply any of these effects repeatedly to increase their effect. Too much sharpening, however, can turn your image into a messy field of high-contrast dots. Too much blurring can turn it into a smeary mess.

Sharpening

Paint Shop Pro offers three sharpening adjustments. Choose Adjust⇨ Sharpness and then choose one of the following options from the menu that appears:

- ✔ **Sharpen:** Does a little bit of metaphorical grinding and filing on the various edges of your photo, boosting the contrast at those edges. No dialog box appears — your image simply gets sharper.

- ✔ **Sharpen More:** The same as Sharpen, but more so.

- ✔ **Unsharp Mask:** Sharpens like its two siblings (Sharpen and Sharpen More), but operates incognito, like the Lone Ranger. No, just kidding. It wears not a mask, but rather an adjustment dialog box. To use this box's controls, refer to Chapter 2, where we discuss unsharp masking when setting contrast and other adjustments in scanning software.

Technically, if your picture is taken out of focus, none of these effects can make it sharp. These effects can, however, give the illusion of doing so in some cases. The detail it restores is fake — but it's a good fake.

Edge enhancing

The Paint Shop Pro Enhance Edge effect is a close cousin to its sharpening effect. Both find adjoining pixels that contrast in lightness (an edge) and then make the contrast stronger by darkening or lightening those pixels. The pixels gradually move toward fully saturated primary colors, plus white and black.

Choose Effects⇨Edge Effects⇨Enhance or its more powerful sibling, Enhance More. Neither uses an adjustment box, but just immediately does its thing.

How do sharpening and edge enhancing compare? The Enhance effect is more dramatic, focusing directly on even the tiniest edge. The Sharpen adjustment makes a subtler change that influences a range of pixels around the edge.

Blurring

Blurring effects, although many and varied, are simple to use. Choose Adjust⇨Blur to access these menu items:

- **Average:** Pops up an adjustment dialog box with a single control, Amount of Correction. Drag right for more blur.

- **Blur:** Applies a moderate amount of blurring. No adjustment dialog box appears.

- **Blur More:** Like Blur, only more so.

- **Gaussian Blur:** Pops up a single-control adjustment dialog box. Drag the Radius control to the right for more blurring or left for less. To the trained eye of the blur aficionado, this blur is a bit more refined than Average blur. To the rest of us, it's just a blur.

- **Motion Blur:** This effect is an artistic one that most people can understand, having tried to take a photo of a fast-moving child, car, or animal and ended up with a motion blur. This effect, using an adjustment dialog box, *produces* a motion blur! Drag the clock-hand-like Direction control in that box to point in the direction you want motion. Then set the Strength slider, moving it to the right if you need more blur (see the following Tip paragraph).

Blur is often most effective when applied selectively to a particular area of your image. Select an area with any of the selection tools we discuss in Chapter 12 and then apply the blur effect. Blur applied selectively can help focus attention on the subject of your photo, and away from a confusing background.

The Motion Blur effect is sometimes best applied to the background area *around* the object you want to appear speedy, so the object of interest isn't blurred. It's a great way, for instance, to make Speedy, your lethargic retriever, appear to live up to his name. Take a photo of Speedy in his fastest pose — moseying toward his dinner bowl, for example. In Paint Shop Pro, select the area around Speedy before choosing the Motion Blur effect. Apply the motion blur in the head-to-tail direction. Your photo looks like your camera tracked Speedy as he sped heroically to save his Gravy Train from a watery demise. Figure 7-7 shows this effect applied to Alex, with a slight feathering to make him blend into the blurred background better.

Figure 7-7:
Speedy
Alex.

Removing Noise (Speckles)

Removing noise from an image sounds a bit illogical, like subtracting apples from oranges or removing odor from a TV program. Okay, you can perhaps imagine ways to do the latter, but apply that same imagination to how your TV looks when you run a vacuum cleaner: The screen is covered with speckles. That's *graphical noise:* pixels altered at random locations and in random colors.

The trick with removing speckles is to avoid removing freckles — and other speckly stuff that's supposed to be in the picture. (Unless, of course, you *want* to get rid of the freckles!) For that reason, Paint Shop Pro offers several choices, depending on what you need. Choose Adjust⇨Add/Remove Noise and then one of these menu selections:

- ✔ **Despeckle:** Removes smaller, isolated speckles altogether. Good for removing a light coating of dust. Speckles that are closer to each other tend to form clumps, however.

- ✔ **Edge-Preserving Smooth:** Gives an effect like rubbing carefully within the shaded areas of a pastel drawing, using your finger. Speckles disappear into a uniform shade, and you keep the sharp edges of those larger areas. This effect is also good for removing the random discoloration of pixels that often results from shooting digital photos in low light. In the adjustment dialog box that appears, drag the Number of Steps slider to the right to make a smoother image.

Edge-Preserving Smooth, turned up high, creates a nice oil-painting-like effect on photos! See Figure C-11 in the color insert in this book.

- ✔ **Median Filter:** Removes speckles by removing fine detail, a kind of blurring process in which each pixel is recalculated to be the average of its neighbors. Contrast is lost at the detail level. An adjustment dialog box appears in which you drag the Amount of Correction slider to the right to remove increasingly large details.

- ✔ **Salt-and-Pepper Filter:** Removes speckles of a particular size (or up to a particular size) you choose. A Salt-and-Pepper Filter adjustment dialog box appears, with these adjustments:

    Speck Size: Adjust this value to match or slightly exceed the size of the speckles you're trying to get rid of. (You may have to zoom in close to figure out how big your speckles are.)

    Sensitivity to Specks: If the right preview window shows clusters of specks remaining, increase this value. Too high a value blurs your photo.

    Include All Lower Speck Sizes: Enable this check box to remove specks of Speck Size and smaller. Otherwise, you just remove specks close to Speck Size.

    Aggressive Action: Enable this check box to remove specks more completely. Otherwise, you may simply reduce the specks' intensity.

- ✔ **Texture-Preserving Smooth:** This effect sounds like a sophisticated grade of peanut butter. Actually, it blurs and reduces the contrast of tiny specks while preserving the larger variations that give texture to grass, wood, water, and the like. The result is sort of like a crunchy peanut butter without small, gritty chunks. An adjustment dialog box appears in which you adjust the Amount of Correction value upward to minimize specks.

- ✔ **Add Noise:** Why would you want to *add* noise? If you're trying to make a photo look older or give it a rusty patina or an overlay of static, you can seed your image with random pixels. Drag the slider to the right to obscure your image in a haze of dots. There are three Add Noise selections, each of which deals with color placement:

    Random: The noise colors are — surprise! — chosen at random from the available color palette. If you have a black-and-white image, don't expect to see red pixels, although you *could* see garish orange and purple pixels in a mostly green picture.

Uniform: The noise colors are all chosen from within the image itself, making this option perfect for "olderizing" a picture.

Gaussian: Choose this option for a more static-like effect.

You can always select an area using the Paint Shop Pro selection tools, in order to add or remove noise from only that specific area (see Chapter 12).

Chapter 8

Creating Artsy Effects

*P*aint Shop Pro has enough wild and crazy effects to satisfy the most *avant garde artistes* (psycho art geeks). The Effects menu in Paint Shop Pro 8 hides more than 70 different effects that you can consider creative. Jasc undoubtedly has even more coming down the pipeline. These gadgets are great fun and incredible timesavers when you need a striking effect in a hurry.

Many of these effects use adjustment dialog boxes, which all have a set of common controls for zooming, previewing, proofing, and other functions. Refer to Chapter 7 for help using these controls. We don't repeat those instructions here.

Paint Shop Pro categorizes its creative effects into these ten major categories:

✔ **3D Effects:** For turning selected areas into raised buttons or cutouts, dropping shadows, or doing anything else that looks like it's raised above or dropped below the page.

✔ **Art Media Effects:** For simulating physical art media, like pencil, colored chalk, and paint brushing.

✔ **Artistic Effects:** For changing your picture into another medium entirely, like a big neon glow, a topographical map, or a tinfoil stamp.

✔ **Distortion Effects:** For warping the surface of your image, by sending gentle ripples across the top of it, making it look like you're looking at it through a big lens, or pixelating parts of it just like they do whenever someone is exposing too much flesh on *Cops.*

✔ **Edge Effects:** For finding the edges within a picture and bringing them into focus or softening those edges into a fine Silly Putty-ish blur.

✔ **Geometric Effects:** For wrapping or distorting the image as a whole. In Distortion Effects, you change the surface, but the picture stays the same size and shape; in Geometric Effects, you can wrap your picture around a can, or stre-e-e-etch it like it was a big rubber band.

✔ **Illumination Effects:** For introducing a sunburst or placing one or more spotlights on parts of the image.

✔ **Image Effects:** A catchall category for creating tiles, moving images slightly, or creating a page-curl effect.

✔ **Reflection Effects:** For holding a mirror — or several mirrors — up to your fabulous image, creating a simple reverse image or a funhouse array of reflections.

✔ **Texture Effects:** For giving your image the effect of being laid on different surfaces, like crinkled paper or leather, or seen through mosaic glass.

Effects, like most other features of Paint Shop Pro, work on whatever layer of a multilayer image is active — and, if you have an area selected, only within that selection. This restriction is designed to let you modify just the portion of the image you want, but it can also be confusing if you forget that you have made a selection or changed layers: Your effect may not appear to work. If your image has multiple layers, choose the layer you want before applying an effect. Effects don't work on Vector or Adjustment layers. If you use an Adjustment layer, you must merge it with your image if you want your effect to act on that adjustment. (See Chapter 14 for more information about layers.) If you haven't created any layers, or added text, lines, or shapes to your image, don't sweat the layer thing.

Effects don't work on 256-color images. If your image has 256 or fewer colors, Paint Shop Pro asks whether it's okay to automatically increase the color depth to 16.7 million. Click OK, and then see Chapter 19 if you want it to stop asking these silly questions.

If you use a certain adjustment often, you can save its settings as *presets;* see Chapter 18 for more details on this timesaver.

Try 'Em On: Browsing the Effects

An easy way to try an effect on your image is to use the *Effect browser*. Choose Effects⇨Effect Browser. The Effect Browser dialog box appears, as shown in Figure 8-1.

Figure 8-1: Browsing gives you a rough idea of an effect's influence on your image.

Choose an effect on the left side; as you can see in Figure 8-1, each of the effects is grouped into folders — which are, conveniently enough, the same categories we list in the preceding section. (Adjustments, as we mention in Chapter 7, can also be found here; click the Adjustments folder to see a constellation of color shifts, blurs, and focusings that improve the quality of your image.)

You can expand a folder by clicking the plus box to the left of it, or you can collapse it by clicking the minus sign. Click in any of the folders to get samples of all the effects within each folder; the preview window on the right side gives you a rough idea of what the effect does to your image. The preview can give you only a rough impression because many effects vary depending on how you adjust them. Figure 8-1 shows all the effects in the Artistic Effects folder applied to an image of trusty Alex.

If your computer is taking a long time to render the effects, check the Quick Render box on the right side, which creates a quick-and-dirty thumbnail version of the effects. If you want the full Monty in finely rendered glory, feel free to uncheck it.

If you have a selected area, or if the active layer contains only one filled-in area, that area fills the preview window. Remember that effects apply to only the active layer.

If you find an effect you think you may like, click the Apply button. If you want to tweak the settings of effect or adjustment, clicking the Modify button displays a dialog box that lets you change the settings, if there are any to change. If you don't like what the image looks like after the Effect Browser finishes up, press Ctrl+Z or click the Undo button on the toolbar.

3-D: Holes, Buttons, and Chisels

Except for the Buttonize effect, you must select an area before you apply any of the 3-D effects. The area you select is what is turned into a button, chiseled, cut out, or beveled inside or outside the selection marquee. Also, if you intend to use background color for the Buttonize, Chisel, or Inner Bevel effect, choose it now.

Choose Effects➪3D Effects. Then, choose one of these options from the menu that appears:

- **Buttonize:** Creates a raised appearance (inside your selection if you have made a selection). Because it's a Web thing, we discuss buttonization in Chapter 17.

- **Chisel:** Creates a raised appearance by making an edge *outside* your selection. In the Chisel dialog box that appears, increase the edge width by increasing the Size value. Choose Transparent Edge to see through the edge, or Solid Color otherwise.

- **Cutout:** Creates the illusion of cutting out your selected area and extending a shadow in two directions. Drag the Vertical and Horizontal sliders left or right to extend the shadow from different edges. Increase the Opacity setting to darken the shadow, or increase Blur to blur the shadow's edge. You can change the color of the shadow or the underlying surface by clicking the Shadow Color swatch or the Fill Interior with Color swatch, respectively. Then choose a color from the Color dialog box that appears.

- **Drop Shadow:** Drops a shadow in any direction from your selected area, as though that area were floating over a surface. In the Drop Shadow dialog box that appears, drag Vertical and Horizontal sliders to change the shadow location — or, if you want something a little more intuitive, you can click the crosshairs in the left window and drag them around the central circle to indicate which way (and how far away) you want the shadow to fall. The Opacity, Blur, and Color settings work exactly the same way as they do in the Cutout section.

✔ **Inner Bevel or Outer Bevel:** Creates an effect like raising a pyramid. The pyramid's sloping sides (the bevel) appear within your selection area for Inner Bevel or outside them for Outer Bevel. A rather complex-looking dialog box appears. Click the Bevel illustration to choose a bevel profile from a gallery. (Each profile is like the cross-sections you see of wood moldings in a hardware store.) To see what other controls do, either fiddle with them or see the section "Common Adjustments," later in this chapter.

Art and Artistic Effects: Simulating Traditional Art Media and Beyond

Paint Shop Pro offers way too many artistic effects for us to discuss them individually here. We show you a couple of examples in this section.

Choose Effects⇨Artistic Effects or Effects⇨Art Media Effects and Paint Shop Pro reveals a large menu of possibilities. (As we said earlier, Art Media tends to simulate things you can do in real life, like turning your picture into a pencil drawing, and Artistic Effects transform your picture into another media entirely, like an old newspaper or hot chrome.) Choose one from the list.

Nearly all these effects display an adjustment dialog box (refer to Chapter 7 for an explanation of the basic controls). See the section "Common Adjustments," later in this chapter, for help regarding more specialized controls. For the most part, your best approach is to fiddle with the controls for a while. A few effects take place immediately. If you don't like the result, press Ctrl+Z to undo it.

Not all the effects capable of making artistic results are neatly categorized on the Artistic Effects or Art Media Effects menu selection! For instance, we find that applying the Edge Preserving Smooth adjustment creates a wonderful painted result, and adding Noise can speckle a picture to make it look old.

Here are a few more general tips for using artistic effects:

✔ If the result is too fuzzy, try decreasing various values (especially density, if that adjustment exists). Most effects do some blurring, so if you turn it down a bit (decrease the effect), the image becomes clearer.

✔ If the result is too speckly or has too many lines, look for a detail adjustment and if you find one, turn it down.

✔ Some effects that do stuff with edges need a little help. Try running the Edge Enhance effect (choose Effects⇨Edge Effects⇨Enhance) or boosting contrast before applying your artistic effect. Or, in the adjustment box for your edge-fiddling effect, look for an intensity control and increase it.

Example 1: Topography

Topography is, for no particularly good reason, one of our favorite artistic effects. Its result is an image that looks like stacked, cut sheets of cardboard or foamboard (like the ones architects use in models to simulate sloping ground). Figure 8-2 shows the creation of Sir Topography.

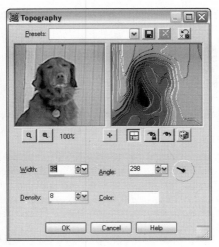

Figure 8-2:
The Topography adjustments control the number of levels and the way the light strikes the stack.

The controls do the following:

- ✔ **Width:** At low Width settings, contours follow the details of the picture more closely. At high Width settings, contours are broad and without sharp turns; detail is lost.

- ✔ **Density:** Density controls the number of layers in the virtual stack of layers. A higher density results in a surface that conforms more to the original detail. A lower density gives a more abstract result.

- ✔ **Angle:** The Angle control in the Lighting section determines the direction from which light is coming to illuminate the side of the stack. Drag its clock-hand-like control to point in the direction you want this light to shine.

- ✔ **Color:** Color determines the color of light that strikes the stack from the side. Originally, the Color control is set to white. To change it, you may either left-click the swatch (to choose from the Color Wheel) or right-click (to choose a basic or recently used color from the Recent Colors dialog box).

Example 2: Brush strokes

The Brush Strokes effect has lots of things to fiddle with, and you probably have to spend some time fiddling to get a result you like. It gives the appearance of applying thin or thick paint with a brush. In real life, the edges of paint strokes catch any incidental light, and in this effect you can simulate that appearance in varying degrees. Figure 8-3 shows a photograph of faithful Alex, who stays there forever as long as you keep stroking his fur.

Figure 8-3:
Brush strokes, one of the more complex effects.

The Brush Strokes controls work as follows:

- ✔ **Length:** Short lengths (low values of Length) create a stippled effect, like someone poking the end of a brush into the canvas. Longer lengths produce visible stroke directions.

- ✔ **Density:** Density determines the number of strokes. The greatest sensitivity of this control is at the very low end. A very low density (1 or 2) gives the appearance of a few strokes made over a photograph. Higher density makes a more abstract effect of many overlaid strokes.

- ✔ **Bristles:** A higher value of Bristles gives the distinct patch of paint that a nice, new, neatly trimmed brush, packed densely with bristles, lays down. A lower value simulates the scratchy result of a brush where the bristles are few or frazzled.

- ✔ **Width:** The Width control determines the width of the brush stroke. A higher value makes a wider brush.

- **Opacity:** The Opacity control sets the density of the paint. A low value gives a blurred effect that is more like looking through frosted glass than anything else. A high value makes paint look like it was applied thickly, as though with a palette knife.

- **Softness:** The Softness control gives a smoother look to the paint surface, with less speckling.

- **Angle:** The Angle control determines the direction of the incident light that glints off the edges of thick paint strokes. Drag the clock-hand-like control to point *toward the source* of the light.

- **Color:** To change the color of incident light striking the paint edges, click the Color swatch and choose from the Color dialog box. (Or right-click to choose from the Recent Colors dialog box.) Black gives no incident light, a dark color (low lightness value) gives a little, and so on. High lightness values strongly emphasize the stroke edges.

Like many effects, if you return to this adjustment dialog box later, it normally resumes whatever settings you last used. This intelligent behavior saves you lots of time returning to settings you like.

If you use this effect often, you may want to save any given combination of settings as a *preset* for later use. See the section in Chapter 18 about presets.

Geometric, Distortion, and Image Effects: Curls, Squeezes, Wraps, and Waves

Paint Shop Pro has enough curls, squeezes, and waves to outfit an entire army of cute toddlers. If you want anything bent, distorted, or wrapped, Paint Shop Pro can tie it up in a knot.

Choose Effects➪Geometric Effects, Effects➪Distortion Effects or Effects➪ Image Effects and then choose from the large list that appears. As with the Artistic Effects, Paint Shop Pro has too many effects for us to try to cover completely. Fortunately, most controls are either self-evident or do something you can easily figure out by playing with them. We give you a couple of examples, though.

Here are a few tips for using Geometric effects:

- Some effects are centered on a particular location. To move the center, adjust the Horizontal and Vertical controls. A setting of zero centers the effect horizontally or vertically. Negative horizontal values are to the left of center; negative vertical values are *above* center.

✔ Remember that you can apply any effect to a particular area by selecting that area first. Using a feathered edge on the selection feathers the modified image into the original image.

Need a thinner face? If you have a portrait on a plain background, Paint Shop Pro can help. First, carefully select the face. Then, equally carefully, remove areas around the eyes, nose, and mouth from the selection. (See Chapter 12 for help with removing areas from a selection.) Apply the Pinch effect on the Distortion Effects menu.

The Page Curl effect is, for some reason, one of the most enduringly popular geometric effects. It seems that we never tire of remarking, "Why, Martha, that photo looks like it's a-peelin' right off the page!" We guess the Page Curl effect (easily accessible by choosing Effects⇨Image Effects⇨Page Curl) is just plain a-peelin'. Figure 8-4 shows this remarkable effect.

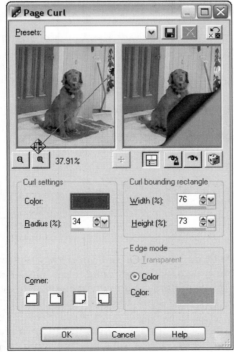

Figure 8-4:
Choose a corner, move the curl line in the left window, and set the radius to get a quick curl.

Here's how to control your curl, with the most important stuff listed first:

- **Corner:** Which corner do you want to curl? Click the button depicting your chosen corner.

- **Curl Bounding Rectangle or Width and Height:** To set the position of the curl, drag the tiny gear-shaped widgets at either end of the black line that diagonally crosses the left preview window. As Figure 8-4 shows, your cursor becomes a four-headed arrow when it's over the line's end. Alternatively, you can adjust the Width or Height values to move those points; watch the line as you do so, and see how the Width and Height values affect it.

- **Radius:** How broad do you want curl to be? The smaller the Radius value, the tighter the corner is rolled up. The smaller the corner you're curling (that is, the lower the X and Y values), the smaller the Radius value usually needs to be.

- **Curl Setting Color:** This setting controls the color that appears on the highlight of the curl (the underside of the curled picture). Paint Shop Pro makes the rest of the curl, the shaded part, the same hue, but darker.

- **Edge Mode:** This setting controls the shade that appears on the flat page revealed by the lifted corner. Click the box to choose a different color from the Color dialog box, or right-click to choose from the Recent Colors dialog box, or select Transparent to do away with any nasty colors.

Bear in mind that besides curling the edge of the entire image, you can select a rectangle — a stamp on an envelope, for example — and curl that. (Other selection shapes don't usually work as well.)

Illumination Effects: Sunbursts and Flares

If you need a sparkle of sunlight, unwrap the Paint Shop Pro Sunburst effect. It places a bright spot on your image, with rays of light and circles of lens flare. The adjustment dialog box appears, as shown in Figure 8-5, on top of the image that it's modifying, to better show the effects.

The controls for the three different components each has its own area: Light Spot, Rays, and the Circle Brightness control. All share the same color setting. Here's how to use these adjustments:

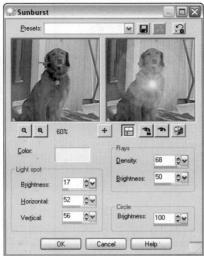

Figure 8-5:
A sunburst placed over Alex's dogtags catches him in midtransformation into his superhero identity.

- ✓ **Color:** Click the Color sample to choose some color other than white from the Color dialog box.

- ✓ **Light Spot Brightness:** Increase to brighten the light spot.

- ✓ **Light Spot Horizontal/Vertical:** Adjust to position the spot. Or, if you can see a tiny set of crosshairs in the left preview window, drag that instead. When your cursor is over the crosshairs, the cursor becomes a four-headed arrow.

- ✓ **Rays Brightness:** Set this option higher to bring out the rays of light you can see in Figure 8-5.

- ✓ **Rays Density:** Adjust this setting lower to see fewer rays or higher to see more rays.

- ✓ **Circle Brightness:** Set this option higher to make the lens flare circles brighter. On light photos, these circles are barely visible, even at full brightness.

Reflection Effects: Mirrors and Patterns

The Reflection effects are a funhouse phenomenon. You can choose a single mirror, or multiple mirrors in various configurations, turning your image into a pattern. Choose Effects➪Reflection Effects, and then one of the four menu items that appear:

✔ **Feedback:** The mirror-reflecting-into-mirror effect you get in barber-shops with mirrors on opposite walls. See "Common Adjustments," later in this chapter, for help with this effect's controls.

✔ **Kaleidoscope:** A humdinger of an effect, like looking at your image through a kaleidoscope.

✔ **Pattern:** Another way, besides Kaleidoscope, to turn your image into a pattern. See the upcoming two sections.

✔ **Rotating Mirror:** Similar to putting a mirror edge-down on your image. You can rotate a reflection to any angle and position the mirror horizontally and vertically on the image.

You can limit any of these effects to a particular area by making a selection first.

Patterns are particularly useful in Paint Shop Pro because you can use them to fill areas. Refer to Chapter 3, where we discuss choosing a pattern to paint with. With the Pattern effect, you can make your own patterns to paint with.

The Pattern adjustment dialog box sets the position, angle, and number of times your image is reflected. Fiddle with these options:

✔ **Center of reflection:** Adjust the Horizontal Offset and Vertical Offset to position the center of your mirror that makes the pattern.

✔ **Rotation angle:** Oddly, this control gives half the rotation it's set to. Set it to 90, for instance, to reflect something at 45 degrees.

✔ **Pattern size:** Set Scale Factor above zero to make the pattern larger than the original, or below zero to make it smaller.

✔ **Number of Columns/Rows:** The pattern is built of repeated rows and columns. Set Columns/Rows values to the number of columns and rows you want.

✔ **Horizontal/Vertical Shift:** Adjust these values to move the pattern within your image boundaries. For instance, to get a horizontally seamless pattern, pixels along the left edge should match those along the right. The Horizontal Shift control helps you do that.

To get a truly seamless pattern requires constant fiddling with two or three controls, especially Scale Factor and the two Shift controls. (Paint Shop Pro comes with some seamless patterns you can use as models. Refer to Chapter 3.)

Texture Effects: Bumpy Surfaces from Asphalt to Weaves

Texture is the neglected third dimension of an image. *Texture,* the surface on which the image is constructed, is a quality most of us don't think about when we think about images, but it's very much a part of the visual experience. An image made up of mosaic tiles, for instance, feels very different from the same image painted on canvas.

To choose a Texture effect, choose Effects⇨Texture Effects and then choose from the extensive menu that appears. Paint Shop Pro has too many textures to cover in detail, but the next few sections should help you sort things out. All effects except one (the Emboss effect) open an adjustment dialog box, in which you should feel free to fiddle while watching the effect.

Relating texture effects to the Material box's textures

You may be a bit confused because Paint Shop Pro gives you two ways to use texture in your images. If you're *painting* an image, you can apply texture by using the Material box (as we show you in Chapter 2). If you already *have* an image, the Texture effects are the way to go.

Texture effects offer more variety and more powerful effects than the Material box does. For instance, you can't paint fur texture or a leather crinkling over an image using the Material box, but you *can* apply it as an effect. Also, unlike Texture effects, which offer scads of ways to change each effect, with Material box textures, you're stuck with three options: the texture, the angle, and the size. That's it; take it or leave it.

If you find that this isn't nearly enough meddling, you can select a sort of superpowered Material box texture from the Texture Effects menu by choosing — surprise — Texture. In that effect's dialog box, you can achieve all kinds of variations using the texture effects you can't achieve within the Material box itself.

(Why didn't Jasc just provide a separate tab for textures in the Material box that had all this stuff in one place, the way it does for gradients and colors? Heck if we know.)

Just as the Texture effect gives you more leverage over the Material box's textures, the Sculpture effect lets you leverage the Color palette's *patterns*. The effect's main job is to turn your image into a sort of etching or embossing, but it also applies patterns. Patterns are sort of like textures, but come with their own colors. The Sculpture effect applies a Paint Shop Pro pattern, allowing you to set a number of variables that are unavailable on the Material Box palette. In the Sculpture effect, for instance, you can give a pattern a (uniform) color or change its size (scale).

Using texture effect controls

Texture adjustments have, in general, two main types of controls:

- ✔ Those for the virtual substance that puts ridges and valleys in the image
- ✔ Those for the light that strikes at some oblique angle and reveals that unevenness

In addition, the virtual substances that make up some textures have optical qualities you can adjust, like transparency and blurring.

If a texture or pattern is unclear at some settings, try zooming out in the adjustment dialog box. (Click the magnifier-with-a-minus-sign button.)

The best way to understand most texture controls is to fiddle with them while watching the right preview window in the adjustment dialog box. (Only the Emboss effect goes to work immediately, without displaying a dialog box.) Some of the more common controls you find in the adjustment dialog boxes are shown in this list:

- ✔ **Length (and occasionally Width) or Size:** The dimensions of the ridges and valleys that make up the texture.
- ✔ **Blur:** The overall fuzziness imparted to the original image.
- ✔ **Detail:** How much detail the lines of texture inherit from the edges of the original image.
- ✔ **Density:** The degree to which ridges and valleys are packed closely together.
- ✔ **Transparency:** The ability to let the original image show clearly through the virtual substance that overlays the image.
- ✔ **Angle:** The direction from which incident light strikes the surface.
- ✔ **Elevation:** The height of the light source above the image. Low elevations show the ridges and valleys more strongly. High elevations make a brighter image. Some textures allow you to set the intensity or luminance and color of the incident light as well.
- ✔ **Ambience:** The overall brightness (ambient light) of the image.

Example 1: The Fur texture effect

A simple texture effect is Fur, excessively applied to Alex in Figure 8-6. The Fur effect causes fibers to radiate from clusters throughout your image, giving a result not unlike the fur of a cat engaged in discussion with a member of the canine profession.

You go fur with this effect if you interpret your controls in the following ways:

- **Blur:** A kind of fluffiness control. Increasing the blur minimizes the visibility of individual hairs and also makes the original image less clear.

- **Density:** Determines the number of hairs; very low settings give a cactus-like, whiskered appearance.

- **Length:** Sets the length of individual hairs. High length values tend to give more of a frosted-glass appearance than a furry one.

- **Transparency:** Determines the extent to which the original image shows through the hair, undisturbed. High transparency values give an effect like hair sprinkled on a photograph.

Figure 8-6:
From the Department of Redundancy Department — giving Alex more fur.

Example 2: The Texture texture effect

The Texture effect you see when you choose Effects⇨Texture Effects⇨ Texture gives you access to the same textures you may use for painting with the Paint Shop Pro Color palette. Here, rather than paint with them, you apply them to an existing image. Figure 8-7 shows faithful Alex, this time receiving a tree-bark texture.

The controls of this dialog box provide enough fiddles to outfit a symphony orchestra. Here's how to make them play in tune:

- ✔ **Texture:** Click here and choose a texture from the Paint Shop Pro gallery of textures that appears.

- ✔ **Size (%):** Make the texture pattern larger by increasing this value above zero. Drag left (make the value negative) for a smaller pattern.

- ✔ **Smoothness:** To blunt the sharp edges of your texture, increase this value.

- ✔ **Depth:** To have deeper valleys and higher hills in your pattern, increase this value.

- ✔ **Ambience:** Adjust this control for a brighter or darker image.

- ✔ **Shininess:** A higher value of shininess puts a bright glint on the edges and corners of your texture pattern.

- ✔ **Color:** Click this swatch to choose a different color of incident light from the Colors dialog box.

- ✔ **Angle:** Drag the clock-hand-like control to point toward the imaginary light source that illuminates the texture.

- ✔ **Intensity:** Higher intensity increases the incident light that reveals the contrast.

- ✔ **Elevation:** Lower values emphasize the hills and valleys; higher values brighten the flat hilltops and valley bottoms. (Reduce ambience to avoid washout at high elevations.)

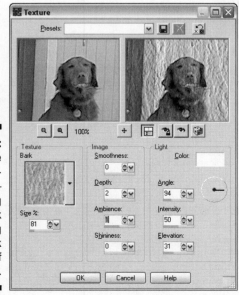

Figure 8-7: More redundancy — making Alex bark (by applying a tree-bark texture, of course).

Common Adjustments

Effects use a wide range of adjustments to set their various variables. In most cases, the function of a control becomes apparent as soon as you fiddle with it, but in complex dialog boxes you may need to understand what does what. This list helps you distinguish one variable from another:

- **Ambience:** General illumination. Determines the image brightness with the incident light source's intensity and elevation.

- **Amplitude:** The degree to which the effect is applied.

- **Angle:** The direction of incident light in the plane of the image. Drag the clock-hand-like control to point toward the source.

- **Blur:** A fuzziness that affects mostly the original image showing through the texture. Makes the texture fuzzier in some textures.

- **Color:** A swatch showing the color of light that glints off the texture's hills and valleys. Click the swatch to choose a new color from the Color dialog box. (To find out how to adjust color, refer to Chapter 2.) Right-click the swatch to choose from the Recent Colors dialog box.

- **Density:** The closeness and number of hills and valleys in the texture.

- **Detail:** The degree to which the texture picks out the detail in the original image.

- **%Effect:** The degree to which the effect is applied.

- **Elevation:** The height of the incident light above the plane of the image. Low elevations show the ridges and valleys more strongly. High elevations make a brighter image.

- **Height:** The height of the hills in the texture.

- **Horizontal/Vertical Center:** The position of the center of the effect.

- **Horizontal/Vertical Offset:** The position of the overall resulting pattern.

- **Intensity:** The strength of the incident light that reveals the texture.

- **Length:** The length of the ridges and valleys that make up the texture.

- **Opacity:** The degree to which the blobs of virtual substance pick up color from the underlying image, as opposed to letting the image's original pixels show through.

- **Presets:** A drop-down list that lets you choose among any named collection of settings you have saved or your Last Used settings. After you change any setting, the Presets selection says Custom.

- **Radius:** The broadness of any curve or curl; smaller radius values make curves or curls tighter.

✔ **Save As:** A button leading to the Preset Save dialog box, in which you enter a name to label your current collection of settings. Choose the name from the Presets list box to recall the setting.

✔ **Shininess:** The glare off the sloping sides of the hills and valleys of the texture.

✔ **Size:** The overall size of the elements of the texture.

✔ **Smoothness:** How rounded the bumps are that make up the texture.

✔ **Symmetric:** A check box that makes an effect work the same way in all directions.

✔ **Transparent/Background color:** Options that either make an edge reveal the underlying image color (Transparent) or color the edge with the current Paint Shop Pro background color.

Framing Your Effects

So you have transformed a picture of Fido into an oil painting, complete with sweeping strokes and a little bit of texture to flesh it out. But you still feel unsatisfied. And that's only natural — after all, what masterpiece is complete without an elegant frame?

Choose Image➪Picture Frame to display the Picture Frame dialog box. Clicking the arrow next to the Picture Frame drop-down menu will display a gallery of frames to choose from, including modern art frames, edge brushings, filmstrip frames, or the ever-popular masking-tape-on-the-corners look. Select a frame to see a preview of your framed image on the right side.

Two radio buttons give you the option to have your frame placed on the outside of your image, or to have the frame jutting into the inside (and potentially obscuring something on the edges of your picture, just like a real frame). Three check boxes allow you to flip, mirror, and rotate the frame, exactly the same as you would flip, rotate, or mirror an image (we show you how in Chapter 11). When you're ready to frame, click OK.

Chapter 9

Adjusting Color By Bits

In This Chapter

▶ Understanding primary color systems

▶ Using hue, saturation, and lightness

▶ Increasing colors

▶ Decreasing colors

*F*or basic painting and image processing, you rarely need to give a hoot about how the computer handles colors. Sometimes, however, understanding a little about the bits behind computer color makes your life much easier and your results better. You likely need to know about bits whenever

✔ Someone gives you, or you have to create, an image file that isn't *full color,* like a GIF file off the Web.

✔ You want to precisely adjust a color.

✔ You want to use a Paint Shop Pro tool that refers to Red, Green, or Blue or Hue, Saturation, or Lightness or some other technical color term.

✔ That little box that follows your cursor when you're choosing a color from the Materials palette is driving you nuts, such as the one shown in Figure 9-1. What do R: 86, G: 147, and B: 7 mean, for cryin' out loud! What are we, playing bingo? No, those are the three color components of the color under the Dropper cursor.

Figure 9-1:
R: 86, G: 147, and B: 7 aren't bingo squares.

Fortunately, the challenge isn't so much understanding the computer as it is understanding the *illusion* of color that humans have been using for about a hundred years to print or display color images. The computer is just the latest step in creating that illusion.

Mastering the Color Illusion

When you look at color in the real world, you're seeing the real thing: the full spectrum of color, from red sunsets to purple mountains plus all the colors of fire engines, new Volkswagen Beetles, and the grassy and flowering plains in between. When you look at *mechanized* color images, however, from printed pictures to TV and computer screens, the colors you see are almost always an illusion!

Understanding why the trick works

Although printed or displayed color images seem to be using a full range of colors, they really use a mix of just three (or, in print, four) colors. They can get away with this trick because your eyes have just three kinds of color sensors: one kind that is most sensitive to blue, another that is biased toward red, and a third that favors green. If truly yellow light from the real world strikes your eye, it has an energy partway between red and green, so it tickles both the red and the green sensors by certain amounts. Your brain says "Aha! Red and green: It must be yellow!"

PC and TV screens use this trick to create the illusion of colors, like yellow: Each pixel on the screen is made up of a red, blue, and green glowing dot, the brightness of which is adjustable. The PC turns the blue way down, cranks up the red and green, and you see yellow because your red and green sensors are tickled equally. To get gray, all three colors are made equal; to make white, they're all at full strength; and to make black, they're all zero. But it's all an illusion. Your PC screen cannot really make yellow, orange, magenta, or anything other than pure red, green, and blue.

Fiddling with the mix

To make use of this inside information to adjust the mix of primary colors, start with the Materials palette. Whenever you're choosing a color in the Available Colors area (refer to Figure 9-1), the primary color values (labeled R, G, and B for Red, Green, and Blue) appear at the bottom of a box that follows your cursor around. (In fact, RGB values for colors appear all over Paint Shop Pro.)

Simply knowing this color's number isn't particularly helpful; but now that you know what these numbers mean, you can use them to fine-tune the color by using the Material dialog box we describe in Chapter 3.

To bring up that dialog box so that you can precisely change your foreground or background material, click the Foreground Material or Background Material square on the Materials palette. A Material dialog box appears, and in that box is a Color tab, as shown in Figure 9-2.

You can fiddle with the color by changing the values for R, G, and B, as described in these examples:

✔ Need a more pastel shade? Decrease the highest value and increase the lower values.

✔ Need a purer color? Decrease the lowest of the three values.

✔ Need a darker or lighter shade? Decrease or increase all three values, keeping the same proportions of each one. White occurs when all values are 255. Black occurs when all values are 0.

✔ Need to move a color toward a given primary color (to make a greener yellow, for example)? Increase that primary value (in this instance, green); decrease the next largest value proportionately to keep the lightness the same.

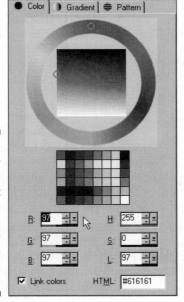

Figure 9-2:
The Color tab lets you adjust the three values. The color here is gray, so R, G, and B are equal.

Of course, you can skip all this by-the-numbers stuff and just click the color you want, but sometimes being precise is useful. You can paint more convincing shadows in outdoor scenes, for example, if you adjust all the values proportionately downward from whatever color you used for the sunlit side and then add just a little blue. (Light in shadows tends to come from a bluish sky.)

Using Hue, Saturation, and Lightness

Fiddling with the primary color values that create the color illusion is okay, but not easy. You may find it tricky to keep proportions adjusted, for example, when you want a lighter shade of a color without changing the basic color of it.

For that reason, clever people came up with a *different* set of three numbers you can use to specify colors: Hue, Saturation, and Lightness (or Luminance), called *HSL*. These values aren't perfectly intuitive either, but they're much closer to how people think about colors than are red, green, and blue. These three values aren't really primary *colors,* but rather a primary color *system:* A few numbers fully describe a color.

You may find yourself using either system in Paint Shop Pro, depending on which controls appear in various places. Some effects, for example, use saturation or lightness. The Color dialog box we describe further in Chapter 3 lets you use either system.

The Materials palette can display color values in either system. Initially, it shows R, G, and B. To make it show H, S, and L, choose File⇨Preferences⇨ General Program Preferences. In the Preferences dialog box that appears, click the Palettes tab and then select the option Display Colors in HSL Format. Click OK.

Here's what H, S, and L are all about:

- ✔ **Hue:** You can think of hue as the basic color. If you and your spouse both want a room painted blue, for example, or even turquoise, you agree on hue. You still have lots of room for disagreement, however, in terms of how pure (saturated) or light that color should be. To a rough approximation, hue is the balance or proportion of primary colors.

- ✔ **Saturation:** Saturation is the least intuitive value. It's the purity, intensity, or richness of a color, independent of its hue or lightness. The most easily understood aspect of saturation is that at zero saturation, any color is a shade of gray (it has equal amounts of red, green, and blue).

- ✔ **Lightness:** Lightness — essentially, brightness — is fairly intuitive. You can change it largely independent of hue or saturation.

To better understand how HSL works and how it relates to RGB, see the Hue color wheel and the Saturation/Lightness box in the Color dialog box described in Chapter 3.

Color Depth and Number of Colors

Because computers use numbers to represent colors, computer images have a unique phenomenon called *color depth,* or a limited maximum number of colors. For some image types, known as *true color* or *24-bit* images, that limit is quite high, like 16.7 million colors. Twenty-four-bit is known as the image's *pixel depth.*

In true color images, the limit of 16.7 million colors comes from the 256 different possible values of red, green, and blue. If you multiply 256 red values by 256 greens by 256 blues, you get 16,777,216, a number that requires 24 computer bits to store; hence, the term 24-bit.

For other image types, called *palette images,* the limit is much less. Imagine painting an image by using an artist's palette that has only 64 little cups for paint. That limit is your image's *palette size.* You can use fewer than 64, or you can change the colors in those cups, but your image can have, at most, 64 different colors. In Paint Shop Pro, no matter how small the palette, any given marker in that palette can be one of 16.7 million colors.

In palette images, the palette size is given in either number of colors or terms of pixel depth. *Pixel depth* refers to how many bits the computer needs to count up to the palette size. It needs 1 bit to count to 2 colors, 2 bits for 4 colors, 3 for 8 colors, 4 for 16 colors, 5 for 32 colors, 6 for 64 colors, 7 for 128, and 8 for 256. An 8-bit image, for example, is a 256-color image.

Most cameras and scanners don't use palette images. On the Internet, however, you may find 256-color palette images, typically of the GIF type. Those files are mostly used for drawings and artwork, like logos. Color photographs these days are usually true-color images in JPEG file format.

Refer to Chapter 1, where we discuss various types of files and files having different numbers of colors.

Checking your image's color depth

To check your image's color depth, press Shift+I or choose Image⇨ Image Information. On the Image Information tab in the dialog box that appears, look at the left-center area for Pixel Depth/Colors.

For all you computer geeks, that value before the slash indicates the depth in bits, and the value after the slash gives a normal human count of colors. A true-color image, for example, reads 24/16 Million.

Increasing color depth to use more tools

For the greatest choice in color and for access to the greatest number of tools, work with a true-color image. Many of the Paint Shop Pro advanced tools don't work with palette images. (Their menu commands are grayed out.)

If you start to use these types of tools on a palette image (on a GIF file, for example), Paint Shop Pro 8 pops up an Action Required dialog box asking whether it's okay to promote (increase) the color depth to 16 million colors. Just click OK.

When you go to save your work as a file, if you save it in its original form as a palette-type file (such as GIF), Paint Shop Pro again pops up a dialog box. This one tells you "It will be necessary to save your work as a single layer and a maximum of (some number) of colors," and asks whether that's okay. Just click Yes.

Unless you're a wild and crazy graphics geek and have something special in mind, if Paint Shop Pro asks permission to adjust the number of colors, you can generally just click OK or Yes.

To manually increase the color depth to 24-bit, or true color, choose Image➪ Increase Color Depth➪16 Million Colors or press Ctrl+Shift+0 on your keyboard. After you have performed whatever tasks you need to do at this color level, you can restore the original number of colors, if necessary (see the following section).

Reducing color depth for speed or size

Images with fewer colors make smaller files, use less memory, and don't slow down Paint Shop Pro as much. Moreover, some image file types, such as GIF (popular on the Web), don't allow more than 256 colors.

To decrease the number of colors in an image, choose the Image➪ Decrease Color Depth option. From the menu that drops down, choose the color depth you want: 2, 16, 256, 32K (32 thousand), 64K, or X Colors, where *X* is any number you choose.

The Decrease Color Depth dialog box appears, offering all kinds of technical-sounding options. Paint Shop Pro now has to decide exactly which colors will be in the palette of the new image — because you're forcing it to eliminate colors — and also decide which colors to give the pixels whose colors are discontinued. Here's how to deal with that box:

- ✔ **The OK button:** Just click OK and don't fret about the other settings if you're not finicky about results.

- ✔ **Palette option buttons:** (These buttons don't appear for the 32K or 64K color depths.) For the best accuracy of broad areas of color, at the expense of less commonly used colors, choose Optimized Median Cut. For the best accuracy of all colors, choose Optimized Octree. For Web images where you want to make sure that even the most out-of-date PC users see accurate color, choose Standard/Web-safe Palette.

- ✔ **Reduction Method option buttons:** For minimal file size, at the risk of inducing blocks of dark and light colors, choose Nearest Color. For color accuracy at the expense of detail, choose Ordered Dither Method (not available unless you choose the Standard/Web-Safe palette option). For the best color at the cost of graininess, use Error Diffusion.

- ✔ **Number of Colors value box:** If you choose the X Colors option for color depth, you must also enter the number of colors you want in the Number of Colors value box.

Don't sweat the other options because they aren't likely to be all that useful to you. In the Decrease Color Depth dialog box, a panel in the upper-left corner shows your original image; the upper-right corner shows what will happen to the image as a result of your choices. Click OK if you're okay with the result.

Chapter 10

Laundering Your Image for Brightness, Contrast, and Color

● ●

In This Chapter

▶ Adjusting brightness and contrast

▶ Adjusting high, low, and mid tones

▶ Getting lighter colors

▶ Getting more intense colors

▶ Tinting and untinting

▶ Creating grayscale and monochrome images

▶ Creating a positive from a negative

▶ Using sophisticated color adjustments

● ●

A common problem with images, especially with photographs, is that they need laundering: better brightness, contrast, or color quality. A wedding photo taken under a canopy, for example, may make everyone look a bit dim. The groom's white shirt resembles his gray tux. Perhaps the problem isn't the whole crowd, but only Uncle Dave — who, as people have been saying for years, is comparatively dim. Or, maybe the poor light makes the colors of the bridesmaids' dresses, actually a charming sea green, look tattletale gray.

The secrets to brightening the family's dirty laundry lie within the Paint Shop Pro color adjustment features. Not all remedies are what you would expect them to be. The remedy for what you may call a brightness problem, for example, may turn out to be something called lightness, or lightness and contrast both.

If you're tweaking photographs and want some simple solutions, check out the automatic controls for contrast, brightness, and saturation (refer to Chapter 7). Paint Shop Pro has some effects that are useful for solving specific photo flaws.

The Paint Shop Pro color features aren't just for fixing problems, however. They're creative tools that can change, for example, a color photo into a sepia one (colorizing) or make your color image look like a silk-screened poster (posterizing).

Most Paint Shop Pro color features appear in two alternative forms; it's your choice which one you use:

- **Adjust menu commands:** Use commands on the Adjust menu if you're not comfortable working with layers. For example, you may use the Adjust menu commands if you're working on a digital photograph, scanned-in picture, or a painted illustration.

- **Adjustment layers:** Use adjustment layers for more flexibility and control. The adjustment layer approach is Jasc's idea of a newer, better way. See Chapter 14 to understand layers before trying to use adjustment layers.

Whether you use the Adjust menu commands or adjustment layers, the dialog boxes containing the color controls are practically identical, so the descriptions in this chapter work no matter which way you go.

Like most Paint Shop Pro effects, color adjustments can be limited to a particular area of an image, like the area occupied by dim, old Uncle Dave. Here are a few points to keep in mind about that phenomenon:

- If you have made a selection, only the selected area is affected by your adjustments.

- If you're using multiple layers in your image, commands on the Adjust menu affect only the selected layer.

- If you're using multiple layers in your image, consider using an adjustment layer so that you can affect color across multiple layers.

- If a feature doesn't appear to be working, check to see whether you have selected an area or have made a particular layer active. If you have, the tool is working only within that selection, or layer, and not necessarily in the area you're trying to change. Read all about selections and layers in Part IV.

Using the Adjustment Dialog Boxes

All the dialog boxes for color and brightness adjustment have similar controls. We summarize those features in this section. The Brightness/Contrast dialog box, as shown in Figure 10-1, provides an example. Note that the slider shown in the figure appears only when you click and hold down the mouse button on the larger down arrow at the far right end of a value box.

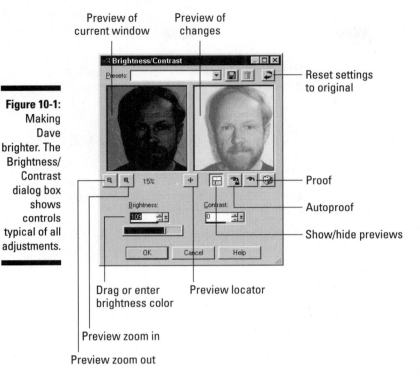

Preview of
current window

Preview of
changes

Reset settings
to original

Figure 10-1:
Making
Dave
brighter. The
Brightness/
Contrast
dialog box
shows
controls
typical of all
adjustments.

Proof

Autoproof

Show/hide previews

Drag or enter
brightness color

Preview locator

Preview zoom in

Preview zoom out

Making adjustments

You have several ways to adjust settings in the dialog boxes:

✔ In adjusting value boxes, you may type a value, click the associated up and down arrows, click in the value box and press the up- and down-arrow keys on the keyboard, or click and hold the larger down arrow to the right of the box and drag the slider that appears.

✔ Some adjustments appear as sliders: Drag sliders to the left or right, up or down. Dragging varies an associated value (number) that appears in a text box to the right of each slider. Dragging left or down reduces that value, and dragging right or up increases it. Alternatively, click a slider and then press the up- and down-arrow keys on the keyboard to increase or decrease its value by one.

✔ To give precise values, double-click in the box where the value appears and type a new value.

✔ To reset adjustments to their original (default) levels, click the Reset to Default button (refer to Figure 10-1).

After you make an adjustment, click OK to apply it to your image. Before you apply it, however, use the proofing or previewing tools that we describe in the following section.

Changes are rarely final in Paint Shop Pro because you can undo them by pressing Ctrl+Z or choosing Edit⇨Command History (refer to Chapter 1).

Proofing or previewing your adjustments

All the color adjustment dialog boxes let you see the effect of your adjustments in the main image window, a feature called *proofing*. The change isn't permanent until you click the OK button. If you cancel out of the dialog box, the change doesn't occur. You have two ways to proof:

- Click the Proof button — the one with the eye icon — after every adjustment.

- If you find yourself clicking the Proof button too often, try using Auto Proof. Click the Auto Proof button — the creepy eyeball with a padlock — shown in Figure 10-1. Paint Shop Pro now shows the effect of your changes in the main image window every time you make a change. For large images, however, you may find this proofing method slow.

The dialog boxes for commands on the Adjust menu also have preview windows that let you see the effect of your adjustments without the long wait that proofing sometimes entails. Here's how to preview your changes:

- To zoom in or out within the preview windows, click the Zoom In button (marked with a +) or Zoom Out button (with a –), as shown in Figure 10-1.

- To move the image in the preview window so that you can see a new area, drag the image in either window.

- To quickly move to a new area of the image, click the Navigate button, as shown in Figure 10-1, and keep the mouse button depressed. A small version of the entire image is displayed, with a rectangle representing the preview area. Drag the rectangle to the area you want to preview and then release the mouse button.

Getting Brighter, Darker, or More Contrast-y

We have been trying for years to be brighter, and now Paint Shop Pro has shown us the light. But just what is brightness? If you increase the brightness of an image, it basically looks whiter. You are, in effect, telling Paint Shop Pro

"More white, please." This whitening affects all shades uniformly, sort of like using bleach in mixed laundry: Lights get whiter, and so do the darks. (Decreasing brightness does the opposite — like washing a new pair of black jeans with your laundry.) This effect also changes your colors — noticeably, if they're very light or dark. Brightness alone rarely does the job you want.

Because brightness alone rarely does the job, Jasc puts the Paint Shop Pro adjustments for brightness and contrast together. Contrast is a bit like a laundry brightener that makes the lights lighter and the darks darker. (It isn't too picky about keeping your colors exactly right, though.)

If brightness and contrast adjustment sounds like the answer to your needs, you have two alternative solutions:

- ✔ **Choose Adjust⇨Brightness and Contrast⇨Brightness/Contrast:** The Brightness/Contrast adjustment dialog box shown in Figure 10-1 arrives, bringing enlightenment.

- ✔ **Choose Layers⇨New Adjustment Layer⇨Brightness/Contrast:** This option adds a Brightness/Contrast layer. The Layer Properties dialog box appears, with the Adjustment tab displayed. See Chapter 14 for help with using layers.

Adjust the Brightness and Contrast % values up or down to see whether you can achieve the results you want. Brightness ranges from –255 to +255; Contrast % ranges from –100 to +100. In Figure 10-1, we turned up both brightness and contrast.

Laundering Lights, Mediums, and Darks Separately

Sometimes, the best way to clean something up is to separately launder what we call three different *tonal ranges:* lights, darks, and midrange colors. Paint Shop Pro gives you several ways to process these different tonal ranges separately:

- ✔ **The Highlight/Midtone/Shadow (HMS) control:** Choose Adjust⇨ Brightness and Contrast to display straightforward control. (It's not available as an adjustment layer, however.) Check out the upcoming section.

- ✔ **The Levels control and the Curves control:** Both are available by choosing Adjust⇨Brightness and Contrast menu and also as an adjustment layer. They are a bit more sophisticated and flexible than the previous control and avoid certain weirdnesses that can arise with the Highlight/Midtone/Shadow control. See the section "Using More Sophisticated Color Adjustments," near the end of this chapter.

The Highlight/Midtone/Shadow controls enable you to adjust separately the darkest regions (shadows) of your image, the lightest regions (highlights), and the regions in between (midtones). To adjust these regions, follow these steps:

1. **Choose Adjust⇨Brightness and Contrast⇨Highlight/Midtone/Shadow.**

   The Highlight/Midtone/Shadow (HMS) dialog box appears, as shown in Figure 10-2.

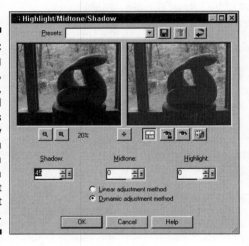

Figure 10-2: Adjusting highlights, midtones, and shadows separately lets you brighten a dark area without washing out other areas.

2. **Click the Dynamic Adjustment Method option, if it's not already selected.**

   The other option, Linear Adjustment Method, is a throwback to an older adjustment method. Jasc included it because some old-time users and experts prefer it. The older method is great for graphics geeks but pretty weird for the rest of us.

3. **Adjust any value downward to darken hues or upward to lighten them.**

   You can think of each value as a sort of brightness adjustment, one each for the shadow, midtone, and highlight areas. To darken shadows, for example, adjust the Shadow value downward. To darken highlights, adjust the Highlight value downward. You can even make dark areas lighter than the light areas, or vice versa. It's a weird effect.

   The more a pixel's value is within a given range, the more the control for that range affects it. The more shadowy a shadow, the more the Shadow control affects it. Likewise, brighter highlights are more affected by the Highlight control, and more midrange midtones are more heavily adjusted by the Midtone control.

Fix Photo Lighting Flaws

Color Plate C-1a: Dave's lovely wife, Katy, overcomes bluish indoor lighting when the Automatic Color Balance effect adjusts "color temperature."

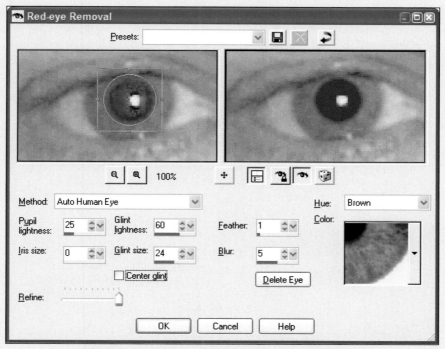

Color Plate C-1b: The Paint Shop Pro automatic Red-Eye Remover effect takes the evil glint from Dave's eye.

Remedy Photo Flops

Color Plate C-2a: The original photo: A nice snapshot taken on a dim day needs some help.

Color Plate C-2b: First, some help from the Automatic Saturation Enhancement effect.

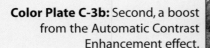

Color Plate C-3b: Second, a boost from the Automatic Contrast Enhancement effect.

Color Plate C-3d: Finally, a fake sky: The original was selected by Magic Wand, and a gradient blue-white fill was added with the Flood Fill tool.

Choose Plain Paint or Fancy

Color Plate C-3a: For simple text, disable the foreground material on the Materials palette. (See the circle-with-a-slash?) The background material does the fill.

Color Plate C-3b: Fancier text. To have an outline, enable the Foreground material on the Materials palette. Here, the background (or fill) uses a pattern. Patterns have their own colors, so the magenta background color is ignored.

Create Image Collisions with Layers

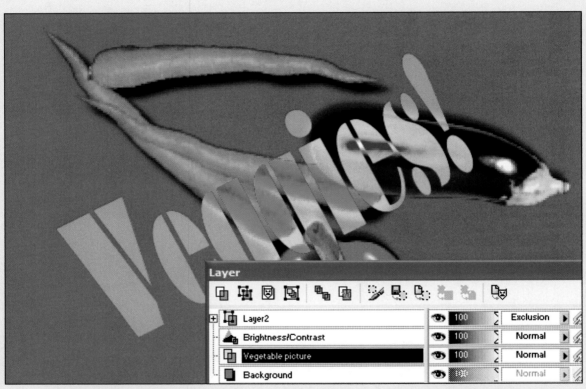

Color Plate C-4: Plain text is added as a separate layer (Layer 2) and rotated, and then a "blend mode" of "exclusion" causes its color to interact with the background.

Color Plate C-5: Text with multicolor gradients is bent to fit a hidden curved line. The skyline has a textured fill.

Stitch Together Panoramas

Color Plates C-6a, C-6b: Two 640 x 480-pixel photographs of Dave's town need to be joined to make a panorama. We opened both photographs in Paint Shop Pro and zoomed out to get working room.

Color Plate C-6c: We created a new image with a white background, wide enough to fit both pictures (1280 x 480). Then we copied each image (Ctrl+C) and pasted it as a new layer (Ctrl+L) in the new image. The images can be dragged around for position.

Stitch Together Panoramas

Color Plate C-6d: Some mismatch is inevitable at the edges because of lens distortions. In this case, having the left image on top of the right one worked better. You can drag layers into different orders by using the layer palette.

Color Plate C-6e: If you're finicky, you can fine-tune the edges. Useful tools are Mesh Warp, to fix distortion; retouch tools, like Lighten/Darken; and the Eraser. Set tools to low Hardness for a soft edge. Here, the Eraser let parts of the underlying image show through.

Straighten Up

Color Plate C-8a: Photos of tall, long, or wide objects may show distortion. Here we take the perspective out of this tall statue.

Color Plate C-8b: We align the Deform tool's bounding box with edges that should be horizontal and vertical. (Image brightened to show the bounding box.)

Color Plate C-8c: Double-click, and the Deform tool adjusts the entire image. But some unwanted distortion creeps in; here, at the top.

Color Plate C-8d: The Mesh Warp tool can tweak the top of the statue to look normal.

Color Plate C-8e: The result.

Change Cardinals to Canaries

Color Plate C-9a: This cardinal's distinctive color makes selecting it easy. Clicking the Magic Wand tool on the red cardinal selects other red pixels. Sometimes, additions to or subtractions from the selection have to be made using other tools.

Color Plate C-9b: After an area is selected, you can do darned near anything to it. In this case, it was "colorized" a bright canary yellow!

Create Paintings from Photos

Color Plate C-10a: The original photograph (Dave's Rusty, looking photogenic in Vermont) in 16.7 million colors.

Color Plate C-10b: Reducing colors (here, to 16) helps make a smaller file (useful for Web work), but also creates an interesting artistic effect.

Create Paintings from Photos

Color Plate C-11: Other tricks for artistic effect: Using the Edge-Preserving Smooth effect, set high, removes fine detail, and then Posterizing reduces colors (here, to 17) and blends, for a watercolor effect.

Put Distant Friends Together

Color Plate C-12a: Alex the golden retriever looking dignified on the front stoop. But he misses his distant friend, Amy. Paint Shop Pro can help put them together.

Color Plate C-12b: With the Paint Shop Pro smart selection tools, Alex can be separated from his favorite front stoop.

Color Plate C-12c: Alex is copied and pasted as a new layer with his pal. He can be scaled up or down as necessary with the Deform tool. A little touchup with retouching tools and color adjustments, and they're picture perfect.

Turn Farmscapes Into Fabscapes

Color Plate C-13: You won't be able to keep 'em down on the farm after they've seen some Paint Shop Pro effects. Here, you see the original, the Colored Foil effect, and the Brush Strokes effect.

Design Your Logo

Color Plate C-14: Layering and fill tricks help make a logo. A photograph of leaves makes a background. Text with an outline only (stroke, no fill) is created in raster form. A new layer is created to contain the white surround. The blank area around the text is selected with the Magic Wand in match mode None. The Fill tool fills the selection with white on the new layer, and the layer is made semitransparent using the Layer palette.

Print Photo Collages and Albums

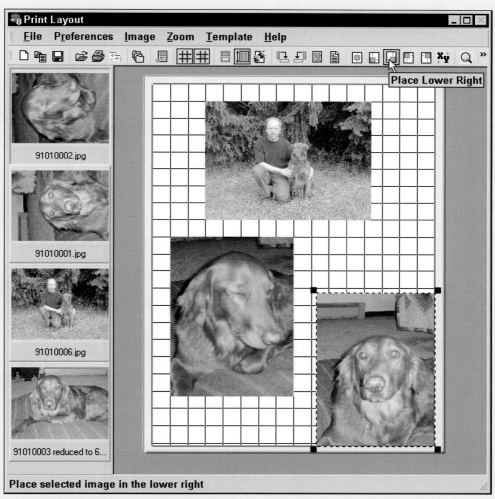

Color Plate C-15: The Paint Shop Pro Print Layout feature lets you lay out, size, and rotate images to create pages for photo albums, simple collages, multiphoto panoramas, and other collections of images.

Smudging and Retouching

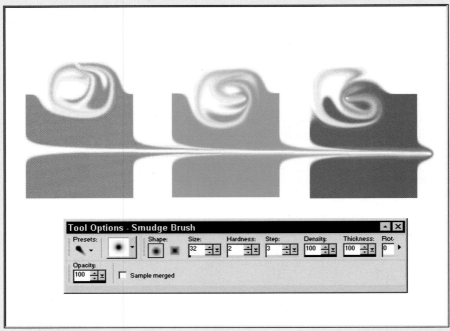

Color Plate C-16a: The Paint Shop Pro Smudge Brush substitutes for your finger in doing artistic smudging and blending. A straight line smudges through the center, and swirls smudge the tops of these colors.

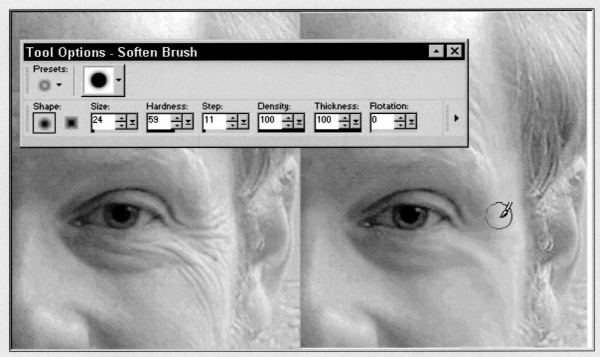

Color Plate C-16b: The Soften Brush makes quick work of the wrinkles this author acquired while writing this book. Balance reasserts itself in the universe.

Equalizing and stretching fix both highs and lows

If your images are either lacking in extremes of highlight or shadow or have too much of both, Paint Shop Pro offers lots of alternatives: contrast, highlight/midtone/shadow (HMS) adjustment, saturation, and gamma, for example. A simple alternative worth trying is to give your image some gentle exercise: equalizing or stretching.

Equalizing gives a more even distribution of pixels from dark to light. Usually, it's the solution you want. Stretching tends to extend the highlights and brighten the overall picture. Choose either Adjust➪Brightness and Contrast➪Histogram Equalize or Adjust➪Brightness and Contrast➪Histogram Stretch. (Each command does its job immediately without providing a dialog box or any other means of adjustment.)

Just as with the Paint Shop Pro Brightness/Contrast control, adjusting brightness can affect the color of an area. If your shadows, for example, have a slightly blue cast, they become noticeably blue if you lighten them. (Many shadows in outdoor photographs are slightly blue because of the incidental light cast by a blue sky.)

Laundering for Lightness, Color Intensity, and Hue

Brightness and contrast are useful, but they're sort of like the laundry tools of yesterday. The way they work, which sometimes can alter colors, doesn't fully address the needs of a color world.

The Paint Shop Pro Hue/Saturation/Lightness control, on the other hand, lets you more safely launder a mixed color load. It gives you brighter colors (lightness) and richer colors (saturation) without risk to your delicate hand-washables, whatever they might be, metaphorically speaking.

To access this modern washday miracle, as with most color controls, you have two choices:

- ✔ **Choose Adjust➪Hue and Saturation➪Hue/Saturation/Lightness:** The Hue/Saturation/Lightness dialog box, shown in Figure 10-3, springs colorfully into action.

- ✔ **Choose Layers➪New Adjustment Layer➪Hue/Saturation/Lightness:** This action adds a Hue/Saturation/Lightness layer. The Layer Properties dialog box appears, with the Adjustment tab displayed. (See Chapter 14 for help with using layers.)

The instructions for how to adjust lightness, saturation, and hue are the same for either method. We give them in the next three sections of this chapter.

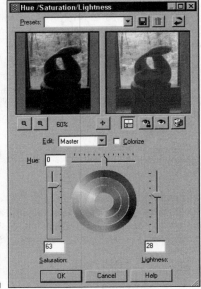

Figure 10-3:
For brighter,
richer
colors, try
the Hue/
Saturation/
Lightness
adjustment.

Hue/Saturation/Lightness (or HSL, to its friends) and Red/Green/Blue (RGB) are two totally different but equally valid systems for specifying colors on a computer. Refer to Chapter 9 for more information about these systems.

Lightness: Brightening without bleaching

Lightness is like a brightness adjustment, only without the bleaching effect on dark colors. Unlike the brightness adjustment, which makes everything brighter by the same amount, the lightness adjustment adjusts proportionately. Dark areas become slightly brighter, and light areas become more bright. A second benefit of this proportional adjustment is that the colors remain more true to the original, except that some are pushed to near-white or near-black.

For a brighter image, increase the Lightness value in the Hue/Saturation/Lightness dialog box. For a darker image, decrease the value. The range is from –100 to +100.

Saturation: Getting more or less intense

Is your image a bit gray and lackluster? For more intense colors (increased saturation), increase the % Saturation value in the Hue/Saturation/Lightness dialog box. Your reds get redder; your greens, greener; your chartreuses, chartreusier; and so on. For less saturation, decrease the value. Values in the Saturation box range between –100 and +100.

The easiest way to understand what saturation does is to go the opposite direction from the way you're probably interested in: decrease saturation. Adjusting saturation downward makes a color image black and white (also called *grayscale*) by degrees.

Hue-ing and crying

We suggest leaving the Hue control in the Hue/Saturation/Lightness dialog box alone because it is not a particularly useful or *For Dummies*-level feature. If you find the idea of adjusting hues attractive, you probably want a completely different control. See the following section about altering the overall tint.

Altering an Overall Tint

Are your overalls the wrong tint? Paint Shop Pro can't fix that laundry problem — unless, of course, you have a picture of your overalls.

Images, whether the subject is overalls or not, sometimes have — or need — an *overall tint.* Portraits taken in a forest setting, for example, tend to make people look a bit green because of the light reflected off the leaves. Or, you may want to add a slight orange tint to a sunset picture.

Paint Shop Pro, as it does with most color controls, gives you several ways to alter tint:

- **Choose Adjust⇨Color Balance⇨Red/Green/Blue:** The Red/Green/Blue dialog box that appears is the simplest control for altering overall tint.

- **Choose Adjust⇨Color Balance⇨Color Balance:** Color Balance and Curves tint shadows, midtones, and highlights separately.

As we point out in Chapter 9, everything you see on your PC screen (or TV screen, for that matter) is made up of a mixture of red, green, and blue, so you can get any tint you like by adjusting the balance of those primary colors.

Choose Adjust⇔Color Balance⇔Red/Green/Blue and the Red/Green/Blue dialog box appears. Like all dialog boxes for commands on the Adjust menu, it has preview windows and proofing controls, plus one sliding control for each primary color: Red %, Green %, and Blue %.

To make your image more red, green, or blue, the solution is straightforward: Increase the value for that color. (Decrease it for less of that color.) Values range from –100 to +100.

Choose Adjust⇔Color Balance⇔Color Balance, and the Color Balance dialog box appears. It works much like the Red/Green/Blue dialog box, but you get to choose whether the controls apply to shadows, midtones, or highlights. Choose by first clicking the corresponding radio button (such as Shadows) for the tonal range you want to change; then move the sliders toward whatever tone you want more of (Red, for example).

Going Gray with a Tint: Colorizing

We all go gray. Some of us try to add an attractive tint when that happens. The same scheme can be even more attractive when applied to images.

Paint Shop Pro calls this process *colorizing*. But, unlike the colorizing you may have seen used to make old black-and-white movies look as though they were shot in color, colorizing in Paint Shop Pro imparts only a single hue to the image. In effect, the result is a grayscale (monochrome) image done in your chosen hue rather than in gray.

The best Paint Shop Pro tool for this process is the Colorize tool, and it works like this:

Choose Adjust⇔Hue and Saturation⇔Colorize to display the Colorize dialog box.

The Colorize dialog box grabs its crayons and reports for duty. The Colorize dialog box sports two adjustments:

✔ **Saturation:** Increase this value to determine how much color is applied. If you set it to 0, the image is strictly grayscale (black and white). At 255, the image has no gray but is purely the hue you choose by adjusting the Hue control.

✔ **Hue:** Click and hold on the tiny down arrow at the right end of Hue value box. A rainbow-colored slider appears. Drag to the hue you want and then release the mouse button.

Going Totally Gray or Negative in One Step

You're just one step away from going gray, or becoming completely negative. The Paint Shop Pro commands for Negative Image and Grey Scale, on the Adjust menu, are simple enough to do their work in a single step: You get no dialog box and have no adjustments to make.

Choose Adjust⇨Negative Image and Paint Shop Pro gives you the negative of your image. Lights become darks, darks become lights, and the colors switch to their opposing colors on the color wheel. Reds become cyan, yellows become blue, and so on. Changing an image from positive (normal) to negative isn't often useful, but sometimes you need to go the other way. That event occurs when you (or whoever is supplying your images) is using a film scanner and scans a film negative. The Negative Image command gives you the normal (positive) image you want.

To turn your color image into shades of gray (like a black-and-white photo), choose Image⇨Grey Scale. Going grayscale affects the entire image, even if you have selected an area. If you want to turn just a certain area grayscale, select that area and, using the Hue/Saturation/Lightness dialog box described earlier, set the Saturation control to the minimum.

Using More Sophisticated Color Adjustments

Paint Shop Pro is, after all, Paint Shop *Pro,* so it offers some sophisticated color adjustments for professional computer graphics mavens. Why, however, should those guys have all the fun?

Here are some rudimentary instructions for using a handful of these highfalutin' controls. They're available in the same two forms as other color controls:

✔ Choose Adjust from the Brightness and Contrast menu. (Just poke around. You'll find 'em.)

✔ Adjustment layers, accessed through the Layers menu or Layer palette (see Chapter 14 for more information about layers).

Levels

The Levels control lets you adjust brightness and contrast within three different tonal ranges: shadows (darker pixels), highlights (lighter pixels), and midtones (pixels in the middle). Choose Adjust⇨Brightness and Contrast⇨Levels to open the dialog box shown in Figure 10-4. The dialog box has two controls: Input levels and Output levels. Each control is a horizontal line, attractively studded with diamonds you can drag.

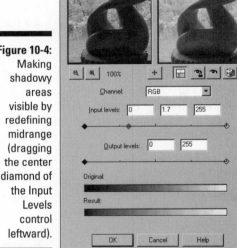

Figure 10-4:
Making
shadowy
areas
visible by
redefining
midrange
(dragging
the center
diamond of
the Input
Levels
control
leftward).

You can think of the Input levels control as a way to adjust contrast and the Output levels control as a way to adjust brightness. (Neither description is perfectly accurate, but gets the idea across without getting *too* technical.) Here's how to use these controls:

✔ To heighten contrast by making shadows darker, drag the leftmost (black) diamond on the Input levels control to the right.

✔ To heighten contrast by making highlights lighter, drag the clear (rightmost) diamond on the Input levels control to the left.

✔ To adjust the midtones, drag the gray (center) diamond on the Input levels control. Drag it left to brighten or right to darken. The midtones diamond also moves a bit when the other two do, so you may need to readjust this diamond after moving the others.

✔ To lighten shadows, drag the black diamond on the Output levels control toward the right. (Shadows and midtones get lighter.) To darken highlights, drag the clear diamond toward the left. (Highlights and midtones get darker.)

Curves

The *Curves* adjustment is a way to change brightness and contrast within a specific range of tones you specify. That range can be anywhere from shadows to highlights to anywhere in the middle. A Curves adjustment can, for example, help you pull out some of the detail that's lost in a specific range of a photograph by increasing the contrast in that range.

Choose Adjust⇨Brightness and Contrast⇨Curves to display the Curves dialog box. The main control (in the dialog box) looks like a chart. (If the chart makes sense to you, great — otherwise, don't worry about understanding it.)

The chart holds a curve — well, initially, it's just a straight, diagonal line between two points. The idea is to bend that line by adding and dragging points.

In Figure 10-5, the three columns show three curve settings. The left column shows the original image that has evenly distributed shades of gray from black to white. The chart underneath shows the straight line that goes with that even distribution. The other two columns show the effect of the curve settings underneath the images.

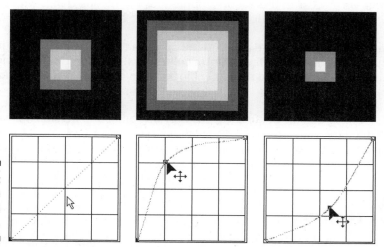

Figure 10-5:
Curve
settings and
their results.

- ✔ On the chart, click that diagonal line in the tone area you want to change the most. Click more toward the left end of the line to adjust shadows and click more toward the right to adjust highlights.

- ✔ Clicking adds a point to the line. For example, to change midtones, click near the middle and add one point. Click in two places to create two points slightly separated from each other. Adding more than one point gives you more control over exactly which tone range you adjust.

- ✔ Drag the point (or points) up to brighten or down to darken. Drag left to move your effect to darker pixels or right to move it to lighter pixels. You can also drag the endpoints of the line: Drag the left end-point to affect shadows, and drag the right endpoint to affect highlights.

- ✔ To get more contrast within a range of tones, drag points so that the curve is steeper (more vertical) in that range.

- ✔ To get less contrast, make the curve flatter. You may need to add points to focus your efforts on exactly the range you want.

- ✔ To remove a point you have decided you don't need, drag it entirely out of the chart area.

- ✔ To adjust contrast and brightness only within a given primary color (red, green, or blue), click the selection box marked Channel and choose your color.

Posterize

The Posterize control isn't in the Adjust menu like the other advanced controls we discuss in this section, but it does interesting things with colors. Choose Effects➪Artistic Effects➪Posterize to launch the Posterize dialog box.

In *posterizing,* an image takes on the appearance of a silk-screened poster, made up of areas of a few uniform colors. Posterizing reduces the number of colors that appear and results in blocks of color, like a paint-by-numbers painting.

The dialog box for posterizing has only one adjustment, named Levels. Reduce the value to reduce the number of colors or increase it to increase colors. The value in Levels determines the number of levels of brightness in the image.

Threshold

The threshold control (choose Adjust➪Brightness and Contrast➪Threshold) gives you images in pure black and pure white. With a threshold control, you're telling Paint Shop Pro, "Turn any pixel with a brightness below a given threshold black, and turn any pixel above that threshold white."

The dialog box for this layer has a single adjustment. Reduce the Threshold value for a lower threshold (more white) and increase it for a higher threshold (more black). You can use a threshold value between 1 and 255.

Part IV
Changing and Adding Content

The 5th Wave   By Rich Tennant

"...and here's me with Cindy Crawford. And this is me with Madonna and Celine Dion..."

In this part . . .

*P*art IV has solutions when you're concerned with an image's content, not its quality. Discover how to pluck out, put in, or move a person, product, or other object in an image. Turn to this part for cropping, resizing, rotating, or distorting an image (or just part of an image). To crop, resize, reproportion, flip, mirror, reorient, bend, spindle, or mutilate an image, turn to Chapter 11.

In Chapter 12, you see how to select parts of an image — the key trick for changing content. Want to abstract your better half from photo A into photo B? Normally, Paint Shop Pro can't tell your spouse from a sofa, so (assuming that *you* can tell the difference) it's up to you to tell Paint Shop Pro, "Pat's the one in green" or to outline Pat by hand. You can even change the color, or other qualities, such as contrast or sharpness, of the selected item. Selecting lets you apply to particular items nearly any of the Paint Shop Pro powers.

After you have selected your spouse, you may want to move, copy, or reshape that person. As inadvisable as such a project may be in real life, it's a simple matter in Paint Shop Pro. Chapter 13 is the place to turn for moving, copying, or other dimensional or reproductive changes.

Adding content is another trick that Paint Shop Pro can help you with. In Chapter 14, we show you how to combine multiple images or create layered images where you can manipulate different objects without affecting the underlying stuff. Layers make later editing much easier, produce cool image overlays, and can even make qualitative changes, such as contrast or saturation, easier to manage.

To add text and shapes to an image, turn to Chapter 15, where we show you how the Paint Shop Pro vector graphics and text tools can give you layers of easily edited material — and we show you how to edit that material.

Chapter 11

Getting Bigger, Smaller, and Turned Around

*I*t happened several times to Alice, of Wonderland fame: She needed to be bigger and smaller or to change her orientation. Fortunately, you don't have to adopt her dubious pharmacological methods — eating and drinking mysteriously labeled substances — to change the size or orientation of your images.

No, to make your pictures bigger, smaller, rotated, or otherwise reoriented, you need to indulge in only a few clicks on well-labeled commands or icons. In this chapter, we illuminate your choices as you navigate the Paint Shop Pro rabbit hole.

If your image appears smaller than you think it should be when you first open it, Paint Shop Pro has probably zoomed the image out to fit your window. To zoom in, click the Zoom (magnifier) tool from the Pan and Zoom toolset and then left-click the image.

Getting Sized

Size may not be everything, but it's certainly one of the things people are often concerned about — or ought to be. You don't need a 1024 x 768-pixel image, for instance (which is full-screen size on many PCs), for a snapshot of your new company CEO on your Web site. If you didn't get an appropriately sized CEO (okay, an image of a CEO) in the first place, you can trim that person down in Paint Shop Pro. Likewise, if you're rushing to prepare the opening screen for a company presentation and the only way you can get a logo is to scan in the tiny one on your letterhead, Paint Shop Pro can help you size it up to a more presentable image.

If you're preparing an image that someone else plans to place in a professionally prepared and printed document, don't scale it down yourself. Let your graphics designer or printer do the scaling to suit the printing process.

Start resizing by choosing Image⇨Resize. The Resize dialog box appears in order to help you size the situation up — or down (see Figure 11-1).

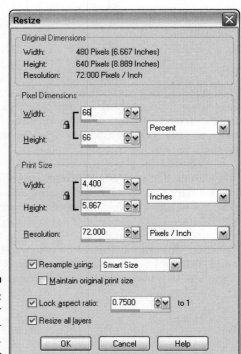

Figure 11-1:
Sizing your
image up —
or down.

Proportioning

The Resize dialog box normally keeps the image's proportions (relationship of width to height) constant while you resize. If you set width, therefore, Paint Shop Pro sets height for you (and vice versa). Keeping image proportions constant avoids distortion.

If you prefer to change the proportions (which distorts your image), you can click to clear (deselect) the check box labeled Lock Aspect Ratio __ To 1, as shown in Figure 11-1, and Paint Shop Pro lets you set width and height independently.

Dimensioning

Using the Resize dialog box, as shown in Figure 11-1, you can adjust the size in one of three ways, all of which do the same thing: change the image's size in pixels. Use whichever way suits your mindset:

- **Specify size in pixels:** If you're using the image on the Web or in e-mail, you probably have a pixel size (probably a desired width) in mind. Select Pixels from the drop-down menu next to the Width and Height controls and then enter a value for Width (or Height).

- **Make it X% of its current size:** Select Percent from the drop-down menu next to the Width and Height controls and then enter a value for Width (or Height). In Figure 11-1, for instance, the setting of 66 makes the image ⅔ (66 percent) of its current size. To double the image size, use 200.

- **Make it *print* bigger or smaller:** Select which measurement you want to use (inches or centimeters) from the menu on the right side and then use the Width or Height controls in the Print Size section to make the image print as large as you want. Paint Shop Pro multiplies this physical size (in inches, for example) by the resolution setting (pixels per inch) in this dialog box and calculates a new image size in pixels. You can also change the value in the Resolution text box to adjust the image resolution (pixels per inch or centimeter). Don't confuse this setting with the printer's resolution (typically 300 to 600 dpi); see Chapter 16 if you *are* confused about printing and resolution!

If your image has several layers and you want them all resized the same, make sure to check the Resize All Layers check box. If you clear that check mark, you resize only the active layer. Click OK to make the resizing happen.

Avoiding degradation

Resizing sounds easy: Just make the image bigger or smaller. What's to think about? Well, usually, you don't have to think about anything. Occasionally, however, your image's appearance degrades after resizing. It has jagged or fuzzy edges. These situations call for a little thought.

Behind the resizing issue is another difference between how computers and humans think. If you want your image to be 25 percent bigger, Paint Shop Pro has to figure out how to spread 100 pixels over 125 pixels. To get an idea of the problem, imagine dividing 100 cookies among 125 kids who don't accept broken cookies. Fortunately, Paint Shop Pro is pretty smart, so you don't have to smoosh up and bake these cookies again yourself. Unless you instruct Paint Shop Pro otherwise, it uses the *Smart Size* feature to make these decisions — it chooses the right way to do it based on what your image looks like.

If your image doesn't look so hot after resizing, try second-guessing the smart resizing that Paint Shop Pro uses by default. Press Ctrl+Z to undo the ugly resizing you just did. Then choose Image➪Resize again. In the Image Resize dialog box that appears, click the Resize Type selection box to see the specific choices of ways to resize. Here's what to do with those choices:

- **Bicubic Resample:** Choose to enlarge a realistic-looking or complex image (like a photo) or to avoid jagged edges.

- **Bilinear Resample:** Choose to reduce a drawn image, one with well-defined edges, or one with text.

- **Pixel Resize:** Choose to enlarge a drawn image or one with well-defined edges. (Paint Shop Pro then simply removes or duplicates pixels in order to resize.)

- **Weighted Average:** Choose to reduce a drawn image, one with well-defined edges, or one with text if the Bilinear Resample option doesn't work out.

Click OK to proceed with the resizing. If your image doesn't look better, press Ctrl+Z to undo the last resize. Choose a different resizing method and try resizing again.

Bilinear and bicubic resampling work for only 24-bit color images (or grayscale images). You can use them on fewer-color images by increasing the color depth to 24-bit, resizing the image, and then reducing the number of colors to the original. Refer to Chapter 9 for help with changing the number of colors.

Trimming (Cropping) Your Edges

Is your image a bit shabby around the edges and in need of a trim? You can improve the composition of many pictures by trimming *(cropping)* a bit off the top, bottom, or sides. Often, for instance, snapshots are taken from too far away, so the subject is too small. You can enlarge the image in Paint Shop Pro, but you also need to trim it so that the overall picture isn't yards wide.

In a layered image, cropping affects all layers.

Paint Shop Pro provides a special tool for your crops. Take these steps to trim your image:

1. **Click the Crop tool (shown in the margin) on the Tools toolbar.**

   The cursor icon displays a set of crosshairs.

2. **Visualize a rectangular area that defines the new boundaries of your image.**

   For instance, if you're cropping a family photo taken in the backyard, next to the trash barrels, visualize a rectangle around the family, excluding the barrels.

3. **Move the crosshairs of your cursor to one corner of that visualized rectangle and then drag diagonally toward the opposite corner.**

   As you drag, a real rectangle forms. The status bar at the bottom of the Paint Shop Pro window gives you the exact pixel column and row where the cursor is positioned, in case you need that information. As you drag, the status bar also gives you the cursor position and the crop's size, as Figure 11-2 shows.

   If the cropping rectangle isn't quite right, you can modify it in one of these three ways:

   • To remove the rectangle and try again, right-click anywhere on the image. The rectangle disappears.

   • To change any side or corner of the rectangle, drag that side or corner.

   • To position the rectangle, move your cursor within that rectangle; the cursor becomes a four-headed arrow and you can drag the rectangle to any new location.

Crop to opaque layer

Crop to current selection   Crop to merged opaque

Figure 11-2:
Cropping a
furry dog.

4. **When the rectangle is correct, double-click anywhere outside the crop area.**

   Paint Shop Pro crops the image. If you don't like the result, press Ctrl+Z to undo the crop and then try these steps again. Rather than double-click, if the Tool Options palette is open (press the F4 key if it's not), you can click the Crop Image button (the green check mark).

Getting Turned Around, Mirrored, or Flipped

We can't tell you how many people we have seen bending their necks to view a sideways image! Apart from providing work for chiropractors, this habit does nobody any good. Paint Shop Pro makes rotating an image simple.

Mirroring or flipping an image is equally simple. Mirrored or flipped images are particularly useful for imaginative work, such as creating a reflection that isn't present in the original or making a symmetrical design, such as a floral border.

Does your image have layers, or have you selected an area? As with many Paint Shop Pro functions, the mirroring, flipping, and rotating commands apply to only the active layer. If you have a selected area, mirroring and flipping also restrict themselves to that area.

Rotating

To rotate an image, choose Image⇨Rotate⇨Free Rotate or press Ctrl+R. The Rotate dialog box appears, with a variety of option buttons:

- ✔ To rotate the image clockwise, click the Right button.
- ✔ To rotate counterclockwise, click the Left button.
- ✔ Choose 90 (a quarter-turn, good for righting sideways images), 180 (a half-turn), 270 degrees (three-quarters turn) of rotation, or Free (see the next bullet).
- ✔ To rotate any desired amount, choose Free and enter any rotation (in degrees) in the highlighted text box.

Although you *can* use the Rotate dialog box to straighten an off-kilter photo, there's a better way: the Straighten tool, which we cover in Chapter 2.

If your image has multiple layers (or if you aren't sure whether it does) and you want to rotate the entire image, click to place a check mark in the All Layers check box in the Rotate dialog box. Otherwise, Paint Shop Pro rotates only the active layer. Click OK to perform the rotation.

To rotate a portion of an image, select that portion first. Or, you can use the Deformation tool rather than the rotation command on the selection. See Chapter 12 for help with selection and Chapter 13 to rotate a selection.

Mirroring and flipping

To *mirror* an image is to change it as though it were reflected in a mirror held alongside the image. To *flip* an image is to exchange top for bottom as though the mirror were held underneath the image. Note that both transformations are unique: You can't achieve the same result by rotating the image!

If your image has layers, mirroring and flipping commands apply to only the active layer. If your image has an area selected, these commands float that selection and then work on only that floating selection. See Chapter 12 for more information about floating selections.

To mirror an image in Paint Shop Pro, choose Image⇨Mirror. Your image is transformed into its mirror image.

To flip an image, choose Image⇨Flip. Your image is turned head over heels.

Taking on Borders

Paint Shop Pro can add a border of any color and width to any image. (If your image uses layers, however, Paint Shop Pro has to merge them. For that reason, borders are often best left as the last thing you do to your image.) To create a border around an image, follow these steps:

1. **Choose Image⇨Add Borders.**

   The Add Borders dialog box appears. (If Paint Shop Pro first displays a dialog box warning you that the layers must be merged to proceed, click OK to proceed and then refer to Chapter 1 for advice on how to turn off these pesky reminders.)

2. **Choose your color.**

   Click the color box to bring up the Color dialog box and then click the shade you want to see surrounding your picture. Click OK. If this strange array of circles and boxes proves too daunting for you, check out Chapter 4, where we explain all.

3. **Set your border widths, in pixels.**

   For a border that is the same width on all sides, leave the check mark in the Symmetric check box and enter your border width in the Top, Bottom, Left, or Right box. (It doesn't matter which one you use; they all change together.) For different border widths on all sides, clear that Symmetric check mark and enter the border widths in all the boxes individually.

Click OK. Your image is now larger by the borders you have set.

Borders are no different from any other area of your image; they're just new and all one color.

Achieving a Particular Canvas Size

Paint Shop Pro enables you to expand the *canvas size* of any image: to add a border area around the image to achieve a particular image width and height. The Canvas Size command has the same end effect as Add Borders.

"But," you say, wisely, "if Add Borders has the same effect, why would I bother with the Canvas Size command?" You would bother if you were looking to have an image of a particular size — and didn't want to do the arithmetic to calculate how much border to add to the existing dimensions.

You might use the canvas size command, for instance, if you were making a catalog using images of various heights and widths and wanted all the images to be of uniform height and width. You couldn't resize the *images* because that would distort them. If you used the add borders command, you would have to calculate border widths to fill out each image to the right dimensions. With canvas sizing, however, you can simply place each image on a uniformly sized background. Here's how:

1. **Choose a canvas (border) color by setting the background color on the Color palette.**

   For example, if you want a white canvas, left-click the Background Material box (the one in the lower-right corner) and select white. (Again, if you want more details about the Material box, Chapter 3 beckons.)

   If your image has any transparent sections, check the Transparent box for a see-through canvas. (It's grayed out if your image is opaque.)

2. **Choose Image⇨Canvas Size.**

   The Canvas Size dialog box makes the scene.

3. **Enter a new width and new height for your image in the Width and Height boxes.**

   These numbers define how big your image will be, with its expanded canvas (borders).

   Paint Shop Pro also has an option that allows you to expand the canvas proportionately; if you make the new canvas twice as wide, the height is doubled. To enable this option, check the Lock Aspect Ratio check box.

4. **Choose where you want your image positioned on the canvas.**

   As you can see in Figure 11-3, you can press one of ten placement buttons to select which corner your image will be flush with. (The button in the center centers your image.)

   If these ten positions aren't good enough for you, you can place your image on the canvas with exacting precision by using the Placement settings. The values in these boxes tell Paint Shop Pro how far away the image should be from each of the four borders, in pixels. For example, if you want to set your image so that it is 20 pixels away from the left side of the new canvas, enter a value of **20** in the Left Placement box.

   Be warned that negative numbers in any of the placement boxes places at least part of the image *outside* the canvas border. For example, a value of –20 pixels in the Left placement box plops your image down so that it begins 20 pixels *outside* the left border of the canvas rather than 20 pixels away from the *inside* of the left border. This action effectively trims 20 pixels off your image's left side.

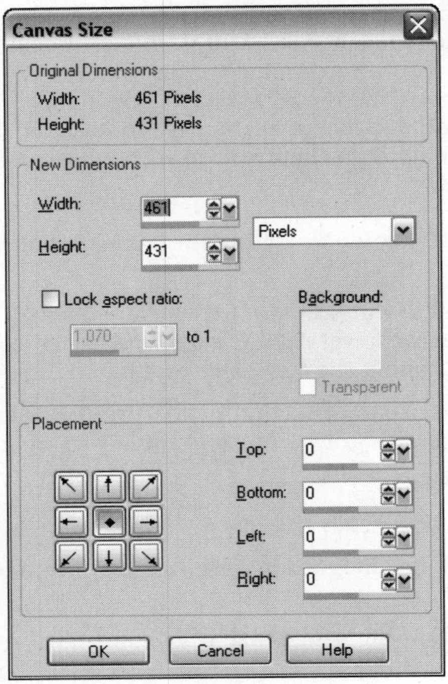

Canvas Size

Original Dimensions

Width: 461 Pixels
Height: 431 Pixels

New Dimensions

Width: 461

Height: 431

Pixels

☐ Lock aspect ratio:

1.070 to 1

Background:

☐ Transparent

Placement

Top: 0

Bottom: 0

Left: 0

Right: 0

OK   Cancel   Help

Figure 11-3:
The Canvas
Size dialog
box.

Click OK and your image is mounted on a fresh canvas of your chosen size and background color. If (as in the catalog example) you're trying to center many images on canvases of the same size, you may find it convenient that your previous canvas size settings remain as you open each image. Just choose Image⇨Canvas Size for each subsequent image and click OK.

Chapter 12

Selecting Parts of an Image

· ·

· ·

*I*f Uncle Dave is looking a bit dark and gloomy in your wedding picture, should the whole wedding party have to lighten up to make up for him? Heavens, no!

If the photographer for your brochure happened to photograph the vile, lime green version of your product, should you now be stuck with that color? Absolutely not.

You should be able to redo your product in screaming magenta or lighten up Uncle Dave, or maybe remove him entirely, while leaving the rest of the image alone. In short, you need to be able to select only that portion of the image you need to work on.

The problem is that Paint Shop Pro hasn't the foggiest idea that your product or your Uncle Dave are in the picture. It's all just colored dots to Paint Shop Pro, so you need a way to tell Paint Shop Pro things like "Select all those lime-green-colored dots" (no, not Uncle Dave) or "Select everything within this line that I'm drawing." After you accomplish that, you can restrict the Paint Shop Pro magic to the selected area and even move or remove selected portions of an image.

Paint Shop Pro has two other features besides selection that help to remove parts of an image, or simply restrict its actions to certain parts: the Background Eraser.

If you're looking to erase just the stuff around Uncle Dave, the Background Eraser is a new feature saves lots of that tedious selecting time. The Background Eraser is smart enough (mostly) to draw a distinction between the interesting stuff in the foreground and the boring stuff in the background, allowing you to wipe away redundant scenery without a single selection! (We show you how in Chapter 4.)

Layers affect the way selection appears to work, and helps to separate portions of an image so that you can move them around easily without affecting anything else — something selections can't offer. (See Chapter 14 for layer information.)

Selecting is a key tool for altering the content of an image. Selecting in just the right way is the key to altering exactly the content you want. Paint Shop Pro lets you be just as selective as you want.

In this chapter, we deal with selecting parts of your image that are bitmap *(raster)* images. We don't, however, deal with the special case of selecting *vector* objects. The text and shapes that the Text, Draw, and Preset Shapes tools make are almost always vector objects. To read about selecting vector objects, see the discussion in Chapter 15 about controlling your objects.

Selecting an Area

Selecting is creating a restricted area in which you want Paint Shop Pro to do its thing — a sort of construction zone. "Its thing" is whatever operation you choose, whether it's moving, changing color, painting, filling, smudging, filtering, erasing, copying, pasting, mirroring — essentially any image change Paint Shop Pro can perform. For instance, you can select an elliptical area around Aunt Elizabeth in a group photo, copy that area to the Windows Clipboard, and then paste it as a new image to create a classical cameo-style oval image.

If you have layers in your image, selection can be slightly more complicated. See "Avoiding Selection Problems in Layered Images," later in this chapter.

The selected area has a moving dashed line around it, called a *marquee*. Figure 12-1 shows Alex the Wonder Dog in his very own marquee.

Paint Shop Pro gives you lots of flexibility in creating a selection, as we describe in this list:

> ✔ **Make a selection:**
>
> • Drag a rectangular, circular, or other regular shape with the Selection tool.

- Draw an outline using the Freehand tool.
- Click an area that has a more-or-less uniform color or brightness using the Magic Wand tool.

Figure 12-2 shows those three tools on the toolbar.

Figure 12-1:
The
marquee
shows your
selection.
We created
this
selection
with the
Freehand
(lasso) tool.

✔ **Add pixels to, or remove pixels from, your selection to modify it.**

✔ **Expand your selection to fill up any specks left in your selection and add more to your selection based on similar colors.**

✔ *Feather* or *antialias* **the edges of a selection to keep natural-looking edges around your selected area.**

The main tools for making a selection are on the Tools toolbar, as shown in Figure 12-2. To make them work exactly the way you want, however, you need to use the Tool Options palette (press F4 if you don't see it).

To make and modify selections, you can use the high-tech selection tools, as shown in Figure 12-2, or give commands from the Selection menu. Because you can add to or subtract from a selection with any selection tool, you may also find yourself switching between tools to build or carve out a selection of a particularly tricky shape.

Figure 12-2:
Three ways
to make a
selection.

Selecting a rectangle or other regular shape

Selecting a rectangular area is particularly useful for copying portions of an image to paste elsewhere as a separate image. It's also useful for working on portions of your image that happen to *be* rectangular. The Selection tool lets you select rectangles, circles, and other predetermined shapes.

To create the selection area, click the Selection tool (refer to Figure 12-2) and then drag diagonally on your image. You determine the shape you drag on the Tool Options palette, as shown in Figure 12-3.

Figure 12-3:
Choose your
shape and
any edge-
smoothing
options
for the
Selection
tool.

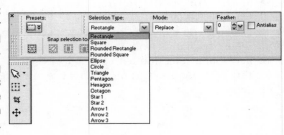

Choose one of the many shape selections from the drop-down menu. Drag diagonally to give your area both width and height. Here are a few tips for making and changing your selection:

- ✔ **Trying again:** After you define a selection, you can't resize it by dragging sides or corners, as you may expect. (Try it and you drag the selection to one side.) Right-click anywhere to clear the shape to try again. Or, you can simply drag a fresh shape if you begin your new drag anywhere outside the existing selection.

- ✔ **Dragging:** After you have selected an area, if you want to move that portion of the image, you can drag it, exposing whatever lies beneath your picture. Unfortunately, this feature also makes accidental dragging very easy! As usual, just press Ctrl+Z to undo an accidental drag (or an accidental anything else, for that matter).

- ✔ **Modifying:** To move, add to, or subtract from the selection, see "Modifying Your Selection," later in this chapter.

Selecting by outlining: The Freehand tool

We find the Freehand tool to be one of the most useful of the selection tools. It lets you define the area you want by outlining. It even helps you with that outlining, so you don't have to scrutinize every pixel you include or exclude.

 On the toolbar, click the lasso icon (the Freehand tool) shown in the margin. The Tool Options palette then looks something like Figure 12-4. (Press the F4 key to flash the Tool Options palette on or off if you have misplaced it.)

Figure 12-4: Four ways to outline your selection with the lasso (the Freehand tool).

The Freehand tool gives you four ways to snare a selection. From the Selection Type drop-down list (refer to Figure 12-4), choose whichever of these methods best suits the area you're trying to select:

✔ **Freehand:** Drag an outline around the area you want to select. At whatever point you release the mouse button, Paint Shop Pro finishes the outline with a straight line to your starting point. This method is best for an area with a complex shape, especially if it doesn't have a clear edge. (If it does have a clear edge, try the Smart Edge method instead.)

✔ **Point to Point:** Click at points around the area you want to select. As you click, the outline appears as straight line segments connecting those points. To close the loop, double-click or right-click, and Paint Shop Pro draws the final line segment from that point back to the starting point. This method works well for areas with straight edges.

✔ **Smart Edge:** If the area you want to select has a noticeable edge — a transition between light and dark, such as the edge of someone's head against a contrasting background — choose this type of selection. To begin, click at any point along the edge. A skinny rectangle appears, with one end attached to your cursor. Move your cursor to another point along the edge so that a portion of the edge is contained entirely within the rectangle and then click. Paint Shop Pro selects along the edge. Continue clicking along the edge in this way; Figure 12-5 shows the result. Double-click, or right-click, and Paint Shop Pro finishes the outline with a straight line back to your starting point.

Figure 12-5:
Alex's coat
forms an
edge that
Smart Edge
can detect.

✔ **Edge Seeker:** This option works much like Smart Edge, except that you can set how wide an area it searches to find an edge (called the Range, it's measured in pixels). As with most Paint Shop Pro elements, you can change the Range on the Tool Options palette. Again, to lose the loop, double-click or right-click.

Here are a few tips for selecting with the Freehand tool:

✔ **Aborting:** You can't abort the selection process after you begin. Instead, right-click (or release the mouse button if you're dragging) to finish the loop, and then press Ctrl+D or right-click again to remove the selection.

✔ **Undoing segments:** If you're in the middle of using Point to Point or Smart Edge, and make a mistake, you can undo segments by pressing the Delete key on your keyboard.

✔ **Being precise:** When using Smart Edge, click directly on or near the edge as you go around the shape. (Put another way, don't overshoot any bends in the edge or let the edge exit the rectangle from the side of the rectangle.)

✔ **Smoothing edges:** The Freehand tool provides antialiasing and feathering, which, if you're going to use them, you should set up before making the selection. See the upcoming sections "Feathering for More Gradual Edges" and "Antialiasing for Smoother Edges."

✔ **Using layers:** If your image uses layers, Smart Edge normally looks for the edge within only the active layer. If you want Smart Edge to look at all layers combined, click to enable the Sample Merged check box.

Selecting by color or brightness: The Magic Wand tool

Sometimes you want to select an area so uniform in appearance that you want to simply tell Paint Shop Pro, "Go select that red balloon" or whatever it is. To you, with your human perception, the area is an obvious thing of some sort. In software, anything that even slightly mimics human perception is often called *magic*. The Magic Wand selection tool is no exception. It can identify and select areas of uniform color or brightness, somewhat as your eye does.

One benefit of this tool is that you can select areas with complex edges that would be a pain in the wrist to trace with the Freehand tool. For instance, a selection of blue sky that includes a complex skyline of buildings and trees would be relatively easy with the Magic Wand tool.

The Magic Wand tool doesn't, however, work as well as your eye. In particular, if the color or brightness of the area you're trying to select isn't uniform or doesn't contrast strongly with the surroundings, the selection is likely to be spotty or incomplete or have rough edges.

Paint Shop Pro gives you lots of ways to improve an imperfect selection. See "Modifying Your Selection," later in this chapter.

Making the selection

To make a selection, select the Magic Wand from the Selection toolset. Your cursor takes on the Magic Wand icon. Click the Magic Wand cursor on your image, and it selects all adjacent pixels that match (or nearly match) the

pixel you clicked. (Note that the selection does *not* include isolated pixels —
pixels that, even though they match, are separated from the place you
clicked by nonmatching pixels.)

To get the selection you want when you use the Magic Wand tool, consult the
Tool Options palette. The Tool Options palette for the Magic Wand tool looks
like Figure 12-6. It lets you define (by using the Match mode list box) exactly
what you mean by match and lets you adjust (by adjusting the Tolerance setting) how closely the selected pixels should match the one you clicked.

Figure 12-6:
Fine-tuning
your Magic
Wand tool
before using
it ensures
good magic.

If your image uses layers, be sure that the active layer is the one containing
the area you want to select. Enable the Sample Merged check box on the Tool
Options palette so that the Magic Wand tool examines all layers combined.
Otherwise, the Magic Wand tool selects a totally wrong area, and you wonder
what's happening!

Choosing Match mode for better results

Click the Match mode list box and you can choose exactly how you want
Paint Shop Pro to select the pixels around the place you clicked. Some of the
choices are shown in this list:

- **RGB Value:** When you choose this option, you tell Paint Shop Pro to
"select pixels that match in both color *and* brightness." Clicking a red
apple using this choice may select only the highlighted side where you
clicked, for instance. Technically, it selects all adjacent pixels with red
(R), green (G), and blue (B) primary color values that match the one you
clicked.

- **Hue:** You're telling Paint Shop Pro to "select pixels that match in color"
when you choose Hue. Hue, however, is somewhat more independent of
brightness than the RGB value. (Refer to Chapter 9 for help with understanding RGB and Hue.) Clicking on a red apple with this choice is more
likely to select the entire apple than if you chose RGB Value. Technically,
it selects all adjacent pixels with hues (in the Hue/Saturation/Lightness
color system, or color wheel) that match the hue of the pixel you clicked.

✓ **Brightness:** Brightness disregards color and selects all adjacent pixels whose brightness matches the one you clicked. This choice is useful for selecting things that are similarly illuminated, like shadows and highlights, or that are in a notably light or dark color compared with the background.

✓ **Opacity:** Opacity, if you're not paying attention, is a measure of how transparent your image is. Opacity mode selects anything that's suitably close to the transparency of the selected pixel.

Opacity is useful only when you're working on layers or images with transparent backgrounds. Even though you can technically paint a low-opacity streak over a white background using the Brush tool, the Magic Wand sees that even though the *paint* is ghostly and transparent, the *background* is 100 percent opaque. It then counts the background as part of the selection and goes on to select the entire image.

✓ **All Opaque:** This option is a special choice for when you're working on an image that has transparent areas — areas of no content whatever — usually displayed with a checkered background. It tells Paint Shop Pro to select the area that has content around the pixel where you clicked. For instance, you may have photos of various air freshener products on a transparent layer, artistically floating over a cow pasture in the background. With this choice, you can just click one of the products to select it in its entirety.

Experiment to get the mode that works best for you! Press Ctrl+D to deselect each failed experiment, change match modes, and click again with the Magic Wand tool.

Setting tolerance to include more or fewer pixels

The Tolerance setting on the Tool Options palette helps you determine how much of an area is selected by the Magic Wand tool. You may have to undo your selection with Ctrl+D, adjust the tolerance, and click again with the Magic Wand tool several times to get the best selection possible. For an easier solution, see the discussion of expanding and filling in selections in the upcoming section "Modifying Your Selection."

Tolerance tells Paint Shop Pro how closely the pixels it selects should match the pixel you clicked — in RGB value, hue, or brightness, depending on which match mode you chose. (Tolerance doesn't matter for All Pixels match mode. A pixel either has content or it doesn't.) Here's how it works:

✓ Lower the tolerance value to make a less extensive selection the next time you click.

✓ Raise the tolerance value to make a more extensive selection the next time you click.

In Paint Shop Pro, low tolerance means that the Magic Wand tool tolerates little variation in color or brightness from the pixel you clicked. The tolerance value itself has no particular meaning; it's just a number.

The Tolerance value box on the Magic Wand tool's Tool Options palette has a clever adjustment feature you find in similar boxes throughout Paint Shop Pro. As with these types of boxes in any Windows program, you can type a value (from 0 to 200) in its text box or click its up or down arrow to adjust the value. We find that the best way is to click the down arrow, or *Clever adjustment feature,* and hold your mouse button down. A tiny slider appears that you can drag left or right to set the tolerance value lower or higher.

Tolerance can be a sensitive and picky adjustment. A small change can sometimes make a big difference in what gets selected. Unless you're trying to select an area well differentiated by color, brightness, or content, you probably have to adjust your selected area afterward. We tell you how to do that in the next section.

Modifying Your Selection

If you didn't select exactly the area you wanted with one of the Paint Shop Pro selection tools, don't despair. You can fine-tune or completely rework your selection in any of these ways:

- ✔ Drag the selection outline to another area of your image.
- ✔ Add to or subtract from your selection by using the selection tools.
- ✔ Expand or contract the selection's boundary by a given number of pixels.
- ✔ Grow the selection to include adjacent pixels of similar color or brightness.
- ✔ Select pixels of similar color or brightness anywhere in the image.

The following sections tell you how to do each one of those modifications. Read on!

Moving the selection outline

To move the selection outline (marquee) to another area of your image, first click the Move tool shown in the margin. Then hold down your *right* mouse button anywhere in the selection area and drag to move the outline elsewhere.

Adding to or subtracting from your selection

You can use the selection tools to add to or remove from your selection. You can add any area at all, using any selection tool — not just the one you used to create the selection — to do any of the following:

- Add or subtract areas around the edge of your selection. You can add cousin Alma's hat to a selection of her head, for instance, or remove it (the hat selection, not her head).

- Select multiple, isolated areas throughout the image. You can select all the buttons on your product, for instance.

- Remove isolated areas from the selection. For example, you can remove a policeman's buttons from a selection of his uniform.

- Use the same tool you used for the initial selection, and also use any of the other selection tools. Although you may have used Smart Edge to select Alex's head, you can add the carpet at the bottom with the Magic Wand tool.

Performing the addition or subtraction is simple as, well, arithmetic — simpler, even. Do either of the following:

- **To add areas to an existing selection:** Hold down the Shift key and, with any selection tool, make a new selection outside of (or overlapping) the original selection. A + sign appears next to the tool's cursor to remind you that you're adding.

- **To subtract areas from an existing selection:** Hold down the Ctrl key and make a selection within (or overlapping) the original selection. A – sign attaches itself to the selection tool's cursor.

Here's an example. In Figure 12-7, we originally clicked with the Magic Wand tool on the blue clothing worn by Dave's wife, Katy, using Brightness for the match mode. (We chose Brightness over Hue because the contrast in brightness between dark blue clothing and white snow was stronger than the uniformity of the blue.) The selection extended over to sled dog Starr's darker markings, however, which we didn't want.

To remove Starr from this selection, we held down the Ctrl key and used the Freehand tool (set to the Freehand selection type) to draw a loop around Starr. Figure 12-7 shows this loop nearing completion. Note the – sign near the lasso cursor, indicating subtraction. When we released the mouse button, Paint Shop Pro completed the loop and subtracted Starr from the selection. We could just as easily have used the Selection tool and (with the Ctrl key pressed) dragged an elliptical selection around Starr. In real life, Starr was never this easy to lasso.

Figure 12-7:
Removing
Starr
from the
selection by
outlining her
with the
Freehand
tool while
pressing the
Ctrl key.

Expanding and contracting by pixels

Expanding or *contracting* a selection in Paint Shop Pro simply means adding or removing a set of pixels around the edge of the selection area. It's like packing snow onto a snowman or melting it away. You can expand or contract a selection by as many snowflakes . . . er, pixels as you like.

Choose Selections➪Modify➪Expand or Selections➪Modify➪Contract. The simple-looking Expand Selection, or Contract Selection, dialog box appears. Set the Number of Pixels control to however many pixels you want to add or remove and click OK.

Removing specks and holes

If you have most of your image selected but it's still got some holes you want to fill in, you can tell Paint Shop Pro to extend its selection to cover any gaps under a certain size. Specks are any small flecks that lie outside of the main body of the selection, whereas holes are flecks *inside* the selection.

After you have your area selected, choose the Selections➪Modify➪ Remove Specks and Holes option. You're presented with an options dialog box, as shown in Figure 12-8, that asks you the maximum size of the speck or hole to be filled in (as measured in pixels, the smallest element of the picture that can be measured). The numbers in the dialog box are a bit confusing, but think of it as a multiplication project: In this setting, because the left number is set to 70 and the right menu is set to 100, any speck or hole smaller than 7,000 pixels is filled in with a selection. You can choose to fill in gaps as small as 1 x 1 (one pixel, obviously) or as large as 100 x 1,000,000 (100 million pixels), which is larger than most people's pictures!

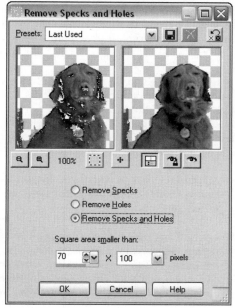

Figure 12-8:
A gappy
Alex,
filled in.

As you can see, the holes in Alex's interior get filled in, but it doesn't expand it out along the border. The danger is that if you select too wide an area, Paint Shop Pro may well decide that your entire selection is one huge gap and erase it.

Selecting similar areas

Selecting all the areas of similar color throughout an image is a pain to do manually. You have to find each spot of similar color and click it with the Magic Wand tool. Paint Shop Pro offers an automatic version of that same task.

First, use any selection tool to select one area. Then choose Selections⇨ Modify⇨Select Similar. Paint Shop Pro selects all pixels similar to the colors within your selection.

How similar? The Select Similar command looks to the Magic Wand tool's Tolerance control to determine how similar to the original color a selected pixel should be. A high tolerance means that a color can be significantly different and still be selected; a low tolerance selects only colors very close to those in your original selection.

A difference between the Magic Wand tool and the Select Similar command is that it asks whether you want to select an area *contiguously*. A contiguous Select Similar action only adds areas that are right next to the current selection; discontiguous selections add parts from all over your image, regardless of where they are.

You can also add or remove selections based on how close they are to certain colors. For example, if you're trying to cut and paste The Artist Formerly Known As Prince Who Is Back to Being Called Prince Again, who is known for wearing purple outfits, you might want to expand your selection to only lavender areas. Choose Selections➪Modify➪Select Color Range and choose a nice shade of magenta in the color box.

If you're selecting areas of a particular color because you intend to change that color throughout the image, consider using the Color Replacer tool instead. Refer to Chapter 4 for instructions.

Sometimes, you don't really want *all* the pixels of similar color — just those within a certain region of the image. Fussy, fussy. For instance, you may want all the sky, including that which peeks through the tree branches, but not the similarly colored pond, thank you. No problem. Just draw a freehand selection around the pond while pressing the Ctrl key to subtract that area.

Feathering for More Gradual Edges

When you copy or modify selected areas, you may notice that the edge between the selection and the background becomes artificially obvious. To keep a natural-looking edge on these types of objects, use feathering in your selection.

Feathering creates a blending zone of several pixels (however many you choose) extending both into and out of your selection. Whatever change you make to the selected area fades gradually within that zone, from 100 percent at the inner edge to 0 percent at the outer edge of the zone. For instance, if you were to increase the brightness of the selected area, that increase fades gradually to 0 at the outer edge of the feathered zone. If you delete, copy, cut, or move a feathered selection, you also leave a feathered edge behind.

You can apply feathering in either of two ways:

- **Before making the selection:** On the Tool Options palette for whatever selection tool you're using, set the Feather value to something greater than zero. When you next make a selection, the feathering is applied and the marquee's enclosed area expands to include the outer feathered pixels.

- **After making the selection:** Choose Selections➪Modify➪Feather and the Feather Selection dialog box appears. Set the Number of Pixels value in that dialog box to the number of pixels you want the selection feathered, and then click OK. The area within the selection marquee expands.

The value you set in the Feather control tells Paint Shop Pro how wide to make the feather zone — how many pixels to extend it into, and out of, the selection. (A setting of 4, for instance, creates a feathered zone 4 pixels into and 4 pixels out from the edge of the selection, for a total of 8 pixels wide.) A larger value makes a wider, more gradually feathered edge. When you feather, the marquee expands to include the pixels that are in the feathering zone.

If feathering in all directions is too clumsy for you, you can choose to feather the edge in one direction only, either into the interior of the selection or feathering out beyond its borders. Choose the Selections➪Modify➪ Inside/Outside Feather option to display a dialog box that offers exactly the same pixel control of the regular Feather control, except that you get to choose which way you feather.

Figure 12-9 shows the difference feathering makes. Normally, Alex is fairly fuzzy around the edges anyway. Feathering makes his edges even fuzzier. From left to right, this is the same image copied without feathering, with feathering in all directions, with inside-only feathering, and with outside-only feathering.

Figure 12-9: Alex, selected and pasted on a white background, with the four types of feathering.

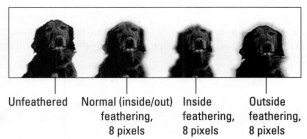

Unfeathered   Normal (inside/out) feathering, 8 pixels   Inside feathering, 8 pixels   Outside feathering, 8 pixels

When you copy or move a feathered selection, you bring along a faint border — feathered copies of the original background pixels surrounding the selection. The image on the far right in Figure 12-9 shows some door background, for instance.

You can defeather your image by choosing Selections⇨Modify⇨Unfeather; unfortunately, this command is not like the friendly Undo button, where it magically undoes any feathering you have added. Instead, this command displays a dialog box in which you can set the *threshold* of how harshly you want to strip any fuzziness from the edges of your selection; a low threshold gives your selection a light shave, whereas a high threshold reduces your selection to a stick-like skeleton of itself.

Because feathering a selection expands the marquee, it gives the appearance of filling in holes in a selection (adding them entirely to the selection). It doesn't really add those holes entirely to the selection, however; the pixels in them are simply feathered. As a result, if you feather a selection that has holes in it and then cut, delete, or move it, you leave behind faint images of those holes. If your selection has holes, try removing specks and holes or smoothing the selection *before* you feather it.

Antialiasing for Smoother Edges

Because computer images are made up of tiny squares (the pixels), when a straight edge of a selection is anything other than perfectly horizontal or vertical, those squares give the edge a microscopic staircase, or sawtooth, shape known as *aliasing*. Any changes you make to the selected area, or any cutting or pasting of the selection, may make that aliasing objectionably obvious.

To avoid aliasing when you next make a selection, click to enable the Antialias check box on the Tool Options palette for your selection tool. Antialiasing is available only for the Freehand tools, not the Magic Wand or the Selection tool. (You can use feathering to reduce most aliasing problems.)

The antialiasing option, like other settings on the Tool Options palette, applies to only selections you make *after* choosing that option, not to a *current* selection. You can't fix an existing aliased selection by clicking that option.

Selecting All, None, or Everything But

Sometimes you want a selection to be an all-or-nothing proposition! To select the entire image, press Ctrl+A or choose Selections⇨Select All.

The easiest way to select complex shapes

Selecting *everything but* and then inverting is a useful trick when you may have a complex object on a comparatively uniform background. Rather than spend lots of effort selecting the object, you can more easily select the uniform background with the Magic Wand tool and then, by pressing Ctrl+Shift+I, invert the selection (which selects the complex object). It doesn't work if the background is complex, but you would be surprised at how much time you can save.

However, if you do have a complex background, you can use the Background Eraser to clear a "moat" of transparent space around the shape you want selected and then switch to the regular Eraser tool to remove everything outside that moat. Then use the Magic Wand to select the transparent space around your image and invert it.

To *select none* (also known as *clearing* the selection or *deselecting*), press Ctrl+D or choose Selections➪Select None. You can also clear selections (except when the entire image is selected) by right-clicking anywhere on the image.

Sometimes you may want to select *everything but* the part of the image that is *not* selected. This process is known as *inverting* the selection. To perform it, choose Selections➪Invert or press Ctrl+Shift+I.

Selecting Alex, and Only Alex

So you have a problem: Your dog (the one in our example is named Alex) is sick of the snow. Sure, you *could* send him to a tropical paradise, but you have decided that it's much simpler to select him so that you can cut and paste him into a picture of the Caribbean. Then you show him the picture and tell him that he was just in the tropics last week.

The genius of dogs is that they require surprisingly little evidence to believe anything you tell them. So how do you do the transfer?

1. **Select the Magic Wand tool from the Selection toolset.**

    Because you're trying to select Alex and he is the only really brown thing in the picture, set the Magic Wand tool options to a match mode of Color.

2. **Set the tolerance of the Magic Wand.**

    Here's the trick: Even we hardened professional Paint Shop Pro experts (we're writing a book on it, aren't we?) *are never sure what number to use for tolerance* — like everyone else, we guess.

We guess 100, which, as you can see in Figure 12-10, turns out to be way too much. Right-click to clear the selection and try again. A little experimenting with the tolerance shows you that 25 tolerance is a solid starting point.

Figure 12-10: Alex, at 25 tolerance and 100 tolerance (selections filled in black for greater clarity).

25 tolerance   100 tolerance

3. Shift-click a few stray selections to clean up the edges.

The Magic Wand selected most of this cuddly retriever, but Alex's ear, the underside of his left foot, and his right rear foot are still not selected. Those are also the areas where the color tends to vary a little more wildly, shifting from almost black to light green, so set the tolerance a little higher, to 50, for example — and then Shift+click in these areas to add those places to your selection. As you can see in Figure 12-11, that action adds the ears and feet, but also adds unwanted portions of the door to your selection.

Figure 12-11: Alex, with more added, and also the door.

4. **Fill in the small gaps.**

   Choose Selections⇨Modify⇨Remove Specks and Holes and set it to 70 x 100 pixels, which automatically chooses any gap smaller than 700 pixels. Look back at Figure 12-8 to see the clear difference; click OK.

5. **Ctrl+click the door away.**

   Although you can do some fancy shenanigans with the Select Color Range option to remove that pesky door, you have a simpler solution: Because it's all in one place, you can just Ctrl+select it away. Remember: Shift+select adds to your existing selection, whereas Ctrl+select subtracts it. In this case, you switch to the Freehand tool, hold down Ctrl, and draw a ring around the door to remove it.

6. **Feather the edges.**

   Now the edges are crisp — *too* crisp, as you can see in Figure 12-12. A little feathering makes it softer and blends it in with any background in which you paste it. Choose Selections⇨Modify⇨Inside/Outside Feather and opt to feather the inside of the selection by two pixels.

Alex before feathering:
Notice the jagged, blocky edge?

Figure 12-12:
The two sides of Alex: pre- and post-feathering.

Alex after feathering, with his edges muted

Avoiding Selection Problems in Layered Images

Layered images can cause both the selection and the editing of those selections to go apparently screwy. The Magic Wand tool and Smart Edge features may appear neither magic nor smart, selecting areas not at all like you had in mind. Also, whatever changes you try to perform to the selected area (such as cutting, copying, or changing color) may apparently not take place. (If you're not sure whether your image has layers, see Chapter 14.)

The basic trick is to work on the right layer. Here are some more detailed rules you can follow to keep the selection and editing process relatively sane:

✔ **Activate the right layer:** Before you make any changes to a selected area (no matter which selection tool you have used to create it), make sure to activate the layer you want to change. You can't change all the layers within a selection at one time — only one layer at a time. You can merge all the layers (see Chapter 14) before making your change, but then you no longer have layers!

✔ **Use Sample Merged for combined layers:** Before you make a selection with the Magic Wand tool or Smart Edge feature, if the object you're trying to select is the result of various layers combined, enable the Sample Merged check box on the Tool Options palette. That way, the Magic Wand tool or Smart Edge feature examines the combined effect, not just the active layer. For instance, if you added a party hat to Uncle Charley's head on a separate layer and now you want to select Charley-with-hat using the Smart Edge feature, you would use Sample Merged.

✔ **Consider the effect of higher layers:** If the changes you try to make to a selected area aren't visible or seem only partially effective, a higher opaque or transparent layer may contain pixels that are obscuring your work. You may have to merge layers, make your changes to the higher, obscuring layer, or rethink your use of layers altogether.

Paint Shop Pro helps keep you sane. The preview window that certain adjustments provide (such as Brightness/Contrast) shows only the area you're affecting: the selected part of the active layer. If the wrong layer is active, you don't see the area you're expecting!

When you make a selection, it extends to all layers — no matter which one is active at the time. *Changes* to selected image areas, however (like painting), affect only the active layer. So you can activate one layer, for example, to make a selection with the Magic Wand tool and then switch to another layer to make changes within that selected area.

Chapter 13

Moving, Copying, and Reshaping Parts of Your Image

In This Chapter

▶ Moving, floating, and deleting a selection

▶ Using the Windows Clipboard

▶ Working with the Deformation tool

*I*n Chapter 12, we tell you how to identify a chunk of your image to Paint Shop Pro by creating a selection. In this chapter, you see how to move, copy, twist, and deform these selections — in short, how to do almost anything that changes the physical location or outline of a selection. (You may also rotate, flip, or mirror a selection, but you have to go to Chapter 11 for those tricks.)

Before you get rolling, take these notes to heart and staple them there:

✔ The instructions in this chapter assume that you know how to make selections. If you don't know how, refer to Chapter 12.

✔ A *selection* is a selected portion of the image, *not* the selection marquee (moving dashed line).

✔ If your image has multiple layers, make sure that you're on the right layer to move, copy, float, or delete the image you want. See Chapter 14 for help with layers.

✔ You can press Ctrl+Z to undo any changes you make. The changes you can undo include selecting, floating, moving, copying, pasting, or defloating. Refer to Chapter 1 for more information about undoing.

✔ The instructions in this chapter deal only with image chunks that are made out of dots (called raster, or bitmap, images). Those selections are the kinds we describe in Chapter 12 and that you make with the Selection, Freehand, or Magic Wand tools. To deal with vector selections (typically text, lines, and geometric shapes), see Chapter 15.

Floating, Moving, and Deleting Selections

After you have made a selection, you can easily move it anywhere within your image, move a copy of it, or delete it altogether. Here's how to do it:

✔ **To move a selection:** Choose any selection tool (Selection, Freehand, or Magic Wand), if you haven't already, and then drag the selection. Selection tool cursors become four-headed move arrows when you position them over a selection, as Figure 13-1 shows. On the Background (main) image layer, dragging a selection in this way leaves behind background color. The image on the left in Figure 13-1 shows the effect.

Simply dragging leaves background color

Figure 13-1:
Dragging a
selection.
Float the
image first
with Ctrl+F
to drag a
copy.

Float, then drag to move a copy

✔ **To float a selection (make it moveable):** A *floating* selection simply means a moveable one. You can float a selection in one of two ways. When you click an existing selection with a selection tool (as though to move the selection), that selection is floated automatically. Alternatively, you can choose Selections⇨Float or press Ctrl+F. Floating a selection in that way (manually) leaves a copy of it behind. (Note that any floating selection also appears on the layer palette.)

✔ **To move a selection and leave a copy behind (as the right side of Figure 14-1 shows):** *Float the selection manually first* (choose Selections⇨Float or press Ctrl+F) and then move it with the Mover tool (the four-headed arrow) or any selection tool.

✔ **To defloat the floating selection (or glue it back down):** To *defloat* a selection, press Ctrl+Shift+F or choose Selections➪Defloat. You can also *deselect* (press Ctrl+D) to defloat. The defloating command leaves the area selected in case you want to do additional work on it. Whichever way you defloat the image, defloating glues the image down. It's now part of the underlying image (or image layer), and its pixels replace whatever was there. If you move the selection again, you find that the original underlying pixels are no longer there.

✔ **To delete the selection:** Press the Delete key on your keyboard. If the image has only one layer (or the Background layer is the active one in a multilayer image), the Paint Shop Pro background color appears in the deleted area. If the selection is on a layer, the pixels within it simply go away. (Okay, technically, they're made transparent — same thing.)

✔ **To move a floating selection to another layer:** Drag the *Floating Selection* layer up or down on the Layer palette. Leave the selection immediately above the layer you ultimately want the selection to join. When you defloat the selection, it joins the closest underlying (raster) layer.

You can also flip or mirror a selection. Refer to Chapter 11 for information on using the Flip and Mirror commands. Both commands leave a copy of the original image underlying the selection.

Cutting, Copying, and Pasting from the Windows Clipboard

To make lots of copies of a selection, use the conventional cut, copy, and paste features that employ the Windows Clipboard. You can use these features for copying selections to or from other Windows applications too because nearly all Windows applications make use of the Clipboard.

If your image has multiple layers, first make sure that you have selected the right layer to cut, copy, or paste the image you want. Click the layer's name on the Layer palette. (Press F8 if the palette isn't visible). See Chapter 14 for more help with layers.

Cutting and copying

In Paint Shop Pro, *cut* and *copy* work much the same as they do in any Windows program. First, select an area in your image. Then, do any of these tasks:

✔ **Cut a selection:** Press Ctrl+X, choose Edit➪Cut, or click the familiar Windows Cut button (scissors icon) on the Paint Shop Pro toolbar. Paint Shop Pro places a copy of the selected area on the Windows Clipboard. If you're cutting on the main (Background) layer of the image, Paint Shop Pro fills the cut area with the current background color on the color palette. On other layers, it leaves behind transparency.

✔ **Copy a selection:** Press Ctrl+C, choose Edit➪Copy, or click the Copy button (two-documents icon) on the Paint Shop Pro toolbar. Paint Shop Pro puts a copy of the selected area (of the active layer) on the Windows Clipboard. Nothing happens to your image.

✔ **Copy a selection on a multilayer image:** The normal Edit➪Copy command copies only from the active layer. If your image is made up of multiple layers, you may want to copy the combined effect of all layers. If so, choose Edit➪Copy Merged (or press Ctrl+Shift+C).

✔ **Cut or copy from other applications:** Most Windows applications offer the same Edit➪Copy and Edit➪Cut commands, so you can place text or graphics on the Windows Clipboard. Paint Shop Pro enables you to paste a wide variety of Clipboard content from other programs, such as text, vector graphics, or raster graphics.

Pasting

After your selection is on the Windows Clipboard, choose Edit➪Paste to paste it into Paint Shop Pro (or nearly any other application). When you choose Edit➪Paste in Paint Shop Pro, however, you get several different paste options, which we describe briefly in this list and in more detail in the following sections:

✔ **As New Image (Ctrl+V):** The Clipboard contents become a whole new image, in its own window.

✔ **As New Layer (Ctrl+L):** The Clipboard contents become a new layer for the current image. See Chapter 14 for a discussion of layers.

✔ **As New Selection (Ctrl+E):** Clipboard contents become a floating selection that you can place anywhere on the image (on the active layer.)

✔ **As Transparent Selection (Ctrl+Shift+E):** This is the same thing as the option named As New Selection, except that this time the background color of the current image is subtracted from the selection. We find this option to be kind of limited, and we suggest that you use the Select Color Range to get rid of a color entirely, as shown later in this chapter, in the section "Removing the background or other colors from your selection."

✔ **Into Selection (Ctrl+Shift+L):** If you have a selected area in your image, this choice fits the Clipboard contents exactly into the selection, scaling the contents up or down as needed.

If you're in the habit of using Ctrl+V for editing in other programs, you need to retrain yourself. In Paint Shop Pro, Ctrl+V creates a new image rather than pastes your selection to the existing image, which is what you probably expect to happen.

Here's one paste selection we cover elsewhere in this book:

✔ **As New Vector Selection:** This command is used for pasting text and shapes you created using the Paint Shop Pro text and shape tools. For more about vectors, see Chapter 14.

If you copy vector graphics from outside Paint Shop Pro (for instance, objects drawn using computer-aided design software, drawing programs, or Microsoft Word's draw feature), Paint Shop Pro converts them to raster graphics when you paste. Paint Shop Pro pops up a Meta Picture Import dialog box in which you can enter either height or width in pixels to determine the image's size. To enter height and width values independently, clear the Maintain Original Aspect Ratio check box.

Pasting to create a new picture: As New Image

The paste As New Image option creates a new image containing the Clipboard contents. The image is just big enough to contain whatever is on the Clipboard. The background of the image is transparent, which means that if your copied selection isn't rectangular, you see transparent areas; erasing also leaves transparency behind.

Choose Edit⇨Paste⇨As New Image or press Ctrl+V (the nearly universal keyboard command for Paste). Your new image appears in a new window.

If you prefer your new image to have a background color or to be slightly larger than the contents of the Clipboard, create the new image first, separately (refer to Chapter 1). Then paste a selection or new layer rather than use the Paste As New Image command.

Pasting on an existing image: As New Selection

The Paste As New Selection option pastes the Clipboard contents as a floating selection on your image. This pasting option is the one most people want for editing an image because it is the simplest and most intuitive.

If your image uses multiple layers, make sure to first activate the layer where you want to paste (refer to Chapter 14).

Choose Edit➪Paste➪As New Selection or press Ctrl+E. A floating selection appears on your image. In the example shown in Figure 13-2, the selection on the right had all the black removed from it, but a small, ugly halo of grayness remains; the figure on the left had the black color range subtracted from it and looks much cleaner.

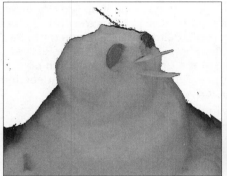

Figure 13-2:
Close, but
not quite.

Because the selection is floating, you drag the selection to move it anywhere in the image. To defloat the selection (paste it down on the underlying layer), press Ctrl+Shift+F. See the earlier section "Floating, Moving, and Deleting Selections," for details about moving and defloating a floating selection.

Pasting for maximum flexibility: As New Layer

Pasting directly on another image is fine, as far as it goes. For maximum flexibility in making future changes, however, paste on a new layer instead. When an image is on a layer, you can modify it to your heart's content without worrying about surrounding or underlying image areas. (In Chapter 14, we discuss the whys and hows of layers in detail.) Here's how:

1. **If your image already has more than one layer, activate (choose) the layer above which you want the new layer to appear.**

   For instance, click the layer on the Layer palette to activate it. See Chapter 14 for more details on activating layers.

2. **Choose Edit⊏>Paste⊏>As New Layer (or press Ctrl+L).**

   Your pasted image appears on a layer of its own.

If the background of the image you pasted was transparent, the underlying image layer shows through those background areas. Otherwise, the pasted image and its background color fill an opaque rectangle. If you want to delete the background (make it transparent), use the Magic Wand tool, or another selection tool, to select it (refer to Chapter 12) and press the Delete key on your keyboard. Alternatively, see the following section.

Removing the background or other colors from your selection

Sometimes you want to be rid of the background behind a selection you have moved or pasted. Often, for instance, a pasted object has a solid white or other colored background — perhaps because you copied and pasted it from the Web. Often, the background may not be perfectly uniform; a tree you moved may bring along some bluish sky around its edge, or a baby may bring along a white blanket with gray folds. You do *not,* however, want the sky or blanket in the new location. Perhaps you're trying to copy the baby to a photo of a hay-filled manger with sheep looking on adoringly — or hungrily, which is easier, given the hay.

One solution is to make the background color transparent, if it's fairly uniform. (If that color appears elsewhere in the image, however, you may get unwanted transparent holes; you can then use the Remove Specks and Holes command to get rid of them, as outlined in Chapter 12.)

With the area you're trying to affect selected in your image, follow these steps:

1. **Choose Selections⊏>Modify⊏>Select Color Range.**

   This step brings up the Select Color Range dialog box, as shown in Figure 13-3.

2. **Click the Reference Color swatch.**

   This step brings the Color dialog box, but you can safely ignore it; instead, click on your image, in the area that has the color you want removed. Click OK.

3. **Select Subtract Color Range.**

4. **Set the Tolerance value to something higher than zero.**

   We know that this instruction is vague, but only experience or trial-and-error can really guide you in this setting. Try a value of 10 to 20 to begin with, if in doubt.

What this does is make transparent any pixel of the color you have chosen, or of a similar color. Low tolerance values remove colors that are almost exactly like your chosen color; higher tolerance values begin to wipe wider ranges of color.

For example, if you chose a baby blue and use a 1 tolerance, only that precise shade of blue is removed; at a 256 tolerance, Paint Shop Pro begins removing dark purples and light browns in addition to all blue shades within the selection.

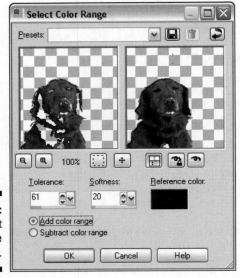

Figure 13-3:
The Select
Color Range
dialog box.

5. **Look at your selection to double-check that it has no ugly fringe.**

If you can see the nonselected areas of your image, clicking the Toggle Selection button to hide them makes this step much easier.

6. **Click OK.**

If the process makes too many or too few pixels transparent, repeat these steps to choose a new tolerance in Step 4, or choose a different background color in Step 1. To make more pixels transparent, increase the tolerance value in Step 4; for fewer transparent pixels, decrease the tolerance.

You can repeat this process as often as you want, removing color after color.

Tips for natural-looking pastes

People frequently use the cut-and-paste feature to put objects in other places; for example, in Figure 13-4, we have cut the faithful Alex out of Dave's snow-covered doorstep and placed him next to Amy, William's daughter, as she kneels next to her fantastic creation: the Snowduck.

Figure 13-4:
Paint
Shop Pro:
Bringing
people (and
animals)
together.

This part of the program is a great deal of fun, and Paint Shop Pro aficionados frequently get hours of enjoyment by inserting themselves into movie posters so that they're costarring with Salma Hayek. In fact, an entire underground Internet movement is devoted to taking pictures from the news and doing as many strange and bizarre things with them as possible. The Web site www.fark.com, for example, holds PG-13-rated contests to see who can "Photoshop" pictures of Alan Greenspan and Ludacris into the funniest places. Some results are quite impressive.

But the problem is that cut-and-paste operations frequently look completely unnatural. Not that you need your photos to hold up to the eye of conspiracy theorists — everyone knows that they're fake, after all — but plopping a picture of you, jaggies and edge halos and all, into some random image just looks amateurish.

With that in mind, we here at the *Paint Shop Pro 8 For Dummies* staff offer the following advice to make your images blend seamlessly:

1. **Use the Magic Wand to select.**

   Yes, it's easier to just draw a line around your target — but unless you have a steady hand and a *ridiculously* exacting eye, the Magic Wand does it better after some fine-tuning. Get used to it.

2. **Get rid of the holes and specks in your selection.**

   This task used to be a difficult, but Paint Shop Pro makes it so easy now with its Remove Specks and Holes command that it's a crime not to do it.

3. **Feather a little.**

   Usually, you want to leave off those crisp edges. Feather one or two pixels on the inside to help the selection blend into the background.

4. **Eliminate the background color entirely.**

   We show you how to do this step in the section "Removing the background or other colors from your selection," earlier in this chapter. Figure 13-2 shows you what happens if you don't. Learn the lesson!

5. **Resize appropriately.**

   When we first put Alex in the picture in Figure 13-4, he only came up to Amy's shoulder, making Amy look freakishly huge. A little upsizing made a large difference.

6. **Match the blur.**

   Most photos aren't perfectly clear, and dropping a crisply focused image into the middle of a slightly blurry pic looks wrong in a way that most people can't quite put a name to. Sharpening or Gaussian-blurring your selection just a tad helps it to blend in.

7. **Adjust the color.**

   Having a sunlit image brought into a fluorescent background makes the image stick out like a throbbing thumb. Adjust the contrast, hue, and brightness to match it as close as you can.

8. **Don't forget the shadows!**

   A touch of low-opacity black paint can serve as a quick-and-dirty fake shadow — as we did in the example shown in Figure 13-4. If you want to go all out, you can even paste in another identical selection as a layer, deform it so that it's twisted sideways and elongated like a real shadow, position it so that it's spreading out from the bottom of the image, erase the layer so that it's transparent — and *then* fill it in with low-opacity paint. But that's a great deal of work for a quick fake!

Resizing, Rotating, Deforming, and Perspective-izing

Okay, so perspective-izing isn't a real word. Perspecting? In any event, you can resize, rotate, deform, or move your selection by using the Deform tool from the Deformation toolset, as shown in Figure 13-5.

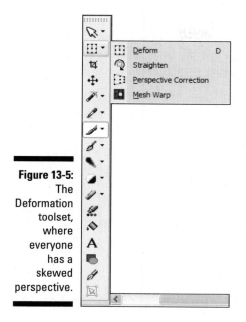

Figure 13-5:
The
Deformation
toolset,
where
everyone
has a
skewed
perspective.

Making a shape look as though it's seen in perspective is one of the cool kinds of deformation you can do. You can make a rectangular area, for instance, look like a wall or road receding into the distance. You can paint a railroad track running vertically, flat, as though it's on a map, and then make it lie down realistically by applying perspective.

Preparing for deformation

The Deform tool is picky: it needs a separate layer (other than the background layer) to work with. If you're trying to deform a selection, Paint Shop Pro asks you whether it's okay to promote that selection to a layer. (See Chapter 19 if you want Paint Shop Pro to do this automatically, without asking you.)

However, you can move the selection to its own layer yourself by choosing Selections⇨Promote to Layer or press Ctrl+Shift+P. For more about layers, see Chapter 14.

The Deformation tool works on the active layer, encompassing all the non-transparent areas in that layer. In other words, if you have a blob of pixels on a layer, the tool encompasses (rather neatly, in our opinion) just that blob. If you have multiple blobs separated by transparency, it encompasses all blobs.

Doing the deformation

The easy and fairly intuitive way to make the deformation is by dragging various parts of the deformation grid with the Deformation tool. See "Deforming by dragging," coming up next.

The geeky, but precise, way to do the deformation is with the Deformation Settings dialog box. See "Deforming by dialog box," a bit later in this chapter.

Deforming by dragging

Select the Deformation tool from the Deformation toolset (if it's grayed out, refer to the earlier section "Preparing for deformation" for instructions), and your cursor turns into that icon. Click your selection to get this cool-looking *deformation grid* with tiny squares (called *handles*) on it, as Figure 13-6 shows.

Drag anywhere inside grid to move selection

Resizing handles

Figure 13-6:
The Deform-ation tool's grid for stretching, rotating, and dragging the victim.

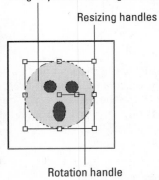

Rotation handle

This figure shows you what to drag for resizing, rotating, or moving the image. Note that you can move the selection with this tool by dragging anywhere *except* on one of the handles. (In areas where dragging is possible, the cursor changes to a four-way arrow.) Here's how to do various operations, using the handles of the deformation grid:

- **Resizing or repositioning sides:** Adjust width and height by dragging the handle in the center of any side. Drag corner handles to change both height and width at the same time. (The Deformation tool provides no way to automatically keep the proportions constant while you drag, so see the following section for help.)

- **Rotating:** Drag the handle, marked "Rotation handle" in Figure 13-7, in a circular motion around the center of the grid. (When your cursor is over the rotation handle, the cursor depicts the pair of curved arrows shown in the figure. The center of rotation is marked by a square that is at the face's nose.) Only the grid rotates until you release the mouse button; then the selection rotates.

Cursor

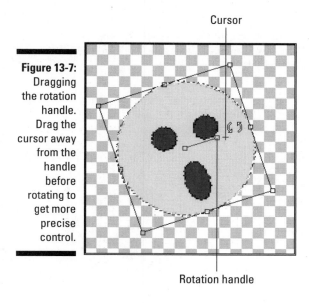

Figure 13-7:
Dragging
the rotation
handle.
Drag the
cursor away
from the
handle
before
rotating to
get more
precise
control.

Rotation handle

✔ **Adding perspective:** In the real world, the farther away an object is, the smaller it appears to your eye. Here's how to create that illusion with your selection so that one end looks farther away:

- To shrink any side of the selection as though it were farther away, first hold down the Ctrl key. With that key down, drag one of the two corner handles that terminate the side; drag toward the center of that side. To expand the side, drag away from the center. The side shrinks or expands symmetrically about the center (both corners move). The perspective this distortion creates is as though your eyes were level with the middle of the selection, as the left side of Figure 13-8 shows.

- To shrink or expand any side asymmetrically (move one corner only), first hold down the Shift key. With that key down, drag a corner handle toward or away from the center handle of that side. When you apply this effect to the left or right side, as shown on the right in Figure 13-8, the result is as though your eyes were at a level above or below center. For instance, to get the illusion of a tall wall, drag the upper corner down.

For a different way to apply simple perspective that doesn't involve as much head scratching, try the Paint Shop Pro Perspective effect. Choose Effects➪Geometric Effects➪Perspective Horizontal or Perspective Vertical. Refer to Chapter 8 for help with effect dialog boxes.

✔ **Shear (or *skew*) distortion:** We got the shear effect of Figure 13-9 by dragging the right side of the selection down. To drag a side of your selection, hold down either the Ctrl or Shift key and drag the center handle on the side you want to move.

Figure 13-8:
Getting
perspective
by dragging
a corner
while
pressing Ctrl
(left image)
or Shift
(right
image).

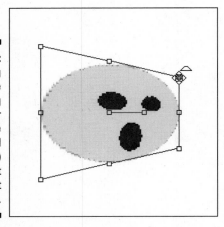 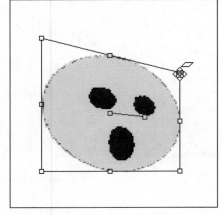

Shear is useful for perspective when you want the virtual horizon (the vanishing point, in drafting terms) to be higher or lower than dead center. Apply perspective distortion to shrink a left or right side first, and then use shear to drag one of those sides up or down. Dragging down, for instance, makes the image appear as it would if a viewer were looking up slightly (it lowers the horizon).

Deforming by dialog box

Dragging handles is convenient and intuitive, but not particularly precise. What if you know that you need to rotate something 31.5 degrees, for instance? Or scale it down to 85 percent of its original dimensions?

Press F4 to bring up the Tool Options palette, and you can type the settings you want. It provides a column for X, or horizontal values, and Y, or vertical values, and rows for each of the various changes that the Deformation tool can make. Here's how to choose the values you need:

✔ **Position:** To move the selection, enter the X and Y coordinates where you want the upper-left corner of the deformation grid to go. (Remember that X and Y both equal 0 at the upper-right corner of the image.)

✔ **Scale:** Enter X and Y scale factors. Enter **80** in the X% scale box, for instance, to reduce the horizontal size of the selection to 80 percent of original. To keep the original proportions, put the same value in both the X and Y columns.

✔ **Shear:** To slide the top edge to the right, enter a positive value; enter a negative value to move the edge the other way.

✔ **Perspective:** To make the right edge appear to recede into the distance by pulling the upper-right corner down and inward, enter a positive number in the Perspective X box. To make the top edge appear to recede, do likewise in the Y box. Use negative values to make those same edges appear to approach the viewer instead.

Figure 13-9:
Shear
brilliance!
Dragging
a center
handle with
Ctrl or Shift
pressed
applies
shear
distortion.

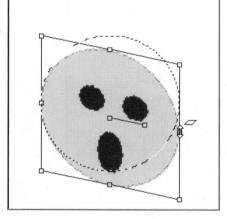

✔ **Pivot:** Normally, when you rotate a selection or layer, it rotates around the center. If you want your image to revolve around a different point — around the upper-left corner of the selection, for example, or even around a point that's outside the selection entirely — adjust the pivot values. The numbers in the X and Y boxes vary, but unless you have changed the pivot in the past, those numbers are the exact center of the image. Lower X numbers move the pivot to the left, whereas higher Xs shift it right; lower Y numbers move the pivot up, and higher numbers drop it down.

✔ **Angle:** To rotate the selection clockwise, enter a positive number of degrees (45, for example) into the text box. Use a negative value for counterclockwise.

Deformation consternations

The Deformation tool can occasionally wrinkle your brow with certain weirdnesses. Here are a few typical problems and solutions:

The tool encompasses the wrong area: You probably have the wrong layer active. Here's what happens: If you're on a layer that's transparent in the selected area, the Deformation tool chooses the nontransparent area instead. Press the F8 key to open the Layer palette and click the layer that contains the image you want.

You can't find the deformation grid; you see only two squares and a connecting line: The grid is there, all right, but you have applied the Deformation tool to a layer or selection that covers the entire image. Change layers or make a new selection.

An annoying background appears in the area the selection outline has vacated: Well, Paint Shop Pro has to put *something* there, and it can't invent a background image. (See "Preparing for deformation," earlier in this chapter, for more information about backgrounds.) If Paint Shop Pro could stretch the surrounding area to stay continuous with your newly deformed selection, that would be nice, but it isn't so. Try dragging your selection elsewhere or filling in the background with the Clone Brush tool (refer to Chapter 5).

Other handy deformities

You should know about three other tools in the Deform toolset:

- ✔ **Mesh Warp:** Using this tool covers your image with a grid of warp points; you can click and drag each of these points to deform your image in specific ways, as you can see in Figure 13-10.

  In the left picture, the grid is untouched; in the right, however, we have moved the warp points around, and the image has stretched itself to fit the new warp points. (You can control the number of warp points by changing the Mesh Horizontal and Mesh Vertical controls on the Tool Options palette; larger values mean more points. As usual, press F4 if you don't see the Tool Options palette.)

  You can accomplish some mighty strange effects with this feature, given time and lots of patience; the most common use is to warp an existing image to fit on another image's contour.

- ✔ **Straighten:** Did you ever spend an afternoon hanging paintings, taking painstaking care to ensure that the bottom edges of the frames were all perfectly parallel with the floor? This tool is an automatic picture-adjuster. Most images are at least a little tilted when they're scanned in, so we discuss this tool in Chapter 2, in the section about scanning into Paint Shop Pro.

✔ **Perspective Correction:** This tool is the reverse of the deform tool; if you have an image that's already a little skewed or sheared, you can use this tool to attempt to *remove* the skew or shear. Dragging the Perspective tool around an image creates a box; you can then drag the points on the edge of the box, just as you would with the Deformation tool — but in this case you're trying to re-create the shear or skew that's already present. When you're done, double-click the image and Paint Shop Pro attempts to remove the shear.

Figure 13-10:
Warping
Amy and
Alex; you
see the left
image when
you first
open the
Mesh Warp
tool; the
right image
shows what
happens
after some
points have
been shifted.

Chapter 14

Layering Images

The old masters of oil painting used layers of paint to give their paintings great depth and radiance. Now, artistic masters (who all work in Paint Shop Pro, of course) use layers for another reason: It makes changing stuff lots easier. It also lets you combine images more easily.

Layers are like transparent sheets of plastic that are laid over an opaque (nontransparent) background. You can put stuff on the background layer or on the other, transparent layers.

As simple as this basic idea is, Paint Shop Pro uses it to give you lots of flexibility and power in creating stunning images. To see what using layers can do for you, read on!

Putting Layers to Work for You

With layers, you can paint, erase, or move things around without worrying about ruining the underlying image. You can erase a line, for instance, without erasing the background. You can move an entire object or see how something looks without permanently committing yourself to it. You can also combine images in various clever ways.

Because Paint Shop Pro layers are electronic, not physical, they can make your life easier in other ways, too. Here are just a few of the special tricks you can do, besides simply painting, moving, combining, or erasing images:

- ✔ Select an object painted on a layer without accidentally selecting other areas of the same color or that underlie that object.

- ✔ Make an image partly transparent, a sort of ghost on the background.

- ✔ Switch image objects into or out of the picture, as needed, or quickly change their stacking order.

- ✔ Combine layers into one layer, if you're certain that no more changes are needed, or lock several layers together temporarily to form a movable group of objects.

- ✔ Make vector layers, which enable you to create basic shapes, text, and other objects in a special form that lets you easily change their shape.

- ✔ Make an adjustment layer (a brightening layer, for example) that affects only the underlying layers and which effect you can vary.

- ✔ Create the frames of an animation by simply moving one or more layers.

- ✔ Make layers interact, for special effects. For instance, you can subtract one layer from another — a way to reveal changes between photographs.

Getting Layers

Your parents probably never explained where layers come from — unless, of course, you grew up on an egg ranch. Here's the real story.

You always have at least one layer: the background layer. That's the layer where nearly everything happens until you add more layers. If you download a digital photo from your camera, for instance, the image is on the background layer. If you happily paint away, ignorant of all knowledge of layers, all your painting is on the background layer.

You can get images with additional layers in a variety of ways:

- ✔ Make a new, blank layer by using the various New commands on the Layers menu (on the menu bar) or by using the Layer palette.

- ✔ Turn a selection into a layer (*promote* it, in Paint Shop Pro terms).

- ✔ Incidentally, make a new vector layer by drawing lines or shapes or by adding text.

✔ Make a new raster layer by using a tool, like the Deformation tool, that requires a layer to work on, and Paint Shop Pro creates one automatically for you.

✔ Paste an image from the Windows Clipboard by choosing Edit⇨Paste⇨ As New Layer.

✔ Open an image file that already has multiple layers, such as many Paint Shop Pro or Photoshop files have.

✔ Add a picture frame with the Image⇨Picture Frame command.

Calling a Pal for Help: The Layer Palette

The first thing you should do when you're working with layers is to call a friend for help. The Layer palette, as shown in Figure 14-1, is your best pal. It's a small pal, hence the name *palette*. See how things make sense, after they're explained?

If it's not on your screen already, call your little pal by pressing F8 on the keyboard or click the Toggle Layers button on the toolbar. Do the same thing to hide the palette again.

One of the not-so-adorable Paint Shop Pro quirks is that sometimes it opens the Layer palette so that the names of the layers (and, hence, the only way to *select* a layer) are hidden. Your Layer palette should look like ours, with at least the Background layer visible on the far left side; if it doesn't, right-click and drag the vertical bar immediately to the left of the Visibility toggle (the little eye) and drag it rightward to reveal all.

Here are a few basic factoids to help you get along with your new and complex-looking pal:

✔ **Each row of the palette represents a layer.** Your view of the image in the image window is down through the layers, from top to bottom (background). The layers' names are on the left side of the palette. You assign names when you create the layers, or else you allow Paint Shop Pro to create a boring but adequate name, like Layer3. Paint Shop Pro automatically calls the initial, background layer (the one that every image starts with) Background.

✔ **To work on a layer, click its name.** Clicking its name makes that layer the active one. Nearly everything you can do to an image in Paint Shop Pro, such as paint, erase, or fiddle with the colors, affects only the active layer. The palette helps you remember which one is active.

New Raster Layer

New Vector Layer

New Mask Layer

New Layer Group

Duplicate Layer

Delete Layer

Figure 14-1:
Your pal,
the Layer
palette, is
at your side
to help you
with layer
tasks.

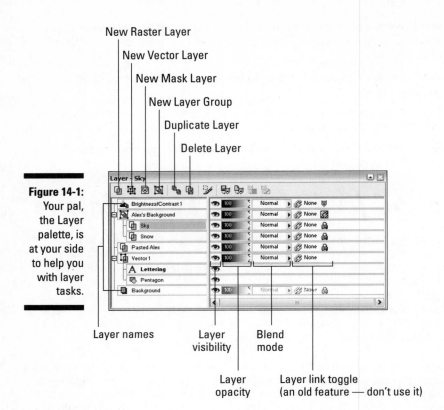

Layer names

Layer
visibility

Blend
mode

Layer
opacity

Layer link toggle
(an old feature — don't use it)

> ✔ **The icon to the left of each row tells you what kind of layer that row represents.** Four kinds of layer exist: raster, vector, grouped, or adjustment. You use raster layers most often. See the following side-bar, "Choosing a layer that's just your type," for details. In Figure 14-1, the rows named Pasted Alex, Sky, and Snow show you a raster icon, the Lettering and Pentagon layers show the vector icon, the Brightness/ Contrast layer displays an adjustment icon, and Alex's Background shows the group icon.

Don't bother trying to understand the palette all at once. We tell you how to use the rest of the palette's features as we go along.

Creating a New, Blank Layer

To create a new, blank layer, follow these steps using the Layer palette:

1. **Choose where, in your stack of layers, you want the new layer to appear.**

   (If this is the first layer you have added to an image, you can skip this step. The new layer appears just above the background layer.)

   Otherwise, on the Layer palette, click the layer that you want the new layer to appear above. In Figure 14-1, for instance, we have clicked the layer labeled Sky, making that layer the active one.

2. **Click the New Layer button or choose Layers⇨New Raster Layer from the menu bar.**

   The New Layer button is in the upper-left corner of the Layer palette, as shown in Figure 14-1.

   If you're savvy about the various types of layer and know that you want a specific type, choose Layers from the Paint Shop Pro menu bar. The menu that appears lets you choose, among others, New Raster Layer, New Vector Layer, or New Adjustment Layer. For more information about types of layer, see the nearby sidebar, "Choosing a layer that's just your type."

   The rather intimidating Layer Properties dialog box appears, trying to scare you. Forge ahead boldly.

3. **Type a name for the layer.**

   The Name field of the Layer Properties dialog box is already highlighted, so you don't have to click there before typing. Whatever you type replaces the rather boring name (like Layer1) that Paint Shop Pro suggests. Enter a name in that field that describes what you will put on this layer. If you're not feeling creative, just skip this step and Paint Shop Pro uses the boring name.

4. **Click OK.**

   Get the heck out of this boring, intimidating Layer Properties dialog box and get on with the fun!

Your image doesn't look any different, so maybe you're wondering "Just what have I accomplished?" Fear not! You have indeed added a layer. The image doesn't look any different because your new layer is transparent and blank. It's just like a sheet of clear plastic placed over a painting.

Look at the Layer palette. You see your new layer, with the name you gave it, highlighted. That means that it's the active layer, and any painting, erasing, selection, or color adjustment you perform now takes place on that layer.

To delete a layer on the Layer palette, click that layer's name and then click the Delete Layer button. Everything on that layer goes away with the layer.

Choosing a layer that's just your type

To make life a bit more complicated, Paint Shop Pro has five different types of layers for different kinds of stuff. Four of those types of layers appear in Figure 14-1, where you can see that they're distinguished by special icons. Here's more about those layers:

 Raster: You use this plain-vanilla type of layer most of the time. Unless you specify otherwise, you get one of these when you create a new layer. A raster layer handles normal images — the kind made of dots, called raster, or bitmap, images. Raster layers are just like the background layer, which you're already familiar with. Raster layers are marked with the icon shown here.

 Vector: This special type of layer comes into play mostly when you use the Paint Shop Pro text, preset shapes, or line-drawing tools. Vector images are made up of lines or curves connected in a connect-the-dot fashion. Paint Shop Pro normally creates text, preset shapes, and lines as vector images, although you can alternatively create them as raster images. Vector images can't appear on a raster layer, and raster images can't appear on a vector layer. Vector images are marked with the icon that appears here.

 Adjustment: This special type of layer doesn't contain any images! It's like a magical coating that imparts a particular image quality to the layers under it. It works almost exactly like color adjustments, so we discuss it some more in Chapter 10. The advantage of adjustment layers is that the enhancement is separated from the image, so changing your mind is easier. Adjustment layers are named according to the kind of adjustment they perform, and each of them has its own snazzy color icon; the one shown next to this paragraph is Contrast.

 Group: Many times, you want to apply an effect to the same two or three layers while leaving the other layers untouched. You can group the layers so that Paint Shop Pro treats them like a single layer, which is awfully handy; we show you how to do this later in this chapter.

 Mask: *Masking* is used to hide certain areas of an overlaying layer's image while letting other areas remain visible. It's a little like masking tape except that rather than cover parts of an image like masking tape does, masking makes areas transparent — just as erasing on a layer does in Paint Shop Pro. That allows the underlying image to show through. It's a handy trick for advanced Paint Shop Pro users, allowing you to cut out shapes with little effort or create transparent areas on the background layer, although it's a little too detailed to go into in a *For Dummies* book. Paint Shop Pro 8 is so brimming with new features that we had to leave out *something*.

When you float a selection, it appears on the Layer palette like a layer and is named *Floating Selection* (in italics). It's not really a full-fledged layer, but you can use Layer menu commands on it, like moving it down in the stack. Refer to Chapter 12 for the details of floating. You can turn a selection into its own layer, as we show you later in this chapter.

Working on Layers

To work on a layer, click its name on the Layer palette to select it (make it active). Then, working on the new layer is very much like working on the background layer. You can paint, erase, adjust color, cut, copy, paste, and make image transformations, such as flipping, filtering, or deforming, and the results appear on only your selected layer. How tidy and organized!

As an artist who is using multiple layers, you're like a doctor who is seeing multiple patients. To avoid mistakes, you must know which one you're operating on. You can't tell what image is on which layer by simply looking at the image. The transparency of layers prevents you. So, instead, keep an eye on the Layer palette to see which layer is active. The active layer is highlighted there. Pause your cursor over a layer's name to see a tiny thumbnail image of the layer's contents. If a tool doesn't seem to be working, you're probably trying to work on something that isn't *on* the active layer. Try turning various layers on and off to find the object you want.

Here are a few peculiarities of working with layers:

- **Moving:** You can use the Move tool (the four-headed arrow) to slide an entire layer around (but not the background layer). Click the Move tool on the Tool palette. Then, in the image window, drag the entire layer by dragging any object on that layer. To move an individual object independently of the others on that layer, select the object before you use the Move tool. (If the object still doesn't move independently, make sure that the object's layer is the active one, reselect the object, and try again.)

- **Selecting:** When you make a selection on a layer, the selection marquee penetrates to all layers. That means that you can select an object on one layer, switch to another layer, and then, for example, fill that selected area (within the selection marquee) with paint on that other layer.

- **Copying:** When you copy, you copy only from the active layer — unless you choose Edit⇨Copy Merged. A merged copy includes all the layers.

- **Erasing:** When you erase or delete on a (nonbackground) layer, you restore the layer's transparency. (On the background layer, you leave behind background color when you erase, or transparency if the image was originally created with transparent background — and for the record, photos are *not* created with transparent backgrounds.)

✔ **Using the Text, Draw, and Preset Shapes tools:** The images created by these tools are, by default, vector-type, not raster-type images. (See the preceding sidebar, "Choosing a layer that's just your type," for more information about these types.) That distinction means that these elements normally can't go on ordinary layers, which hold only raster-type images. As a result, if you're not already using a vector layer when you choose one of these tools, Paint Shop Pro automatically creates a new vector layer for you. See the section "Using Vector Layers," later in this chapter, for more information about what happens in layers when you use these tools.

Seeing, Hiding, and Rearranging Layers

When you view a multilayer image, you look down through all the layers just as you would look down through a stack of plastic sheets with stuff painted on them. To control which layers you see and also adjust the order in which they're stacked, use these techniques:

✔ **To see just the active layer:** Choose Layers➪View➪Current Only.

✔ **To see all layers:** Choose Layers➪View➪All.

✔ **To see specific layers:** On the Layer palette, click a layer's Layer Visibility toggle, known to its friends as the eyeglasses icon. Each layer has this icon, to the right of the layer name. Click it once to turn the layer off (make it invisible) and click again to turn it on. When a layer is off, an X appears through the eyeglasses icon.

✔ **To move a layer up or down in the stack:** Drag it up or down in the left column of the Layer palette. While you're dragging, the layer itself doesn't move; instead, a black line follows your cursor to tell you where the layer will go when you release the mouse button. An alternative to dragging is to click a layer and then choose Layers➪Arrange➪Bring to Top, Move Up, Move Down, Send to Bottom, Move Into Group, and Move out of Group.

Pinning Layers Together: Grouping

After you have carefully positioned objects on different layers, it's nice to pin those layers together so they can't reposition themselves. If you have painstakingly put Uncle Tobias's head on the neck of a giraffe, for instance, you want to keep them together while you get creative with other layers.

The first thing to do is to select the first layer you want to add to your group and then click the New Layer Group button near the upper-right corner of the palette. This action brings you to the ever-so-titillating New Layer Group dialog box, which looks almost exactly like the New Layer dialog box, and you should do the same thing you did there: Ignore all those scary options and just type a friendly name for your group. Then click OK. (As with the New Layer dialog box, if you leave it to Paint Shop Pro, it chooses something delightfully undescriptive, like Group1.)

As you can see in the Alex's Background group shown in Figure 14-1, you now have a group in your Layers palette, complete with the layer you selected neatly tucked under it. (You also should see a tiny box with a – next to it; if you don't want to see all the layers contained in this group, click the – to hide them. Click the + sign next to the group to reveal them again.) To add another layer to your group, click on the name of the layer, drag it back up to just underneath the name of the layer (it turns into a small black bar), and let go. Your layer is now a part of the group! (If only high school had been this easy.) To remove a layer from a group, simply drag it above the group name.

Layers with the same group name behave as though they were pinned together: When you move one layer with the Move tool (the four-headed arrow thingy), you move the entire group. Members of a group keep their independence in other ways, though. If you change the appearance of a layer (make it brighter, for example), its fellow group members don't change.

Gone but not forgotten: Layer links

In the old days of Paint Shop Pro, you didn't have the handy-dandy Layer Groups command; instead, you used *layer links,* which were clumsier, harder to remember, and you could have only 12 of them. In a nod to older Paint Shop Pro .psp files that may not support layer groups, Paint Shop Pro 8 also allows you to use layer links in addition to groups.

Click the layer link toggle to assign a layer link number to your layer; layers that share the same layer link number act exactly like groups. Click the Layer Link toggle button to assign a given layer to layer link 1, and click it again to raise the number by one each time, all the way up to the number of layers you have within your image — at which point it goes back to having no layer link. You can tell whether a layer is assigned to a layer link because it has a small number next to the tiny chain image.

Honestly, the new Group Layer feature is so handy that we're only letting you know about this ratty ol' layer link feature in case you open a Paint Shop Pro 7 (or earlier) file that uses it. You don't want to *know* what happens if you start mixing layer links and layer groups. (But it's much like mixing tequila and rum.)

The upshot is that if you have a layer that you could *swear* you have grouped properly but just doesn't seem to be affected by something that changed the rest of the group, check to see that it doesn't have a layer link number. If it does, click the toggle enough times to set the layer link to None and then group those layers. You'll thank us in the morning.

Using Layers to Separate or Combine Images

The main reasons for using layers are either to break an image apart into several layers for more flexible editing or to combine multiple images into one. This section describes how to do both.

Combining entire images

Do you have two entire images to combine? To combine an entire image file with the image you're working on, follow these steps:

1. **On the Layer palette of the image you're working on, click the name of the layer above which you want to insert your new image.**

   If the image doesn't have multiple layers, skip to Step 2.

2. **Choose File⇨Browse and open the image browser to the folder containing the image file.**

   Thumbnail pictures of the images in that folder appear. (Refer to Chapter 1 for more information about how to use the image browser.)

3. **Drag the thumbnail picture of the image file to the image you're working on.**

   Paint Shop Pro inserts the new image as a layer, above the layer you selected in Step 1. (If the image you're dragging contains multiple layers, all its layers are grouped together.) The cursor turns into a four-headed arrow to indicate that Paint Shop Pro has selected the Move tool for you.

4. **Drag the new image to position it where you want it.**

After dragging, we often click the Arrow tool (at the top of the tool palette) or some other tool to avoid accidentally dragging the selection when we move the mouse again.

Separating image parts into layers

How do you get an object separated out and on its own layer? One answer is that you can select the object and turn it into a new layer, called *promoting a selection*. Take these steps:

1. **Select the desired chunk of any existing layer (the background layer, for example) using any of the Paint Shop Pro selection tools.**

   We cover selection tools for normal (raster) images in Chapter 12. To select an object on a vector layer, click the object with the Object Selector tool (at the bottom of the Tool toolbar).

   Is your selection tool not selecting on the object you want? Remember that selection works within only one layer at a time. Your object may be on a different layer than the active one. On the Layer palette, click the layer where that object lives to make that layer active. Then try selecting again. If you're not sure where that object lives, pause your cursor over each layer's name, one at a time, and look for your object in the thumbnail image of the layer's contents.

2. **On the Layer palette, click the layer that you want the new layer to appear above.**

3. **Choose Selections↔Promote to Layer from the Paint Shop Pro menu bar.**

   A new layer, cleverly named Promoted Selection, appears on the Layer palette. Although nothing appears to change in your image, your selection is now on that Promoted Selection layer.

Your object is now on its own layer. A copy of that object remains on the original layer. You can now deselect the object; press Ctrl+D or choose Selections↔ Select None.

If you would prefer that no copy be left behind when you promote a selection, drag the selection slightly after Step 1. On the background layer, this action leaves behind an area filled with the background color. On other layers, the area becomes transparent.

Another way to separate image chunks into layers is to select the chunks and then cut and paste the chunk as a new layer (see the following section).

Copying, cutting, and pasting with layers

A good way to get an image or chunk of an image onto a layer is to copy (or cut) it and then paste it as a new layer. This approach uses the same, familiar Windows Clipboard system that other applications use, which is a great way to combine multiple images, even if the additional images come from a program other than Paint Shop Pro. In the following sections, we tell you how to copy, cut, and paste a selected image as a new layer.

Copying or cutting the image

You can copy or cut images from a variety of sources. Here's how to do it:

- **From a program other than Paint Shop Pro:** First, open that program and display the image you want. (You don't need to close Paint Shop Pro.) Exactly how to copy or cut an image from that program varies somewhat from program to program. Copying from a Web page in Internet Explorer, for instance, you can right-click the image and then choose Copy from the menu that appears. In many programs, click the image to select it and choose Edit➪Copy to put a copy on the hidden Windows Clipboard.

- **From another layer within your Paint Shop Pro image:** On the Layer palette, click the layer containing the object you want. Select the image chunk you want with any of the Paint Shop Pro selection tools. (Refer to Chapter 12 for help with selection tools. If the layer is a vector layer, use the Object Selector tool at the bottom of the Tool palette.) Then choose Edit➪Copy (or Edit➪Cut, if you want to remove the chunk from its current layer).

- **From another image file:** Open that file in Paint Shop Pro (refer to Chapter 1). A new window appears, displaying that image. Use any of the Paint Shop Pro selection tools to select your chosen chunk. Choose Selections➪Select All if you want to select the whole image. Choose Edit➪Copy to copy from the active layer. To copy combined images from all layers, choose Edit➪Copy Merged.

Pasting the image as, or on, a new layer

After you have copied (or cut) an image to the Windows Clipboard, you can paste it *as* a layer or *on* an existing layer. Here's how to paste it as a layer:

1. **Click the title bar of the window in Paint Shop Pro where you want to paste.**

   This step makes sure that you paste it in the right place.

2. **On the Layer palette, click the layer that you want the new layer to appear above.**

   To put a layer above the background layer, for instance, click Background. If your image has only one layer, you can skip this step because Background is already selected.

3. **Choose Edit➪Paste➪As New Layer or press Ctrl+L.**

   Your image appears as a new layer, and the Paint Shop Pro cursor appears as a four-headed arrow. That cursor tells you that Paint Shop Pro has automatically selected the Move tool for you.

(If you copy a vector object from outside Paint Shop Pro, such as a Microsoft Draw object from Microsoft Word, Paint Shop Pro converts it to a raster layer when you paste it. First, however, Paint Shop Pro displays a dialog box labeled Meta Picture Import. In that dialog box, set Width in Pixels and Height in Pixels to the sizes you want for the pasted image and click OK.)

4. **Drag your newly pasted image where you want it.**

When you're done dragging, consider clicking the arrow tool (at the top of the tool palette) or some other tool to avoid accidentally dragging the selection with subsequent mouse motions.

Paint Shop Pro assigns a clunky name, such as Layer3, to your new layer on the Layer palette. To change that name, double-click the layer's current name. When the Layer Property box appears, type a new name in the Name field (already selected, for your convenience) and click OK.

You can also paste an image on an *existing* layer rather than paste it as its own *new* layer. After you have copied or cut the image to the Windows Clipboard, click the existing layer's name on the Layer palette and choose Edit⇨Paste As New Selection or press Ctrl+E. The image appears; drag it where you want it and then click to make it a floating selection. Press Ctrl+D to deselect the image.

Copying entire layers from one image to another

When you start using layered images, you may find that a layer you created in one image is useful in another image. To copy a layer (or layers) from one image to another, you drag the layer from the Layer palette of the source image to the destination image. To do so, take these detailed steps:

1. **Open both images in Paint Shop Pro.**

   Each image gets its own window. Arrange the windows so you can see at least part of both images. (For instance, choose Window⇨Tile Vertically.)

2. **Click the title bar of the destination image.**

   By destination image, we mean the one where you want the layer to go.

3. **On the Layer palette, click the layer above which the new layer is to go.**

   Clicking makes that layer the active one.

4. **Click the title bar of the image containing the layer you want to copy.**

5. **On the Layer palette, click the name of the layer you want to copy and drag it to the destination image.**

   Drag the layer directly into the middle of the destination image, and not onto the title bar of its window. When you release the mouse button, the copied layer appears.

Blending images by making layers transparent

Double your pleasure, double your fun. One popular effect is a sort of double exposure, which you do by making an overlaying layer on which the image is partially transparent. For instance, you may want to overlay a diagram on a photograph or add a faint image of a logo to a picture.

Figure 14-2 shows a few tasty vegetables overlaid with the word *Veggies*, perhaps to be used as a sign for a vegetarian buffet. (It looks much more appealing in color — see Figure C-4 in the color section of this book.)

Note that Layer 2, which contains the text *Veggies*, is at 52 percent opacity.

Figure 14-2: Making Veggies transparent makes them clearly a good menu choice.

To make a layer transparent, you merely adjust one little setting, Layer Opacity. Each layer has a Layer Opacity setting on the Layer palette (the shaded bar shown in Figure 14-2). Until you change it, the setting for every layer is 100 to indicate that the layer is 100 percent opaque (you can't see through the image on the layer).

At the far right end of each bar is a pair of pointers (triangles). Drag that pair to the left to make the layer more transparent. Drag the pair to the right to make the layer more opaque. The number on the bar changes as you drag, between 100 and 0. In Figure 14-2, the layer containing the text *Veggies!* is set to 52 percent (roughly half-transparent).

Blending images in creative ways

Sometimes, simply overlaying one image on the other doesn't give quite the effect you want. For instance, if you overlay colored text on an image that has like-colored areas, you can't read the text in those areas.

In that case, the result may be better if the layer could, for example, lighten or darken the underlying image — or perhaps change the underlying color, no matter what color it is. With Paint Shop Pro, you can create those effects, and more, using *layer blending*. Layer blending is determined by two settings: *layer blend mode* and the *layer blend levels*.

To use blend modes with forethought and skill requires pondering all kinds of technical stuff about computer graphics. So, do like we do: Use blend modes with reckless abandon rather than with forethought and skill. Try one mode, and if you don't like the result, try another!

The right side of the Layer palette contains layer blend mode settings you can change for each layer. Until you change a layer's blend mode, it's normal, which means that the paint on that layer simply overlays the paint on lower layers, like paint on transparent plastic (see Figure 14-3).

Click the Blend Mode control for your chosen layer and choose a blend mode from the menu that appears. To restore the original appearance, choose Normal from the list of modes.

Here are a few tips:

  ✔ For maximum contrast between underlying and overlying images, try Difference mode.

  ✔ Try making the color of the overlying layer lighter or darker, if you can't get the results you want otherwise.

✔ Make a layer more transparent if you want to reduce the effect of any blend mode, producing a more subtle result.

✔ For a speckly, spray-painted look, try Dissolve mode and also make the layer partly transparent.

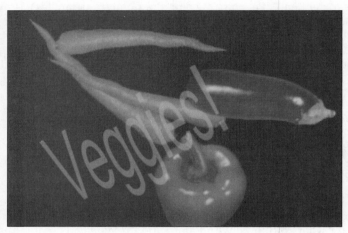

Figure 14-3: To make veggies tastier, try another way of blending. Here, the blend mode is Exclusion, which is how some kids prefer their veggies.

Using a blend mode on a group may or may not work, depending on what layers are in it; having a group with mixed raster and vector layers will almost certainly reject the attempt. If you're trying to blend a group and it's not "taking," try removing layers one by one from the group until it works.

Creating and Using Adjustment Layers

An adjustment layer is sort of like a perfect facial makeup. It doesn't cover anything up; rather, it magically changes the appearance of underlying layers. Changes include brightness or contrast, color, and other effects.

Many of these effects you can create in other ways — with commands on the Colors menu, for example. In fact, the dialog boxes for adjustment layers are *so* much like those for commands on the Colors menu that we cover them both with one set of instructions in Chapter 10.

So, why use an adjustment layer rather than a command on the Colors menu? Here are a few good reasons:

✔ Adjustment layers can affect the entire, combined, multilayer image (if it's placed on top of all other layers). Most commands on the Colors menu, on the other hand, affect only the active layer.

✔ Adjustment layers are useful when you're using different layers to combine two images. One image may have lower contrast than the other, for instance. You can put a contrast-adjustment layer above one image and put the second image above that adjustment layer so that it remains unaffected.

✔ An adjustment layer lets you make changes that are later easily reversible. You can simply delete the layer or change its settings if you later find that the adjustment is wrong. Otherwise, you need to counter your earlier adjustment — a trickier job than undoing or changing it.

✔ You can paint the layer to apply the effect in different strengths in different places! This process is admittedly a bit mind-boggling, but if you can imagine being able to paint brightness (rather than a color), for example, you have the idea. Rather than paint, you can copy an image to the layer, and the brightness of each pixel of the image determines the strength of the effect.

Adjustment layers change only the *appearance* of the underlying colors, not the *colors* of the layers. For instance, when you use an adjustment layer, the colors that the Dropper tool picks up and displays on the Materials palette are the real colors — the color of the paint in the layer, not the apparent color caused by the adjustment layer.

Creating an adjustment layer

To create an adjustment layer, follow these steps:

1. **Open the Layer palette (press the F8 key) if it isn't already onscreen.**

2. **On the Layer palette, right-click the name of the layer above which you want to add the adjustment layer.**

3. **Choose Layers⇨New Adjustment Layers.**

4. **Choose the type of adjustment layer you want from the menu that appears.**

   See the following section for choosing adjustment types. The Layer Properties dialog box appears.

5. **Click the Adjustment tab near the top of that dialog box.**

   The tab shows various sliders, and other adjustments appear, depending on your choice of layer type.

6. **Make your adjustments and click OK.**

   We describe how these adjustments work in Chapter 10.

You can delete or move adjustment layers just as you do other layers. See "Working On Layers," earlier in this chapter, for instructions. To rename an adjustment layer, double-click its name on the Layer palette; when the Layer Properties dialog box appears, click the General tab, enter a new name in the Name field there, and click OK.

To change these adjustments after you create a layer, double-click the layer's name on the Layer palette. You find these adjustments on the Adjustments tab of the Layer Properties dialog box that appears. It's the same dialog box that appears when you create a new adjustment layer (refer to Step 5 in the preceding list).

Choosing the type of adjustment layer you need

The Paint Shop Pro adjustment layers give you lots of different ways to fiddle with the color, contrast, and brightness of the underlying layers of your image. Here are some suggestions for what to use to achieve various results:

- To adjust brightness or contrast, use the Brightness/Contrast layer.

- The Brightness/Contrast layer affects *all* three major tonal ranges — shadows, highlights, and midtones — at one time. To independently adjust *any* of these three ranges — to just get darker shadows, for example — try a Levels layer.

- If shadows, highlights, and midtones aren't precise enough for your brightness and contrast adjustment — you need better contrast only within *specific* shadows, for example — you can adjust brightness or contrast within *any* range of tone by using a Curves layer.

- For richer/grayer or lighter/darker colors, try a Hue/Saturation layer. The Hue/Saturation layer also lets you colorize underlying layers (give them a monochrome tint).

- To make a negative image, choose an Invert layer, set the blend mode to Normal (if it isn't already) and set the opacity to 100.

- To reduce the number of colors, resulting in a kind of paint-by-numbers effect, try a Posterize layer.

- To get a truly black-and-white (two color, no shades of gray) effect, choose a Levels layer.

Applying adjustments to only certain areas

One cool feature of adjustment layers is that you can apply their effects selectively, to certain areas of your image. Paint Shop Pro uses paint on the adjustment layer to accomplish that result.

After you create the adjustment layer, you can paint out the areas on that adjustment layer where you *don't* want the effect, using black paint. Apply the paint to the adjustment layer with any painting tool, such as the Paint Brush tool. The paint doesn't show as black, but only as a masking out of the effect. Use gray paint to screen out the effect. (You can also use a texture in the Material box while you do this to create some neat-looking effects.)

You can also paint in an area with white or gray, if that area is painted out. Notice that black, white, and shades of gray are the only colors the Materials Box palette gives you to paint with when you're working on an adjustment layer.

Using Vector Layers

Most people discover vector layers accidentally. They use the Text, Draw, or Preset Shapes tools to create vector objects, and Paint Shop Pro automatically (and without telling them) creates a vector layer to contain the vector objects these tools produce. (We explain the difference between vector and raster images and layers in the sidebar "Choosing a layer that's just your type," earlier in this chapter.) See Chapter 15 for more information about using these tools.

You can also create vector layers intentionally, as we describe in the section "Creating A New, Blank Layer," earlier in this chapter. After you create a vector layer, you can use the Text, Draw, or Preset Shapes tool to add objects to that layer. You can also copy and paste to move these objects from one Paint Shop Pro vector layer or image to another. (Refer to Chapter 13 for more about copying and pasting.)

You can convert a vector layer to a raster layer. The command to choose is Layers⇨Convert to Raster Layer. Converting an image to raster form allows you to apply any of the raster paint tools to your vector shape to get cool effects, such as graduated fills or airbrush spraying. The drawback is that you can then no longer edit the shape by adjusting the lines and points that make up a vector object. You can't convert a raster layer to a vector layer.

However, if you copy the vector layer before converting it, you have a backup copy of it. Simply hide it when it's not needed.

As you add vector objects to a vector layer, each object gets its own entry on the Layer palette. The left side of Figure 14-4 shows the Layer palette with two layers: the background layer and a vector layer, Vector1. To see each individual object in the vector layer, click the white box with the + sign to the left of the vector layer's icon. That action reveals the individual vector objects, indented under the layer. (To hide the objects, click that same white box again, which now holds a – symbol.)

Figure 14-4:
Clicking the
+ symbol
next to
Vector1 has
revealed
individual
objects on
the layer.

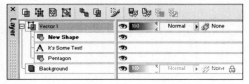

Paint Shop Pro has three kinds of vector objects: line objects, text objects, and groups of objects. Each kind of object has its own icon, as Figure 14-4 shows. Vector1 contains a line object named New Shape, a line object named Star 2 and a text object named "Hello, you fine readers you." Star 2 is a single, multisegment line that is part of the Preset Shapes object library (see Chapter 15).

Having objects listed on the Layer palette lets you select, delete, hide, or reposition them in the stack, just as you would a layer — the main difference is that each object is grouped within a vector layer, just like regular layers are grouped in layer groups.

Clicking an object on the palette selects it and displays its name in bold type. (Hold down the Shift key as you click to select multiple objects.) Pressing the Delete key deletes the selected object. Dragging it moves it up or down in the stack, enabling you to place it over or under other objects. Double-clicking it reveals, one of two things: If it's a text object, it displays the Text Entry dialog box; if it's a shape, it displays the Vector Property dialog box. See Chapter 15 for more information about managing vector objects.

Merging Layers

Using multiple layers usually makes working with images easier. Sometimes, however, you would rather have (or need to have) everything on one layer. For instance, you may want to use one of the commands on the Colors menu on the entire image, but the command works on only a single layer. Or, if you try to save your image as something other than a Paint Shop Pro file, Paint Shop Pro may offer to merge all the layers for you. (Merging can sometimes be necessary because not many file types support multiple layers.)

If Paint Shop Pro merges layers when you're saving a file, it merges layers only in the file you're creating on your disk drive. It doesn't merge the layers in the image you're working on in Paint Shop Pro.

Paint Shop Pro gives you two ways to merge layers into one layer. To merge all the layers (including those whose visibility is switched off), choose Layers⇨Merge⇨Merge All. To merge only the visible layers (leaving the hidden ones as layers), choose Layers⇨Merge⇨Merge Visible. To merge a group into one handy layer, choose Layers⇨Merge⇨Merge Group. Choosing Layers⇨Merge⇨Merge Down merges the selected layer with the one underneath it.

What happens when you merge? Nothing *visible* happens to your image when you merge. The merged layers, however, become one normal (raster) layer, named Merged, that you see listed on the Layer palette. Any vector layers (typically text, lines, or preset shapes) are converted into raster images, so you can't edit them any more with the text, drawing, or shape tools. When adjustment layers are merged, they no longer simply affect the image appearance; rather, they modify the underlying colors.

Chapter 15

Adding Layers of Text or Shapes

· ·

In This Chapter

▶ Vectorizing versus rasterizing

▶ Playing with text

▶ Fiddling with lines and shapes

▶ Changing colors, fills, and whatnot

▶ Positioning and arranging objects

· ·

Given a paintbrush, most of us would have trouble making nice, neat text, regular shapes like circles, or even straight lines. We would clamor for a typewriter, template, ruler, or some other special tool that gives nice straight edges and shapes.

Clamor not. Paint Shop Pro offers three tools for creating such stuff and one to help you manage the stuff you create. Figure 15-1 shows those four tools as they appear at the bottom of the Tools toolbar.

Figure 15-1:
Three tools
to create
text and
shapes,
and one to
move them.

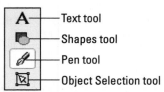

Text tool
Shapes tool
Pen tool
Object Selection tool

Unless you tell Paint Shop Pro otherwise, these tools create text, lines, and shapes in a special vector form that makes them easier to change. Images in this form are known as *vector objects*. Unlike the other things you can paint or otherwise create in Paint Shop Pro, vector objects aren't a collection of pixels (colored dots). Instead, they're shapes that have color, line width, and other properties. These shapes can exist only on special *vector layers*.

Antialiasing for smoother edges

Shapes with nice, sharp edges tend to look a bit ragged when those edges run in any direction other than perfectly horizontal or vertical. They develop an objectionable staircase look called *aliasing. Antialiasing* is a process of filling in those steps with a little bit of color, which gives the illusion of a straighter, if slightly fuzzier, edge. To antialias objects, place a check mark in the Antialias check box on the Tool Options palette.

So, you ask, "What's the upshot?" Here's the bottom line:

- **Creating stuff as vector objects:** If you use the Paint Shop Pro text, line, or shape tools in the normal, vector way, your creations are easier to modify — but you have to know how to deal with layers and the special features of vector objects. See Chapter 14 for help with layers, and we explain vector features in this chapter.

- *Not* **creating stuff as vector objects:** If you don't want to bother with vector layers and special vector object features, you can create text, lines, and shapes as though they were painted with a brush. This form is called *raster* form. If you're such a dedicated, um, rasterfarian, you must do this: If you use the Draw or Preset Shapes tool, look at the Tool Options palette (press F4 if you don't see it) and then click to clear the check mark in the Create As Vector check box. If you want text as a raster selection, choose Selection or Floating from the drop-down Create As menu on the Tool Options palette. Eh, but we talk about it in the next section. Your choice of raster remains unless you change it. No problem, *mon.*

If you need to work on vector objects with raster tools (like the Paint Brush or Eraser tools), you can convert a vector layer to a raster layer. Choose Layers⇨Convert To Raster Layer. You can't convert back, however (though you can use the Undo function if you have done it recently).

Keeping Track of Objects and Layers

Here's the most important thing to remember about adding text, lines, or shapes: If you try to add these types of vector objects to a normal, raster image (such as a digital photograph), Paint Shop Pro automatically, and quietly, creates a vector layer to hold the new object.

If you want to return to the rest of the image, you have to switch to the layer on which the image lives. So, for instance, if you add text to a photograph (which usually appears on the background layer), you need to press F8 to see the Layer palette (if it's not visible already) and then select the background layer.

To add text, lines, or shapes in a nice, controlled fashion, where you know exactly what layer every object is on, create or select a vector layer before you create or paste a vector object. See Chapter 14 for help with creating and choosing layers. As you put vector objects on a vector layer, each object is listed separately, indented under the vector layer's name on the Layer palette. Click the + sign to the left of the layer's name to display these objects individually. From within the Layer palette, you can select, reorder, rename, or delete objects; refer to the discussion of using vector layers in Chapter 14.

Adding and Editing Text

Text in Paint Shop Pro isn't just your grandfather's plain old letters and numbers. Oh, my gracious, no. Although you can certainly have plain text in a straight line, you can also have it filled or outlined with colors and patterns, bend it around curves, or rotate it into a jaunty angle. It's truly the cat's pajamas!

Creating, placing, and editing text

Text has two parts: an outline, set by the color palette's foreground controls, and a fill, set by the background controls. You can have both or either.

If you already have a vector layer (one that has text, lines, or shapes on it), you may put your text on that same layer; just choose the layer now on the Layer palette. Or, you may create a new vector layer on which to put your text. If your active layer is a raster layer (background, for example), Paint Shop Pro creates a new vector layer for you in the following steps. If you're not familiar with layers, don't worry about all this layer stuff for now.

Here's how to create basic text:

1. **Click the Text tool (as shown in the margin) on the toolbar.**

2. **If you want outlined text, do the following:**

a. Choose a background color (the inside color) by left-clicking the Background Material box. A small dialog box pops up, giving you a wealth of colors to choose from. You can either fake it and click OK, which we heartily endorse (remember that just clicking things and hitting OK is an entirely valid way to learn a program), or if you want us to walk you through it, you can turn to Chapter 3, where we show you how to choose a specific color.

If you want to have *just* an outline, leaving the middle of the letters completely see-through, click the Transparency button under the Background Material box. (It's the rightmost button, and should have the international circle-with-a-slash No sign in it.) The box turns gray and contains an international No sign of its own, meaning that the background color is now set to no color. (If this confuses you, refer to Chapter 3 to understand these kooky Material boxes.)

b. Choose a foreground color (the outline) by left-clicking the Foreground Material box. On the Tool Options palette, set the value in the Stroke Width dialog box to the width of the outline you want, in pixels. For instance, for an outline 4 pixels wide, set it to 4.

3. If you want solid (filled) text:

a. Click the transparency button under the Foreground Material box. (It's the rightmost button, and should have the international circle-with-a-slash No sign in it.) The box turns gray and contains an international No sign of its own.

b. Choose a background color by left-clicking the Background Material box and selecting one from the Material dialog box.

In Paint Shop Pro, a *material* is a combination of a color, pattern, and texture. It's just as easy to use gradients and patterns as the foregrounds and backgrounds of text as it is to use colors, as we show in Figure 15-2 — and it makes things look *so* much snazzier! Again, refer to Chapter 3 to unveil all the mysteries of the Material boxes.

Figure 15-2:
Have it your way: text, antialiased, with outline and gradient fill. Hold the pickles.

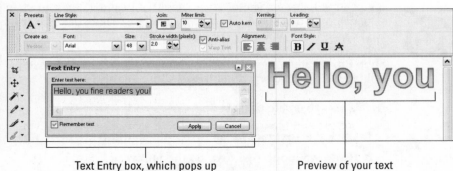

Text Entry box, which pops up after you click with the Text tool

Preview of your text

4. **Click your image where you want the center of your text.**

   The Text Entry dialog box appears, as shown in Figure 15-2. Note that a preview of your text, as it appears when you click OK, appears on your image. You can change your choices here by changing what's in the Foreground and Background Material boxes.

   Figure 15-2 shows how the Tool Options palette controls the width (and style) of the text outline. It also shows, on the Layer palette, that the text object appears indented under the vector layer after you click the white square at the far left end of the object layer (originally containing a + sign). If you don't see the Tool Options palette, press F4.

5. **Choose a font from the Font drop-down menu on the Tool Options palette.**

6. **Choose a font size from the Size selection box or manually enter any other size you want, in points, on the Tool Options palette.**

7. **Enter your text in the big box that is ingenuously labeled Enter Text Here.**

   The text appears in your chosen font and size. For long, multiline text, you can press the Enter key to start a new line. If you have multiple lines of text, decide how you want them aligned (left-justified, centered, or right-justified) by clicking the appropriate button in the upper-right corner of the Tool Options palette.

   If you know that you'll be using the same text the next time you use the Text tool, you can check the Remember Text check box next to the OK button.

8. **To selectively apply any font style (bold, italic, underlined, or strikethrough), drag across the text you want styled to highlight it. Then click the B, *I*, U, or A (strikethrough) buttons on the Tool Options palette, just as you would in most word processors.**

   You can also selectively change the font or size of any text by highlighting the text and then choosing a new font or size.

9. **For vector text, remember to choose Vector from the Create As menu on the Tool Options palette.**

   If you prefer raster text, choose Selection to create a nonfloating selection (or Floating to create a floating selection). Refer to Chapter 13 to understand the minor difference between those selection types. If you don't care, use Vector.

10. **Click the OK button when you're done.**

    While you're using the Text Entry dialog box, it displays a continuously updated preview of your work in the image window.

Your text appears attractively displayed in a rectangular frame that has squares *(handles)* around it. This *selection frame* means that your text object is selected. You can do several things to the text object now, including move, resize, rotate, or delete it. See the section "Controlling Your Objects," later in this chapter.

You can also edit your text. With the Text tool chosen, double-click directly on the body (outline or fill) of the text. The cursor turns into a four-headed arrow when your cursor is properly positioned; clicking and dragging allows you to reposition it, whereas double-clicking brings up that darned Text Entry dialog box all over again, where you can change the text or its appearance.

You can turn text into shapes, if you like. For instance, you may want to alter the shape, rotation, or other attributes of a text character in a creative way. Select the text you want to convert and then choose Objects⇨Convert Text to Curves. Then, to make each character an individually selectable, movable, rotatable object, choose As Character Shapes. If you want the characters to remain part of a single object, choose As Single Shape.

Bending text to follow a line or shape

Is your theatre company performing the *Wizard of Oz?* Before you can click your heels together three times and say "There's no place like home," you can make the text on your advertising posters follow the yellow brick road — or any other (vector) shape or line in Paint Shop Pro. Figure 15-3 shows a before (top) and after (bottom) picture of fitting text to a line.

Here's how to do your own:

1. **Create your (vector) text.**

   See the preceding two sections for help with text.

2. **Create your shape or line.**

   See the rest of this chapter for help with lines or shapes. Bear in mind that if a line is created from left to right, text ends up on top of that line. If a closed shape is created clockwise, text ends up on the inside. In both instances, the opposite direction gives opposite results.

3. **Click the Object Selector tool.**

   If you just want to shape the text — you don't really want the line (or shape) itself to appear — take one additional step before proceeding to Step 4. The selection frame is still around your shape or line from its creation, and you have chosen the Object Selector tool. Now, click the Properties button on the Tool Options palette. In the Properties dialog box that now appears, click to clear the Visible check box and click OK. Your chosen shape becomes invisible, and the selection frame remains.

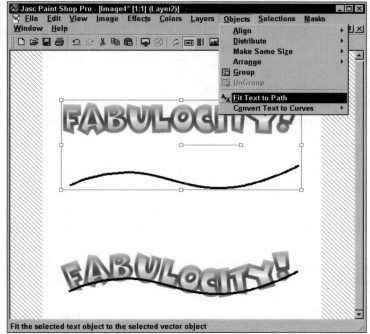

Figure 15-3:
Bending text
around a
shape —
whee!

Fit the selected text object to the selected vector object

4. **Hold down the Shift key and click the text so that both line and text are now within the selection frame.**

   The top illustration in Figure 15-3 shows this stage of the game.

5. **Choose Objects⇨Fit Text to Path.**

   Zap! Wanda the Good Witch puts your text safely on the yellow brick road to Oz. The bottom part of Figure 15-3 shows the result of fitting text to the path.

Don't use solid-color-filled shapes if you intend for your text to be on the inside of the shape — the fill hides your text! A gradient, textured, or patterned fill, however, usually allows your text to be seen.

Drawing Lines and Shapes

Paint Shop Pro is a quirky little devil. It makes drawing lines and shapes so darned easy that it's not even funny, allowing you to draw point-to-point like a connect-the-dots, to draw freehand like a crayon, or even a combination of the two. And if you want shapes, hoo-boy! You can select stars, diamonds, and lucky clovers (not really) from a drop-down menu. Simple!

Setting line and fill color for lines and shapes

To determine how lines and outlines look, choose a foreground color, style, and/or texture on the Color palette before creating the line or shape. To determine how fills look (unless you're making a single straight-line segment, where fill doesn't apply), choose a *background* material from the Background Material box before creating the line or shape. (Remember that a *material* is a combination of a color, pattern, or gradient and any textures you choose to add to it.)

Note that for open shapes (a curvy line, for example), if you use fill, it fills the area between the starting and ending point of the shape. In many such cases, you may want to turn off background (fill) material altogether: Click the Transparent button on the right side, just underneath the Background Material box.

If you have already created a line or shape and want to change its appearance, see the "Changing Colors and Other Properties" section, later in this chapter.

Now, what about *adjusting* those lines and shapes when you have drawn them? That's a bit trickier and involves adjusting things called nodes — but we walk you through that process in the next section — never fear. After all, we're professionals: professional dummies.

Straight, single lines

To draw a straight (vector) line, click the Pen tool on the Tools toolbar and then follow these steps:

1. **Choose a foreground color, style, and/or texture.**

   Left-click the Foreground Material box on the Color palette. Refer to Chapter 3 for more help.

2. **Set the mode to Drawing, as shown in Figure 15-4.**

   Press F4 to bring up the Tool Options palette if you don't see it.

3. **Choose the Line Segments button under Segment Type from the Tool Options palette.**

   Press F4 to bring up the Tool Options palette if you don't see it.

4. **Also on the Tool Options palette, set the Width value to the width (in pixels) of the line you want.**

   All the Paint Shop Pro value boxes offer a nifty way to adjust them: Click and hold the big down arrow on the right side of the value box and drag left or right in the slider that appears.

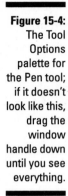

Figure 15-4:
The Tool
Options
palette for
the Pen tool;
if it doesn't
look like this,
drag the
window
handle down
until you see
everything.

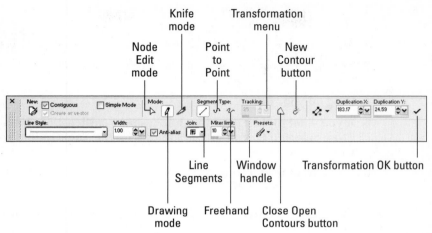

You can also choose a line style (like dashes or barbed wire) for your line at this time by choosing a style from the Line Style drop-down menu, also on the Tool Options palette.

5. **Drag.**

Your line not only appears, but it also appears with square dots (handles) on each end. If you want lines drawn at perfect 90-degree or 45-degree angles (perfect horizontal, vertical, or diagonal lines), hold down the Shift key before you drag, and Paint Shop Pro snaps your lines to the nine compass points.

Drag any of the handles around to resize or reorient your line. To move it, rotate it, or deform it, see "Changing Colors and Other Properties," later in this chapter.

Freehand lines or shapes

Freehand lines are basically any old scribble you want to make (or almost so). Here's how to scribble in high-technology land. Click the Pen tool on the Tool toolbar, choose your color (together with any textures, patterns, or gradients) from the material boxes, and then follow these steps:

1. **On the Tool Options palette (if the window isn't onscreen, press F4), set the mode to Draw.**

2. **Also on the Tool Options palette, set the Segment type to Freehand.**

3. **Also on the Tool Options palette, set the Width value to the width (in pixels) of the line you want.**

4. **Drag on your image.**

5. **If you want to turn your line into a shape (with a closed line), click the Close Selected Open Contours button on the Tool Options palette when you're done.**

6. **If you want to start a new line elsewhere on the canvas, click the New Contour button on the Tool Options palette.**

Paint Shop Pro has this *adorable* habit of keeping everything you draw with the Pen tool joined. Even if you draw a squiggle in one corner, start a new contour, and then draw a loop on the other side of the screen, Paint Shop Pro thinks of them as one big shape — even if they're not connected. If you want to draw two entirely separate shapes so that you can apply separate fills and strokes to them, right-click the screen and choose New Drawing Object from the context menu that pops up. You can go back to your old drawing object by selecting it on the Layer palette.

When you release your mouse button, your line appears with square dots (handles) around the perimeter. Drag any handle around the outside of the rectangle to resize or reorient your line.

The line is a clever, automatically constructed, connect-the-dots line. If you want to drag a line that follows your tight turns more smoothly, you need dots that are closer together. For a line more obviously made up of line segments that connect dots, the dots need to be farther apart. On the Tool Options palette, you can set that closeness by adjusting the Curve Tracking value: smaller for closer dots and larger for more widely spaced dots.

Connecting dots

A game that many of us loved as children endures in Paint Shop Pro: connect-the-dots. In this case, however, because you're a grown-up now, *you* place the dots and Paint Shop Pro draws the lines.

The Pen tool's connect-the-dots system can be as simple as child's play, but it can also go way beyond crayons. The Pen tool can give you straight lines between dots or a snaky line passing through the dots in a smooth fashion you control. It can also remove dots, break the line into multiple lines, and more.

To play connect-the-dots with Paint Shop Pro, choose the Pen tool on the Tools toolbar, choose your foreground (stroke) and background (fill) material, and then follow these steps:

1. **Select Draw mode on the Tool Options palette.**

2. **Also on the Tool Options palette, set the Segment type to Point to Point.**

3. **Set the Width value, yet still within the Tool Options palette, to the desired width of your line (in pixels).**

4. **Set the Background Material box to transparent if you want just a line or outline, or select a material if you want it filled.**

   To make it transparent, click the Transparent button on the right side, just underneath the Background Material box.

5. **Make a sequence of clicks on your image, leaving dots *(nodes).***

   As you do, Paint Shop Pro connects the nodes with straight lines. If you prefer nicely curved lines, see the following section.

   As you create this line, if you discover that you have placed an earlier node in the wrong position, you're free to return to the node at any time and drag it to another position.

   Technically, you're in Node Edit mode during this process. See "Picking at Your Nodes," later in this chapter, for more information about this node mode.

6. **If you want a shape (with a closed line), click the Close Selected Open Contours button when you're done.**

   Your line now appears in all its colorful, patterned, or textured glory.

Connecting dots with curved lines

To connect your dots with curved lines, don't just click when you place your dots — click where you want the dot, but then keep your mouse button down and drag a little. As you drag, you pull out an arrow by its tip. Your line no longer bends sharply at the dot. Here's how that arrow works for you:

- ✔ As you drag the arrow longer, the curve gets broader at the dot. If you make the arrow shorter again, the curve gets sharper at the dot.

- ✔ When the arrow appears, you can release the mouse button and make your adjustments by dragging either end of the arrow.

- ✔ If you drag either end of the arrow around the dot, your line rotates to stay parallel to the arrow where the line and arrow pass through the dot.

Figure 15-5 shows the effect of dragging the tip of the arrow. On the left, a curved line is created and the arrow appears for the latest dot. On the right, the arrow's tip is being extended and dragged upward a bit. You can see how the curve broadens and changes angle to follow the arrow's direction.

Figure 15-5:
Making a curved line. On the right, dragging the arrow's tip to adjust the curve.

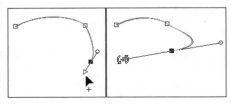

Adding preset shapes

Need a square? Need a star? The Paint Shop Pro Preset Shapes tool lets you choose from a wide range of predetermined shapes, including circles, rectangles, stars, triangles, and cool icons.

To use a preset shape, click the Preset Shapes tool, as shown in the margin. The tool lives near the bottom of the Tool toolbar.

Preset shapes are normally vector objects (as are text, lines, and arbitrary shapes). If you prefer them as raster (normal, bitmap) objects, make sure that the Vector option box is cleared on the Tool Options palette. If you create any vector object, it must be on a vector layer. If your active layer isn't a vector layer, Paint Shop Pro adds a vector layer for you and places the shape there.

If you like, you can edit the shapes of preset shapes after you have placed them in your image. Follow the instructions in the section "Picking at Your Nodes," later in this chapter.

When you're done adding preset shapes and you want to work on other parts of the image, you may need to change to another layer — probably the background layer. Otherwise, refer to Chapter 14 for the skinny.

Dragging a shape

The Preset Shapes tool can deliver a shape from its library of shapes in any size, proportion, color, gradient, pattern, or texture you like! Like text and drawn shapes in Paint Shop Pro, preset shapes have two parts: the outline and the fill. Follow these steps:

1. **Click the Preset Shapes tool on the Tools toolbar.**

2. **If you want your shape to have an outline, do the following:**

   Click the Foreground *(Stroke)* Material box and choose a color from the dialog box that pops up. For a gradient or patterned outline, switch to the appropriate tab; refer to Chapter 3 for help on how to set gradients, patterns, or textures.

   On the Tool Options palette, set the value in the Width dialog box to the width of the outline you want, in pixels. For instance, for an outline 4 pixels wide, set it to 4.

   If you want to use a styled outline (like arrows or dashes) to surround your shape rather than a solid line, choose a custom line from the drop-down Line Style menu, also on the Tool Options palette.

   If you want no outline, click the Transparent button on the right side underneath the Background Material box.

3. **Select a background for your shape:**

   Click the Background *(Fill)* Material box and choose a color from the dialog box that pops up. For a gradient or patterned outline, switch to the appropriate tab; refer to Chapter 3 for help on how to set gradients, patterns, or textures.

   If you don't want your shape filled (that is, you want just the outline of a shape), click the Transparent button on the right side underneath the Foreground Material box.

4. **On the Tool Options palette, click the down arrow next to the Shapes preview box and choose a shape in the gallery of preset shapes that appears.**

   The Tool Options palette and its gallery of shapes appear.

5. **If you want to use the colors, styles, and textures you chose in Steps 1 and 2, make sure that the Retain Style check box is cleared on the Tool Options palette.**

   Otherwise, if that box is checked, Paint Shop Pro uses the colors, line width, and other properties of the original shape that is stored in the shape library.

6. **Drag diagonally on your image.**

   As you drag, your chosen shape appears and expands. (The colors and other style attributes don't appear until you release the mouse button.) If you drag more horizontally than vertically, the shape is flattened. Likewise, dragging more vertically gives you a skinny shape. Hold down the Shift key as you click and drag to create a shape with the original proportions that's not skinny or fat.

When you release the mouse button, your shape appears fully colored and filled according to your choices. The shape appears within the usual Paint Shop Pro object selection frame, which means that you can redimension the shape by dragging any of the handles (squares) around the edge of that frame. To rotate your shape, drag the handle at the end of the arm that sticks out from the center of the frame. A star is born: Figure 15-6 shows the various elements we have discussed in the preceding steps.

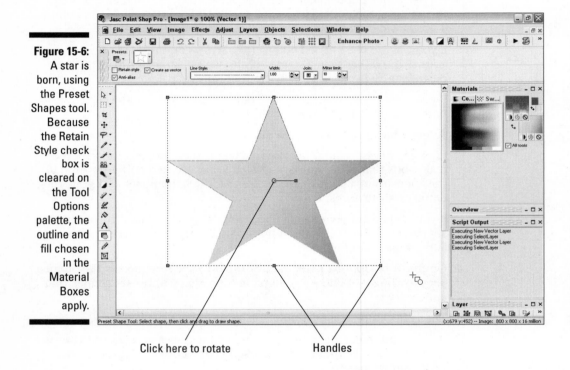

Figure 15-6:
A star is born, using the Preset Shapes tool. Because the Retain Style check box is cleared on the Tool Options palette, the outline and fill chosen in the Material Boxes apply.

Click here to rotate   Handles

Picking at Your Nodes

Paint Shop Pro users have an old saying: "You can pick your friends and you can pick your nodes, but you can't pick your friend's nodes." It's not true, of course, but that doesn't keep users from saying it. You can freely pick, or pick at, all your nodes — including your friend's nodes, if that person gives you a Paint Shop Pro file with vector lines or shapes in it.

If you want to alter a shape or a line after you have drawn, you need to get down and dirty and start changing the nodes. *Nodes* are the dots that Paint Shop Pro plays connect-the-dots with to create lines and shapes; you can move nodes, remove them, or change how the line passes through them. The secret to picking at your nodes in this way is to enter Node Edit mode.

To start fiddling with nodes, you need to select the Pen tool and click the Node Edit button on the Tool Options palette.

When you have the Pen tool selected, even if you're not in Node Edit mode, you still have some node-editing options available (either by dragging or right-clicking), making a fine distinction between Node Edit mode and the Pen tool in general a little fuzzy to the casual user — or even to the writers of *For Dummies* books, for that matter. You can tell that you can edit nodes if you can see the nodes (tiny squares) along the line. Also, your cursor turns solid black.

To enter Node Edit mode, follow these steps:

1. **Select the Pen tool.**

2. **From the Tool Options palette, choose Node Edit mode, as shown in Figure 15-4.**

After you're in Node Edit mode, you can manipulate your nodes all you want. Here are some changes you can make:

✔ To select a node for any action (like deleting, dragging, or changing its type), click it. You know that you can select it when a four-headed arrow appears under the cursor; you know that a node is selected when it's solid black.

✔ To move a node, drag it. You can move multiple nodes at one time as long as they're all selected.

✔ To delete a node, press Delete.

✔ To select several nodes, hold down the Shift key while clicking them.

✔ To select several nodes at one time, make sure that you're in Node Edit mode (this action doesn't work if you're in Drawing or Knife mode) and draw a square around the nodes you want to select.

✔ To select *all* nodes, right-click a node and choose Edit⇨Select All from the context menu that pops up.

✔ To join two line segments that are part of the same object (for instance, if they were created by cutting a line in half with the Pen tool in Knife mode), select the two ends you want to join by Shift+clicking both of them and then right-click your image and choose Edit⇨Join.

If your vector shape is the only vector layer in your image, you may be able to select nodes in it, regardless of which layer you're in — which is a direct reversal of everything we have told you in all the other layer sections. (Paint Shop Pro loves to make us look foolish.) However, if you have more than one vector layer in an image, you can select nodes from only the vector object you have selected. For more information on what these layers are, look to Chapter 14.

Note that a line has *direction,* based on the order in which you create the line. The control arrow that appears on a node in Node Edit mode points in the line's direction. The word Start or End that appears when you pause your mouse cursor over end nodes of a line also tells you the direction. A few things you do may be dependent on direction, such as aligning text to the line or shape.

The Pen tool is mightier than the Sword Tool — or would be, if a Sword Tool existed. Ironically, though, Knife mode is a part of the Pen tool, and it's mightier than the *rest* of the Pen tool, slicing the lines and shapes you have drawn in half.

Select Knife mode from the Tool Options palette and drag a line through your vector object. This separates your object into two separate sets of nodes, cut cleanly where you drew through them with the knife. Be warned that even if you separate an image in two with the knife, both still count as one vector object.

Changing Colors and Other Properties

Don't like the color or some other look of your vector text, shape, or line? No problem. Put on colored glasses — or use the Vector Properties dialog box. Sound like fun? No? Well, it *is* fun. Follow these steps:

1. **Click the Object Selector tool at the bottom of the Tools toolbar.**

2. **Select the object or objects you want to modify.**

   The selection frame appears around your chosen object or group of objects. See the following section for different ways to select objects.

3. **Right-click the object and then choose Properties from the context menu that drops down.**

The Vector Properties dialog box, as shown in Figure 15-7, makes the scene. With this puppy onscreen, you can change all kinds of features.

Here's a list of what you can change:

- ✓ **Object name:** If you have lots of different objects in your image, you may find naming them useful. Enter a name in the Name text box, if you like.

- ✓ **(In)visibility:** Clear the Visible check box to make your object invisible. What good is an invisible object? It's useful mainly as a hidden curve for text to follow. See "Bending text to follow a line or shape," earlier in this chapter, to find out how to make text follow a curve.

✔ **Aliasing (staircasing):** Place a check mark in the Antialias check box to avoid the jaggies (jagged edges) that afflict the edges of computer-generated shapes.

✔ **Color/gradient/pattern/texture:** The Styles and Textures swatches work just like the ones in the Material boxes, except that you can't make them transparent from here.

✔ **Thickness of line or outline:** For a thicker line, adjust the Stroke Width value upward.

✔ **Dashed line or outline:** Click the Line Style drop-down list and choose something appropriately cool.

Figure 15-7: Change color, or darned near anything else, in the Vector Properties dialog box.

The rest of the controls have to do with joins. The term *join* refers to the point that forms where line segments meet. Paint Shop Pro offers three basic types of join, which you select by clicking the arrow next to the Join drop-down list box and then choosing one of these options:

✔ **Miter:** A miter join (what Paint Shop Pro normally creates) is one that ends in a point. It *tries* to end in a point, anyway. If the lines meet at an acute angle, Paint Shop Pro gives up in disgust and creates a flat (beveled) end. The point at which it gives up is controlled by the value in the Miter Limit value box. Fiddle with it this way:

  • If you want a point, increase the Miter Limit value.

  • If you want a flat end, decrease the Miter Limit value.

✔ **Round:** A round join is one that is, well, round at the point. Enough said.

✔ **Bevel:** A bevel join is one that is flat at the point, like a miter join that has reached its miter limit (or a computer user who has reached her limit and has been banging her head against the wall).

These join settings are available when you first create a line or shape, on the Tool Options palette.

Controlling Your Objects

Creating objects is one thing; getting them to do what you want is another — sort of like having kids. If the time has come to discipline your vector objects, Paint Shop Pro can make them straighten up and fly right.

Lots of illustrations need objects that are precisely centered, balanced, or distributed evenly. You can certainly arrange objects by dragging them and rotating them. For drill-team precision, however, you should also check out the Paint Shop Pro vector object positioning talents.

Selecting and grouping vector objects

To do anything to an existing object, you need to select it first. Vector objects (the usual Paint Shop Pro form of text, lines, and shapes) have their own selection tool — the Object Selector tool. The Other Paint Shop Pro selection tools (the Magic Wand, Freehand, and Selection tools) don't work on vector objects.

Click the Object Selector tool that appears on the Tools toolbar and then do one of the following:

✔ **Click your vector object to select it:** If the object has gaps in it (spaces between letters, for instance), don't click the gaps. Even if the object isn't on your active layer, the tool selects the object. Your layer selection doesn't change.

✔ **Drag around one or more objects.** Whatever vector objects you drag around become selected. Selecting multiple objects lets you treat them as a group for many purposes: You can change their color, change other properties, or use the Paint Shop Pro automatic arrangement features.

✔ **Hold down the Shift key and click multiple objects to select a group.** To remove objects from that selection, hold down the Ctrl key and click them.

You don't need to use the Object Selector tool. With the Layer palette open, you can click the object's name on the list of layers. Refer to the discussion of using vector layers in Chapter 14.

A selection frame appears around your object or group of objects, with squares (handles) you can drag to move, resize, or rotate the object or group.

To create a single object out of multiple objects, select them all and choose Objects⇨Group. To ungroup them again, select the group and choose Objects⇨UnGroup.

To deselect, press Ctrl+D or choose Selections⇨Select None from the menu bar. To select all objects, press Ctrl+A or choose Selections⇨Select All.

Paint Shop Pro selects an object automatically after you create it so that you can move, resize, or rotate the object. You can tell that the object is selected by the rectangular frame that appears around it. Even though the object is selected, however, you can't access the same context menu (the thing that pops up when you right-click) that you could access if you had selected the object with the Object Selector tool! For instance, you can't change the object's color unless you first select the object with the Object Selector tool.

Deleting, copying, pasting, and editing

As with nearly any Windows program, you can delete, cut, copy, or paste selected objects in Paint Shop Pro using the Windows Clipboard. First, select the object with the Object Selector tool. Next, do any of the following:

- ✔ **Copy, cut, or delete:** Use the conventional Windows keystrokes (Ctrl+X to cut, Ctrl+C to copy, and the Delete key to delete) or the familiar toolbar buttons Cut (scissors icon) or Copy (two documents icon).

- ✔ **Paste:** You can use the conventional Paste command (Ctrl+V) and Paste button (Clipboard-with-document icon). These conventional methods, however, create an entire, new image from the Clipboard contents. More likely, you want to paste the object as a new object on the current layer. For that, choose Edit⇨Paste⇨As New Vector Selection or press Ctrl+G on your keyboard. Your copied object appears and is selected so that you can position it; click to anchor it. Another alternative is to paste your object as a new layer: Choose Edit⇨Paste⇨As New Layer or press Ctrl+L.

Positioning, arranging, and sizing by hand

To move an object (or group of objects), select it with the Object Selector tool. You can then position it in the following ways:

✔ **Move it:** Click anywhere on an object (on the outline or fill, but not in gaps like the spaces between letters), and then you can drag it anywhere. Or, you can drag the object by the square handle in the center of the selection frame. You can tell when your cursor is properly positioned over the square handle because the cursor displays a four-headed arrow.

✔ **Resize or reproportion it:** Drag any corner of the frame, or any side of the frame, by one of the square handles to resize the object or group. By default, Paint Shop Pro keeps the proportions constant; if you want to drag one corner away to skew your shape, hold down the Shift key as you drag, and if you want to change the perspective, hold down Ctrl. These work pretty much like the Deformation tool, described in Chapter 13.

✔ **Place it on top of or underneath another object:** Vector objects can overlay one another, so sometimes you need to control which object is on top of which. Envision them in a stack and the following menu choices on the Objects⇨Arrange menu make sense:

 • Bring To Top (puts your selected object on top of all)

 • Move Up (raises your object in the stack)

 • Move Down (lowers your object in the stack)

 • Send to Bottom (puts your object on the bottom of the stack)

Alternatively, you can see the stack of objects on the Layer palette and adjust an object's positioning by dragging it up or down. Refer to Chapter 14, where we discuss using vector layers.

✔ **Rotate it:** Sticking out from the center square is an arm that ends in a square handle. Pause your mouse cursor over that handle so that the mouse cursor displays a pair of circling arrows. Drag the handle around the center square to rotate your object.

✔ **Delete it:** Press the Delete key on your keyboard.

Part V
Taking It to the Street

The 5th Wave — By Rich Tennant

©RICHTENNANT

NATIONAL ENQUIRER PHOTO IMAGING WORKSHOP

"Remember, your Elvis should appear bald and slightly hunched.-- nice Big Foot, Brad.-- Keep your two-headed animals in the shadows and your alien spacecrafts crisp and defined."

In this part . . .

*I*n the end, you probably want your image to appear somewhere else besides Paint Shop Pro: on a piece of paper, on the Web, or as part of an animation. Check out this part for help in taking your image that last mile.

For printing on paper, we show you in Chapter 16 how to get the size and proportions right. We also tell you how to print multi-image pages for photo albums, collages, and portfolios.

Web work often involves getting the right kind of file and making some trade-offs. In Chapter 17, we tell you how to choose and create the best image file type, including special Web effects, such as transparency and different kinds of fade-in as an image downloads. We also show you how professional Web designers create Web pages and how Paint Shop Pro can create an HTML page for you.

When you have successfully learned all that Paint Shop Pro 8 has to offer, Chapter 18 shows you two handy new tricks that can save you tons of time: scripts, which record your actions and play them back at super-speed, and presets, which save your tool settings and reload them with a click.

Chapter 16

Printing

· ·

In This Chapter

▶ Sizing and positioning the print on the paper

▶ Printing a single image

▶ Printing thumbnail images from the browser

▶ Creating multi-image pages

▶ Adjusting print speed and quality

· ·

All this electronic image stuff is just fine, but in the end many of us want our images printed on dead and flattened, bleached trees — paper. As a good friend once said, "The paperless office of the future is just down the hall from the paperless bathroom of the future." Paper will be around for a little while yet.

Paint Shop Pro has some great features for making the printing job easier: automatically fitting the image to the page, printing a collection or album page of images, printing browser thumbnails, and more. Read on for ways to make paper printing work better and faster for you.

Fitting Your Print to the Paper

"Let the punishment fit the crime," said Gilbert and Sullivan's Mikado, who prescribed the death penalty for flirting. With the help of the few hints in this section, your image should fit your page with far less pain.

If you have multiple images open in Paint Shop Pro, click the title bar on the window of the image you want to print. That makes it the active window.

You can find all the controls for sizing and positioning your print on paper by choosing File⇨Print to bring up the Print dialog box and then clicking the Placement tab if it's not already shown. You can see the handy-dandy Placement subscreen, as shown in Figure 16-1, and then consult the following bulleted list for help.

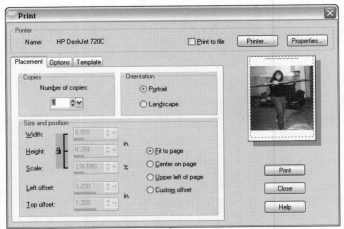

Figure 16-1: The Placement tab fits your print to the paper. A preview window shows the current setup.

Keep in mind that when Paint Shop Pro changes the size of your *print,* it's not changing your *image.* It's only resizing the printed output; the image itself isn't changed in any way. If your image is 500 pixels across, it remains 500 pixels across.

Use these options in the Placement dialog box to fit your print to your paper:

- ✔ **Number of Copies:** This option is self-explanatory. You can print as many as a hundred copies at a time, but we wouldn't advise it unless you have *lots* of ink hanging around.

- ✔ **Printing sideways (orientation):** Paint Shop Pro initially sets you up to print in *portrait* orientation on the paper, in which the paper's long dimension runs vertically. For prints that are wider than they are high, however, you may want to print sideways, or in *landscape* orientation. Click either Portrait or Landscape to choose orientation.

- ✔ **Centering:** Often, you want your print centered on the page. Click the Center on Page radio button to do just that.

- ✔ **Filling the page:** To fill the page with your image (to the maximum extent possible), click the Fit To Page radio button, and your print is enlarged until it fills either the width or height of the paper, within the allowable margins of your printer.

- **Upper Left of Page:** What else can we say? It's in the upper-left corner.

- **Offset:** If having your image in the middle or the upper-left corner isn't good enough for you, selecting the Custom Offset value allows you to position your image on the paper wherever you want it. The Left and Top Offset values — which are grayed out unless you specifically choose Custom Offset — control how far your image is placed from the left or top margin. Enter however many inches you want your image to be shoved away from either side, and the result shows in the preview window.

- **Making the image larger or smaller:** You can print your image as small as .025 percent of its original size or scale it up to a Godzilla-size 1000 percent (ten times larger). Adjust the Scale value in the Size and position area to whatever percentage you want. A setting of 100 percent means that the image's resolution, assigned at its creation, is observed. An image 144 pixels wide, for instance, at a typical resolution of 72 pixels per inch, is printed 2 inches wide. (This option is grayed out in the Fit to Page feature, which scales your image automatically.)

Another method of scaling your printed image is to specify a specific size, in inches, at which the image is printed. Enter a value for either the width or the height; the image scales proportionately, so if you double the width, the height is also doubled.

When you print an image at a scale much greater than 100 percent, your pixels may begin to show. Scandalous! Rather than scale your print, try closing the Print dialog box (click Close) and scaling your *image* by that same percentage, resampling it via Smart Size. Refer to Chapter 11 for help with resizing. Your image may be a bit blurred, but it doesn't look as pixelated.

Printing in Grayscale and Other Options

If you're looking to save some color ink, you can choose File⇨Print to bring up the Print dialog box and then click the Options tab. It gives you a choice of three colors in which to print: Color, Greyscale (black and white), and CMYK separations. (Don't worry about printing CMYK separations unless you're a professional artist — if you are, you know what to do when you see it.)

If you're going to print lots of images, you may want the filename of the image on the print. If so, enable the Image Name check box. (If you have entered a title on the Creator Information tab in the Current Image Information dialog box, that title appears in place of the filename.)

In some instances, you may want to trim the margins off the print when you're done. If your image has a white background, however, finding those margins may be hard. To solve that problem, enable the Print Corner Crop Marks and Print Center Crop Marks check boxes.

Printing an Image

After you have set everything to your liking, it's time to get printin'!

1. **If you haven't already, choose File⇨Print, press Ctrl+P, or click the Print button on the toolbar.**

   The Print dialog box appears.

2. **If necessary, choose your printing options.**

   By clicking the Properties button, you can adjust the usual controls that come with any Windows program: the printer you're using, the number of copies you want, and a Properties button that takes you to the printer's driver software. (That's where you can set the print quality, speed, paper type, and other variables. Refer to the section "Printing at Different Speeds or Qualities," later in this chapter.)

3. **Click Print after you have set all the options you want.**

Shortly, you have hard copy of your hard work.

Printing Collections or Album Pages

One of the most popular Paint Shop Pro features is the ability to print multiple images. It's a great way to create album pages or make collages of photos to celebrate an event.

First, select in the image browser the images you want to print (hold down the Ctrl key and click them — or refer to Chapter 1 for another way), and then choose File⇨Print Layout. Your entire Paint Shop Pro window changes to the multi-image printing tool shown in Figure 16-2.

The multi-image printing tool occupies the entire Paint Shop Pro window. To exit from it and return to the normal window, choose File⇨Close Print Layout. Unless you have saved your layout (see the section "Saving and reusing your template," later in this chapter), closing the tool discards your layout.

Figure 16-2:
Composing
a multi-
image page.

With the multi-image printing tool onscreen, here's the basic procedure:

1. Choose the page orientation.

Paint Shop Pro initially gives you a portrait-oriented page (long dimension vertically). If you want a landscape- (sideways-) oriented page, choose File➪Print Setup and then click Landscape in the Print Setup dialog box that appears. Click OK.

2. If you want to use a template for your images, choose File➪Open Template.

A *template* is a prefab layout you can use to arrange your photos to save time. As a bonus, templates look nicer than dragging pictures helter-skelter onto the page (well, better than the way *we* drag them, anyway). Paint Shop Pro gives you a dialog box with three categories of templates you can choose from: Avery, Combinations, and Standard Sizes. Click a category to bring up a gallery of templates:

• **Avery templates:** Intended for the industry-standard Avery labels — sheets of precut stickers you can use in your printer. Yes, you can print stickers with your baby on it! Each Avery template has a number underneath it, like Avery 8386; this number refers to the product number of a specific Avery label sheet, which you can buy at your local office supply store. Use the right sheet with the right template, and you have perfect stickers.

- **Standard sizes:** Templates in which all the images are one size: 5x7, wallet-size photos, miniwallets, and the like.

- **Combination sizes:** Templates with mixtures of sizes, generally one or two larger photos at the top and a bunch of smaller ones at the bottom.

Each template has a small thumbnail that shows you what its layout is like; click a template and click OK to apply it, or click Cancel to escape.

3. **Drag images, one at a time, from the left column onto the page.**

If you have a template applied, drag the photo into each of the boxes; Paint Shop Pro automatically resizes the photo so that it fits as best it can into the box.

If you don't have a template applied, you have to resize the photos manually. If the images are too large for the page, Paint Shop Pro asks if you want to scale it. If you click Yes, your image appears with handles (square dots) at the corners that you can drag to resize the image. Choose No if you want to use the Paint Shop Pro autoarrange feature (see Step 4) to place and size the image for you.

If an image is rotated 90 degrees the wrong way, drag it to the page and click the 90+ (clockwise) or 90– (counterclockwise) button on the toolbar to rotate the image.

4. **If you haven't applied a template and want to position the images yourself, drag them into position.**

If you don't want to use a template but still want everything lined up neatly, you can choose Preferences⇨Auto Arrange, which lines up your images for you sans template.

5. **To print your page, click the Print icon on the toolbar or choose File⇨Print.**

Neither choice gives you a Print dialog box, but immediately sends the page to your printer. If you need to change any printer settings, do so before sending the page to the printer. Choose File⇨Print Setup and click the Printer button in the Print Setup dialog box that appears.

If you're done, return to the normal Paint Shop Pro window by choosing File⇨Close Print or click the Close button on the toolbar (the door-with-arrow icon).

If you're using a pregenerated template and Paint Shop Pro asks "The current template has changed, would you like to change it?" when you exit, *do not accept the default name if you choose to save it.* (Avery templates in particular do not like being fiddled with — and by just clicking OK, you're overwriting the template, potentially changing vital placement information.)

Fooling with the pictures and layout

You can fiddle with the pictures and their arrangement all you want, after they're on the page. Most controls for fiddling are duplicated on the menu bar, the toolbar across the top of the window, or, if you right-click an image, on the context menu that appears. Nearly everything can be done fastest by the right-clicking approach, so that's mainly what's in the following list. Here are some basic fiddlings you may want to do:

- To select a picture so that you can do something with it, click it. (Handles appear at its corners.)
- To move a picture, drag it.
- To position a picture in the center or at any of the four corners of the page, click any of the five positioning buttons at the far right end of the toolbar. The icon indicates the position the button delivers. Pause your cursor over the button for a text indication of its positioning.
- To resize a picture, drag any of its handles.
- To remove a picture from the layout, either click it and press the Delete button on your keyboard or right-click it and choose Remove from the context menu.
- To rotate a picture, right-click it and choose Rotate 90+ or Rotate 90– from the context menu that appears (+ is clockwise).
- To see an alignment grid, right-click the white page background and choose Show Grid from the context menu. (Repeat to turn the grid off; this action doesn't work if you have a template loaded.)
- To make photos snap to the grid when you move them, right-click the white page background and choose Snap To Grid from the context menu. (The grid must be on first, or else this command is grayed out.)

Saving and reusing your template

To save this attractive arrangement of photos, choose File➪Save Template. In the Save As dialog box that appears, enter a name for your layout in the filename text box. Unless you tell Paint Shop Pro otherwise, it saves the layout as a set of empty boxes, forgetting what photos were there; you can tell it to remember the photos by checking the Save with Images check box.

To reuse this layout, reopen the Print Layout screen and then choose File⇨ Open Template. Select your template in the Open dialog box that appears.

When you open a template, it brings up the image in its current condition, whatever that may be. For that reason, be sure not to move any images to other folders or rename them because then the multi-image print tool can't find them.

Printing at Different Speeds or Qualities

Paint Shop Pro itself doesn't have much to do with choosing the quality or speed of printing your printer delivers. That falls in the province of the software that runs your printer, known as its *driver*. To access that piece of software, click the Properties button in the Print dialog box. Because what happens next depends on your printer, we can't tell you exactly what you see from then on.

Speed, size, and ink

Quality comes at the cost of speed and of ink. Most printers have *draft* and *quality* settings. If you want just a general idea of how your image will look and want to save time and ink, choose Draft. Your image is printed lighter and fuzzier than if you choose the quality (or nondraft) setting, but is printed more quickly.

The size of your printed image also costs you time and ink. Doubling the size increases the amount of ink you need by four.

Many inkjet printers do a much better job on special photograph-quality paper. In that case, the printer driver generally has a setting where you can tell it that you're going to use special paper.

Printer and image resolution

One aspect of print quality is *resolution,* or dots per inch. A higher resolution generally gives a better-quality image. That resolution number is often confusing because your image has resolution too, in pixels per inch. The two don't match, either. The printer resolution is always a higher number than image resolution.

What's going on? Your printer creates its range of colors by putting out tiny dots in four colors: cyan, magenta, yellow, and black. It needs many tiny dots to make a pixel of a particular color, so your printer needs many more dots per inch (dpi) than your image has pixels per inch. Dave's printer, for instance, can print 1440 dpi. So, each pixel of a 72-pixel-per-inch image covers an area of 20 x 20 dots of ink. For an image twice that resolution, Dave gets an area of only 10 x 10 dots, giving him one-fourth the number of possible colors.

The bottom line? Although using a higher image resolution when you create your image gives you more detail in your prints, don't push it too high and don't try to match your printer's resolution. If you use a higher image resolution (pixels per inch), each pixel uses fewer printer dots, so color accuracy may suffer. Your printer driver does a few tricks to keep things accurate, but the laws of physics eventually win.

Chapter 17

Creating Web Images

· ·

· ·

*T*he Web makes special demands on graphics. Images have to be stored as particular file types, and they can't take too long to download or else people get bored.

What's more, popular tricks and techniques have been developed for Web graphics. On some pages, you can click different spots of an image to go to different Web pages. Other pages provide rollover graphics that respond to the viewer's mouse position and actions. These techniques aren't part of the images themselves, but are part of the Web page. The Paint Shop Pro Webtools feature lets you create these Web page features.

In this chapter, we show you how to make your Web images look their best while downloading as fast as possible. We also show you how to use the Paint Shop Pro automated Webtools to quickly generate Web pages and rollovers.

Paint Shop Pro offers a special Web toolbar for the Web features we discuss here. With the Web toolbar enabled, you simply click a button for an effect rather than use the menu commands. To enable the toolbar, choose View⇨ Toolbars⇨Web.

Making Images Download Faster

The key trick with images on the Internet is to make sure that they don't take any longer to download than they have to. Web users are fickle: If you make them wait, they don't stay around. Images download faster when their files are smaller, which is especially handy when you're sending pictures via e-mail. The following list describes a few general tips for making sure that your images download as fast as possible — some you do when you're creating the Web page and others you do in Paint Shop Pro:

- ✔ **Reduce image size:** The main mistake made by beginners is to use excessively large images on their Web pages. Web page authoring tools sometimes give the illusion of having made an image smaller, but in fact they just squeeze a large image into a small space. Size or resize your image in Paint Shop Pro to exactly the size you need on the Web page; refer to Chapter 11 for details.

- ✔ **Repeat images:** In your Web page authoring software, if your page uses the same image over and over again (for a bullet icon, for example), insert exactly the same image file each time. Don't use multiple files that are identical copies of the same image.

- ✔ **Reduce colors:** If you're painting or drawing an image in Paint Shop Pro for Web use, don't use any more colors than you have to.

- ✔ **Use solid colors:** Gradient fills, dithered or airbrushed areas (hues made up of multicolored pixels), and scanned printed images (made up of visible dots) require larger files. Paint with solid colors wherever possible if you want to keep file size down. Noise effects, such as Edge Preserving Smooth on the Paint Shop Pro Effects menu, can help reduce dots to uniform colors.

Exporting Images for the Web

The images that appear on Web pages are almost always stored as one of two main types of file: GIF or JPEG. Sometimes, they're stored as PNG files, a new and improved type of file, but that type is still rarely used. To make your image viewable on a Web browser, all you have to do is make sure to save a copy of the image as one of these file types.

To create a Web file from your image, you can go either of two ways:

- ✔ Save the image *as* a particular type of file (choose File➪Save As or File➪ Save Copy As, as we describe in Chapter 1).

- ✔ *Export* the image to a particular type of file.

Exporting takes you immediately into an optimizer dialog box for that type of file, where you choose features and tradeoffs.

Always store your image as a Paint Shop Pro file before you create Web image files from it. Paint Shop Pro files retain lots of features that are lost when you store an image as a Web image.

Choosing features and file types

Each file type has its own advantages and features. Table 17-1 lists attributes you may want, and the file type or types that are generally best to use. *Best* considers both image quality and speed of downloading (file size).

Table 17-1   Images, Image Features, and What File Types to Use

Image Attributes	*File Type to Use*	*Notes*
Is (or is like) a photograph	JPEG	Color photographs are much smaller in JPEG than in GIF.
Uses patterns or textures	JPEG or GIF	More complex patterns or textures are better as JPEG.
Uses mainly solid colors	GIF or PNG	Solid-color images, like cartoons or text, often have thin or sharp edges, all pixels of which are entirely preserved in GIF or PNG.
Has transparent areas	GIF or PNG	Transparency lets the page background show through (see Figure 17-1).
Fades in during loading	GIF, JPEG, or PNG	Fade-in *(progression)* is an optional feature.

Figure 17-1: Transparency, a popular Web feature, allows this slanted-text image to float over a Web page's background image.

Creating GIF files

GIF files are the most widely used graphics files on the Web. They offer certain popular features, such as transparency, but are also limited to 256 colors. To export a GIF file from your image, follow these steps:

1. **Choose File➪Export➪GIF Optimizer.**

   The GIF Optimizer dialog box (the *optimizer*) appears, containing five tabs of settings that we cover throughout the next few sections. The optimizer has before and after preview windows (left and right, respectively) that show what effect your choices have. To zoom in or out, click the Navigation icons. Click the magnifier with the + to zoom in, or the one with the – to zoom out.

2. **Click the OK button.**

   The familiar Save As dialog box appears.

3. **Choose a filename and folder for the file and click OK.**

You can (and should) make image files smaller so that they download faster; see the section "Reducing download time," a little later in this chapter.

Creating transparent areas

To prepare an image to have transparent portions on the Web, first save your image as a Paint Shop Pro file. Then choose *any one* of the following alternative approaches to mark a transparent area — whichever approach seems easiest to you:

- ✔ **Color:** If all the pixels in the area you want to become transparent are roughly the same color (a white background, for example), you don't need to do much more in preparation. Just make sure that your chosen color does *not* appear in any pixels where you *don't* want transparency, such as the whites of people's eyes. If the color *does* appear elsewhere, try one of the two following approaches instead.

- ✔ **Selection:** Select either the object that you want to be visible (opaque) or the background that you want to be transparent.

- ✔ **Transparency:** If the object (your logo, for example) that you want to be visible (opaque) isn't already on its own layer or layers, select it and promote it to a layer. On the Layer palette, turn off the visibility of the background layer and any other unwanted layers, and the transparent portions of the logo layer are apparent (display a checkerboard pattern).

To have edges of a selected area blend gradually into the Web page's background, contract the selection by a certain number of pixels (4, for example). Then feather the selection by that same number of pixels. (Refer to Chapter 12 for help with contracting and feathering a selection.)

Opening and using transparent GIF files

If you open a transparent GIF file in Paint Shop Pro, you may be surprised at what you see: Areas that appear transparent in a Web browser are filled in with a color. That result occurs because GIF transparency is a special trick used mainly in Web browsers. Paint Shop Pro shows the reality behind the trick.

GIF files achieve transparency by designating as transparent a particular color on the palette. Web browsers pay attention to that designation and show the underlying Web page background where that color occurs. Paint Shop Pro, however, shows the color itself — unless you tell it otherwise.

To tell Paint Shop Pro to show the transparency, choose Image➪Palette➪View Palette Transparency. Repeat the command to return to viewing the color.

If you want another color on the file's palette to be displayed as transparent, choose Image➪Palette➪Set Palette Transparency. In the Set Palette Transparency dialog box that appears, click the option Set the Transparency Value to Palette Entry ___, and then click your chosen color in the image window. To turn off transparency, choose the No Transparency option. Click OK when you're done.

Be careful when choosing a color. It may be used in places where you're not expecting it — white, for instance, may appear in someone's eyes, giving a spooky result when the whites of their eyes become transparent! Likewise, you may find that the area you want transparent is composed of more than one color, leaving an unseemly halo of not-quite-your-selected color around everything else in the image. To fix it, you have to select the area and tell Paint Shop Pro to make it transparent; refer to Chapter 12 for an example of this halo problem and how to select it properly.

Remember that GIF files are palette-type files, so many Paint Shop Pro features don't work unless you convert the file to 16.7 million colors first. (Press Ctrl+Shift+0.)

A tab in the GIF Optimizer dialog box lets you translate your chosen area into a transparency. In the GIF Optimizer dialog box, click the first tab, Transparency. This tab asks "What areas of the image would you like to be transparent?" Your choices are shown in this list:

- **None:** Choose this option if you want no transparent areas whatsoever.

- **Existing image or layer transparency:** Choose this option if your image already has transparent areas (appearing as a gray checkerboard pattern) that you want to remain transparent on the Web page. This is the Transparency approach in the preceding bulleted list.

- **Inside the current selection:** Use this option if, using the Paint Shop Pro selection tools, you have selected the area (the background, for example) that you want to become transparent (the Selection approach in the preceding bulleted list). If you have selected instead the area that is to remain opaque, choose Outside the Current Selection.

✔ **Areas that match this color:** Choose this option (the Color approach in the preceding bulleted list) if the areas you want transparent are all the same color. If the color that is already displayed in the adjoining color swatch is *not* the one you want to make transparent, move your cursor outside the dialog box, over the image, and click any area of your chosen color. The result appears in the right preview window. Increase the Tolerance value to make a wider range of similar colors transparent or decrease it to narrow the range of colors made transparent.

Choosing image fade-in

As GIF images download, they build gradually onscreen. You can choose whether they build from top to bottom or fade in from fuzzy to increasingly detailed. For small images that download quickly, the choice doesn't matter much. To choose a method, click the Format tab.

On the Format tab, choose Non-Interlaced if you want the image to build from top to bottom. Choose Interlaced if you want the image to fade in. Leave the option labeled What version do you want the file to be? set to Version 89a unless someone specifically requests a file of Version 87a.

Reducing download time

For GIF files, you can reduce download time in two ways: Reduce the physical size of the image, and reduce the number of colors in it. (We tell you how to resize in Chapter 11.) Removing unused colors saves time, which makes sense — why send 256 colors across the Internet when you can send only 40?

To reduce colors, select the Colors tab of the GIF Optimizer. You have several options:

✔ **How many colors do you want?** The lower the number of colors, the quicker the file downloads. Take out too many colors, and the image may start to look grainy or choppy. Experiment with this value, setting it as low as you can until you find something acceptable in the preview window.

✔ **How much dithering do you want?** It sounds like if you set this option high, Paint Shop Pro would just waste your time, saying "Oh, I don't know — what do *you* want?" In reality, though, if you have removed a bunch of colors, this setting controls how much Paint Shop Pro attempts to simulate those removed colors by filling them in with the colors it *does* have. That helps to make a low-color image look smoother, but at high values it may add weird moiré patterns or make it look spotty. Again, experiment to find the right value for you.

✔ **What method of color selection do you want to use?** There are only two you need to be concerned with:

- *Existing Palette*: Uses the colors in the original image, although they may not look right on other computers.

- *Standard/Web-safe*: Ensures that the image looks the same on all computers, although it may not look quite like what you originally created.

When you're done selecting all these options, you can select the Download Times tab to see a chart of how quickly your image loads at various speeds. People with modems are generally running at 56 Kbps; unless you know for a fact that the people who will be viewing these images have something other than a modem, *assume that they use a modem.*

The GIF Wizard

Alternatively, you can choose to click the Use Wizard button at the bottom of the GIF Optimizer dialog box. The GIF wizard asks you five questions dealing with palettes, backgrounds, and quality, all of which we detail earlier.

Creating JPEG files

JPEG files tend to be smaller than GIF files for many kinds of images, so they download faster. The main tradeoff is that JPEG files are *lossy.* They lose some detail in your original image, and the clean lines of text can look fuzzy. You can choose how much detail to trade off for a reduction in file size, however.

The second tradeoff is that JPEG files can introduce *artifacts:* blurs, spots, and rectangular blocks that weren't present in the original image. Again, however, you can choose how many artifacts you're willing to live with to get a smaller file.

To export to JPEG, follow these steps:

1. **Choose File⇨Export⇨JPEG Optimizer.**

   The JPEG Optimizer dialog box appears. It has three tabs. It also has before-and-after preview windows (left and right, respectively) that show the effect of your choices. To zoom in or out, click the magnifier icons. Click the magnifier with the + to zoom in or the one with the − to zoom out. To view different parts of your image, drag in a window.

2. **Click the Quality tab to trade off file size for quality.**

   Adjust the Set Compression Value To __ value box to a value from 1 to 99. Higher values make the file smaller, but give it lower quality. You can see changes in the file size under the right preview window, in the line Compressed: __ bytes. As you can see in Figure 17-2, you can save *lots* of time with comparatively little loss in image quality.

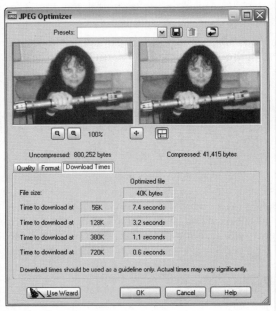

A menu offers Chroma Subsampling options. This is deep juju that tells Paint Shop Pro when to average the color information for any given block of pixels, and the best subsampling approach is a subject of debate among graphics professionals. To make things simple, we just say that you should go with the default value (unless you feel like experimenting).

To see estimates of how fast your file downloads, depending on the viewer's Internet connection speed, click the Download Times tab. A table there gives estimated download times for various connection speeds. Unless you have specific knowledge that the people who will view this image have anything faster than a modem, *always assume that they're running at 56Kbps.*

If you can't get your image to download fast enough, don't forget that resizing, as shown in Chapter 11, saves *lots* of time. Do people really need to see a poster-size picture of your baby?

3. **Click the Format tab to control how the image fades in.**

   JPEG files normally assemble themselves from top to bottom as they download to a Web browser. If you would rather have your image fade in from blurry to detailed, choose Progressive on this tab. Otherwise, leave the choice set to Standard.

4. **Click the OK button.**

   The familiar Save As dialog box appears.

5. **Choose a filename and folder for the file and click OK.**

The JPEG Wizard

Interestingly enough, the JPEG Wizard is available at the bottom of the JPEG Optimizer, but it involves clicking more times than the regular JPEG Optimizer. Our advice is to skip the wizard and just use the Optimizer, which allows you to see your download time in one click, as opposed to three.

Doing Common Webbish Tricks

Unless you're Spider-Man, creating Web pages is a complex business. But Paint Shop Pro can make some aspects of Web design much easier! This section describes two tricks that Paint Shop Pro can help you with.

Creating buttons

Paint Shop Pro offers an effect that's great for creating graphical buttons for Web pages. The *buttonize* effect makes any image (or selected part of an image) look like a raised button by shading around the edges.

Choose Effects⇨3D Effects⇨Buttonize. The Buttonize adjustment dialog box that appears offers two styles of button. Click the Solid radio button for a button that has flat sides (and then choose your color in the palette box), or choose Transparent Edge for a button with rounded sides. The Buttonize dialog box also offers three adjustments:

- ✔ **Height and Width:** These controls adjust the vertical and horizontal dimensions, respectively, of the top surface of the button.
- ✔ **Opacity:** Increasing opacity makes the edges of the button darker, obscuring the underlying image more.

The right preview window in the Buttonize dialog box shows the result of your choices.

Matching image colors to HTML colors

You may want to match colors used in your image to colors used in the text of your Web page — or vice versa. Text colors are often given in cryptic, geekish codes called *hexadecimal* in the HTML code used to write Web pages. They're written like this: #FFC0FA. These codes always begin with a # symbol, followed by six characters — digits or the letters A through F.

If you're creating a Web page and want to match the text color to a color in your image, the Material box can help. Click the Dropper tool on the Tools toolbar and then click your chosen color. Next, click the Foreground Material box and select the Color tab. Use the HTML code at the bottom in your Web page authoring software to set the color of your text.

If you're creating an image and want to match a color in your image to a text color, the solution is similar: Click the Material box to bring up the Material dialog box. In the HTML code value box on the Color tab, enter the HTML code you obtained from your Web page authoring tool. Click OK and your chosen color swatch now matches the HTML document's text color.

Creating Interactive Web Pages from Graphics

Paint Shop Pro not only creates static Web images (images that just sit there), but can also create the interactive graphical portion of the Web page itself. For instance, Paint Shop Pro can help you

- ✔ Slice a single image into a multi-image grid and create the Web page that assembles the pieces into a grid and makes each image a hot link.

- ✔ Create graphical *rollovers* — images that change as you pass your mouse cursor over them — and write the Web page code to make the rollover happen.

To accomplish its Webbish wonders, Paint Shop Pro writes HTML files (Web pages), not just image files. You can then use these HTML files on their own or copy their HTML code (including JavaScript code) into other Web pages.

You probably need to understand how Web pages, hot links, and rollovers work before trying to use Paint Shop Pro to make these features. Check out the Wiley Web site, at www.wiley.com, to find various books on Web pages and design.

Creating image slices

Professional Web designers rarely design in HTML; instead, they create a picture of how they want their Web page to look, using multiple layers and futzing with it until it looks perfect. Then, when they're done, they *slice* that image into multiple images (known as *cells*) and assign a link to each cell. Paint Shop Pro creates the HTML code (a table) that's necessary to hold the images in a grid and also creates a series of new images from your original, single image.

You can use another technique, called *image mapping,* but it has two major disadvantages: The entire image has to download at once before the viewer can do anything (and haven't we *told* you about the importance of speedy downloads?), and you can't use rollovers effectively. We advise skipping it unless you have a pressing need.

To slice an image, follow these steps:

1. **Choose File⇨Export⇨Image Slicer, as shown in Figure 17-3.**

2. **Zoom and position your image in the Image Slicer so that you can see the whole area you intend to slice.**

   To zoom, click either of the magnifier icons just below the image: + to zoom in or – to zoom out. To position *(pan)* your image, click and hold your mouse button on the Pan icon and drag in the preview window until you see what you want.

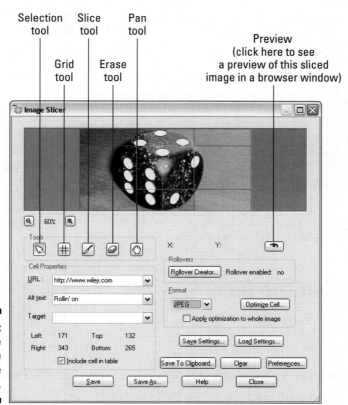

Figure 17-3: Slicin' dice with the Image Slicer.

3. **Click either the Slice tool or the Grid tool.**

   The grid divides your image using a grid of evenly spaced lines. You can adjust the lines and their positions afterward. The Slice tool, although tricky to control, enables you to slice wherever you like.

4. **Slice your image.**

   If you use the Grid tool, click anywhere on the image. In the Grid Size dialog box that appears, enter values for the number of rows and columns in your grid.

   If you use the Slice tool, click where you want the center of your cut to be and drag either horizontally or vertically; the Slice tool creates a horizontal or vertical cut that expands in both directions from where you originally clicked. You don't need to drag entirely across the image; the line automatically extends to the image edge or to the next line it encounters.

   Note that you can use both the Slice Tool and the Grid tool to provide extremely fine control; for example, you can create a grid of boxes, and then subdivide each of those boxes with the Slice tool.

5. **With the Delete tool, remove any extra lines.**

   Click the Delete tool in the Tools area and click lines you don't want.

6. **With the Arrow tool, drag any lines that need moving.**

If your image has any solid white cells, you can improve the Web page's downloading speed by not placing an image in that cell. With the Arrow tool, click the cell and then clear the Include Cell in Table box. This trick also works for other solid-color areas, but you have to edit the resulting HTML file to set the background color to match the image color.

At this point, you're ready to enter the hyperlink (Web address) information that describes what Web page appears when the person viewing your page clicks a cell (see the following section).

Entering the links

After you have created your hot spot areas or cells, the next step is to enter the Web address you want each hot spot or cell to link to when someone clicks it on the Web. Follow these steps:

1. **Choose the Arrow tool (in the Tools area) and click a hot spot or cell.**

2. **Enter the URL (address of the Web page) you want to link to in the URL text box.**

   If you intend for the page to appear in a named frame of the current page, enter the frame name in the Target area.

3. **Enter a text description of that new page in the Alt Text text box.**

4. **Repeat Steps 1 through 3 for all the cells you have created.**

You may also want to save the work you have done so far, which we describe how to do in "Saving and reloading your work," later in this chapter.

Optimizing the cells

Unless you tell it to otherwise, Paint Shop Pro saves all your cells as GIFs, which can create grainy images and horribly lengthy download times. A little compression can make all the difference; remember that the JPEG used earlier took *four minutes* to download before it was squeezed down. Is your page so cool that you would watch a blank screen for five minutes before you saw it? (Studies have shown that people don't wait for longer than 12 seconds.)

To optimize your images:

1. **Choose the Arrow tool (in the Tools area) and click a hot spot or cell.**

2. **Choose whether your cell will be a GIF or a JPEG image.**

   Refer to Table 17-1 for a comparison of formats. (You *can* use PNG, but not all browsers support it.)

3. **If you want to optimize the image — and you should — click the Optimize Cell button.**

   This step brings up the GIF or the JPEG Optimizer, as discussed earlier this chapter; pay special attention to the Download Times tab. If you want all your cells to be optimized the same way, check the Apply Optimization to Whole Image box.

4. **Repeat Steps 1 through 3 for all cells you have created.**

Saving and reloading your work

You may want to go back and change your hot spots, cells, or links later, or perhaps use similar settings on a slightly different image. For those reasons, save your work as a file. (Note that this file isn't the Web page file or an image file; to create those, see the following section.)

Click the Save Settings button. The Save Slice Settings dialog box that appears works just like any other file-saving dialog box. Enter a name and choose a folder for your file, and then click Save.

If you want to use or edit your settings later, open the Image Slicer tool as before and click the Load Settings button. Open your file in the Load Slice Settings dialog box that appears. The hot spots or cells you defined earlier are now set up for the current image.

Saving the result as a Web page

For all this slicing and dicing to be of any use, you need to transform it into a Web file. The Paint Shop Pro Webtools output the two kinds of file you need for your Web page: one or more image files (in GIF, JPEG, or PNG format) and a single HTML file. You output as many image files as you have cells. The Web page (HTML) file you output incorporates those image files and provides the links, hot spots, and other programming that makes it all work.

Before you output the final files, you can test your Web page by viewing it in your Web browser. In the Image Slicer, click the Preview button. Your Web browser launches and displays the result. You can test all the hot spots or other features you have created.

To output your Web files, click the Save or Save As button. If you haven't created any Web files since you launched the Image Slicer, the Save As dialog box appears. As with the Save As dialog box in any program, you enter a filename and choose a folder. The name and folder you choose is the name and location of the HTML, or Web page file, you're creating. (The Save As dialog box doesn't appear if your Web page file already has a name and folder.)

Paint Shop Pro creates a series of cell images in the same folder as the HTML file; although each cell file's name begins with the name of the original image file, Paint Shop Pro appends additional characters to distinguish the cell.

Making rollovers

Rollovers are images (typically buttons) that change appearance whenever you position your mouse over them or whenever you do various other mouse or keyboard actions. For instance, a button may get darker. Rollovers are popular Web page features because they provide immediate feedback to the user's cursor motion.

The basic *mouseover* rollover, which we describe here, simply changes as the mouse passes over it. It requires two images: the original image (a button, for example) and the one that substitutes for the original when a mouse cursor passes over it (a darkened version of the button, for instance).

To create a rollover, follow these steps:

1. **Prepare the pair of images for each rollover.**

   For each rollover, you need the image that first appears on the Web page and the image that takes the first image's place. If you like using sliced images, first use the Image Slicer to slice a large image into separate cell images and save your settings. Close the Image Slicer, load into Paint Shop Pro all the cell images created by the slicer, and modify them in some way; for instance, you can make them darker. Save each one with a modified file name so that the original cell images remain unchanged.

2. **Open the original image in Paint Shop Pro, if it isn't already open.**

   For instance, open the large image you originally sliced in Step 1.

3. **Launch the Image Slicer and load your earlier settings.**

   Load the settings you saved in Step 1 to restore the slicing.

4. **With the Arrow tool, click in the Image Slicer the cell you want to program with a rollover.**

5. **Click the Rollover Creator button.**

   The Rollover Creator dialog box appears.

6. **Click the Mouse Over check box.**

7. **Click the file folder icon on the same line as the Mouse Over check box.**

   The Select Rollover dialog box appears.

8. **Choose the image file you want to appear when the mouse passes over and click Open.**

   For instance, this file is the darkened version of the original file.

9. **Click OK in the Select Rollover dialog box.**

10. **Repeat Steps 4 through 10 for each cell or hot spot.**

Proceed to save your settings and output your Web files as we describe in earlier sections in this chapter.

Chapter 18

Automating Paint Shop Pro

- -

In This Chapter

▶ Saving tool and effect settings as presets

▶ Recording scripts

▶ Running scripts

▶ Advanced scripting

- -

*T*his timesaving chapter shows you two terrific tools to use when you need to save time: Scripts record your actions and play them back at super-speed, and presets save your tool settings and reload them with a click.

Saving Tool and Effect Settings As Presets

Paint Shop Pro has *lots* of options for each of its tools and effects, and setting them all by hand can be tedious. If you painstakingly set the opacity, shape, blend mode, stroke width, and thickness to get a watercolor-style effect from the Brush tool, you can save those settings as a single *preset*. Then, the next time you want to paint in watercolors, you can load all your carefully tweaked tool options with a single click — as opposed to having to not only remember each of the controls' settings, but also having to set each of them individually.

You can find presets in two separate places, depending on whether the settings you need to save are in a tool, like the Magic Wand, or whether they're in a dialog box that pops up whenever you try to apply an effect or adjustment, like the Mosaic effect or the Automatic Color Balance.

✔ In Effects and Adjustments, the preset controls are along the top of the dialog box, as shown in Figure 18-1.

✔ For tools, the presets are in the upper-left corner of the Tool Options palette. Click the small arrow next to the tool's icon to display the drop-down Presets menu.

Preset menu   Delete Preset

Save Preset

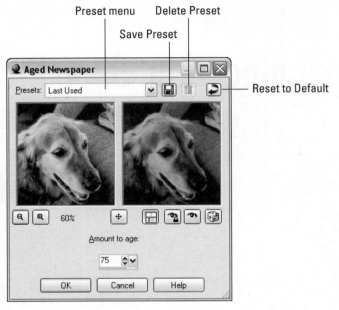

Reset to Default

Figure 18-1:
The Preset
controls,
coming to
the top of a
dialog box
near you.

To save a particular group of settings, set all the dials, slider bars, menus, colors, and other options to the settings you want to remember — but don't do anything else! When you have everything tweaked to perfection, press the Save Preset button (the one with the little floppy disk) and enter a memorable name for the effect. Then, the next time you want to call up a group of settings, just choose it from the drop-down menu and it automatically enters all the numbers you saved.

The preset always comes with at least two entries, in addition to any others you add to it (although one may be hidden):

- **Default:** Resets any changes you have made since Paint Shop Pro was installed, bringing this effect back to its pristine, untouched state.

- **Last Used:** Automatically saves the settings you used the last time and loads them the next time you open them. This preset doesn't show up on a Tool preset, but it saves your settings nonetheless.

To delete a preset, select it from the list and click the Delete button. You can't delete the Default or Last Used presets.

If you feel that you have made too many changes and want things back to the way they were originally, click the Reset to Default button, which sets the controls back to the way they were when you first installed Paint Shop Pro.

The Material dialog box has no presets, but you can save textured gradients and colors as *swatches,* which are similar to presets; refer to Chapter 3 for details.

Scripting 101

Scripts are a new Paint Shop Pro 8 feature that allows you to automate repetitive tasks. If you have a bunch of commands you need to do over and over again — you want to resize an image, buttonize it, and then change its color to fuchsia, for example — you can record them all as one script and save them for future use. Then, the next time you need to resize, buttonize, and fuchsia-ize, you can select the script from a list and click Run. Paint Shop Pro then replays those commands as you entered them, saving you valuable time. If you have ever used macros in Word or Excel, the concept is the same.

Scripts have two major advantages over doing tasks by hand: Scripts perform tasks more quickly than you could ever do them, and the tasks are done flawlessly (assuming that you completed the task flawlessly when you recorded it, of course).

Recording a script

To have Paint Shop Pro record everything you do in order to play it back later, the process is as simple as following these steps:

1. **If you don't see the Script toolbar, as shown in Figure 18-2, choose View➪Toolbars➪Script.**

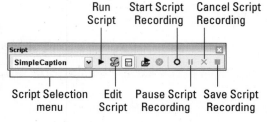

Figure 18-2: The Script toolbar.

2. **Click the Start Script Recording button.**

3. **Perform the sequence of actions you want recorded, just as you would normally do in Paint Shop Pro.**

   Keep in mind that the settings for the tools you use are saved within the script; for example, if you paint a circle with a 50 percent opacity and 25-pixel brush, that script always draws with a 50 percent opacity, 25-pixel brush regardless of what the Brush tool may be set to.

4. **If you need to pause recording in the middle of a task to do something you don't want replayed later, click the Pause Script Recording button.**

   Click the button again to continue the recording where you left off.

5. **When you're done, click the Save Script Recording button and enter a name, and then click OK.**

   Or, if you have done something wrong and you don't want to save the script, click the Cancel Script Recording button.

You have two options when saving, but only one is worth mentioning (the other involves lots of non-*For Dummies* information): To ensure that the script draws with the material (the color, gradient, or pattern) you used when you recorded the script, thus ensuring that a red line is always a red line, check the Save Materials check box. Leaving it unchecked causes this script to draw with whatever materials are selected at the time you run it.

You can also, if you're so inclined, click the Description button and enter the author, copyright, and description of your script. This option is handy if you expect to pass the script on to someone else.

Scripts are saved by default in the folder named My Documents\My PSP8 Files\Restricted-Scripts. You can send them to other users, who can put them in their folders and run them as though they had been recorded on their own PCs.

Running a script

Running Paint Shop Pro scripts is *much* simpler than recording them:

1. **Select from the drop-down list on the Script toolbar the script you want to run.**

   Note that scripts are already there. Paint Shop Pro has added several scripts to automate common tasks, like creating thumbnails; feel free to experiment to see what's there.

2. **Click the Run Selected Script button.**

Certain advanced scripts may have dialog boxes that ask for user input, but most just zip through and go about their business in no time.

Advanced scripting

Paint Shop Pro scripts are written and recorded in *Python,* a powerful free-ware scripting language that helps drive much of the Google search engines and helped to create the special effects in *Star Wars, Episode II: Attack of the Clones.* (Note that although Python is a scripting language, it had nothing to do with the *script* for *Episode II;* that's George Lucas's fault. Who dresses up in a leather backless bustier to break up with her boyfriend, anyway?)

Computer programmers can tell you that Python is a "simple" scripting language, but it means that Python is simple *to a programmer.* To Joe Average, it's a darned complex piece of work. Still, if you're well versed in Python or you just like a challenge, you can hand-write complex scripting programs that automate Paint Shop Pro to ridiculous extremes.

If you're interested in delving into Python, `www.python.org/doc/Newbies.html` is a great place to start.

Part VI
The Part of Tens

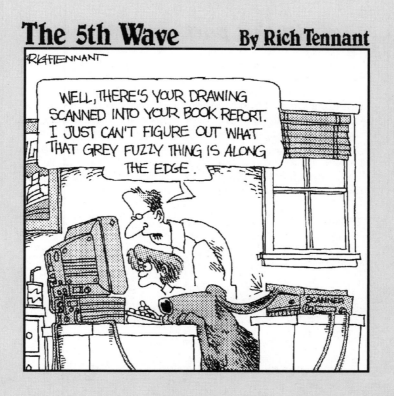

The 5th Wave   By Rich Tennant

WELL, THERE'S YOUR DRAWING SCANNED INTO YOUR BOOK REPORT. I JUST CAN'T FIGURE OUT WHAT THAT GREY FUZZY THING IS ALONG THE EDGE.

In this part . . .

If you find yourself throwing your hands in the air in despair, your ten fingers are telling you something: "Turn to The Part of Tens!" You can find in this part quick solutions for common problems and issues. We give you, in Chapter 19, remedies for the ten most common headaches that afflict new users of Paint Shop Pro. In Chapter 20, we give you ten quick fixes for the most common photographic failures. If the solution isn't here, turn off your PC, take a walk, and join millions of others in reciting the comforting (and true) mantra "I am smart; software is stupid."

Chapter 19

Ten Perplexing Problems

*I*n real life, your paint brush doesn't suddenly start painting in plaid, your canvas doesn't double in size, and (unless you have kids) your tools don't suddenly become unavailable. In software, however, all the laws of nature are repealed and then reformulated by people whose idea of a good time is to *make* your brush paint in plaid: software engineers.

When the bright colors you see before you are the result of a migraine and not paint, this chapter is a good place to start. Take a deep breath, get a chocolate chip cookie, and repeat, "I am smart, software is stupid. I am smart, software is stupid." Then read on.

"The Tool or Command Doesn't Do Anything"

If a tool or command doesn't seem to do anything as you apply it to an image, the cause is probably related to selections or layers. Specifically, the problem may be one of the following:

✔ **You have in your image a selected area (called a *selection*) that you're unaware of.** Tools and commands are almost always constrained to working within a selection, if one exists. Probably you're either not working on, or not looking at, that selection. If you don't really want to be working within a selection at the moment, simply press Ctrl+D to remove the selection.

One reason you may be unaware of this selection is that you have somehow hidden the selection *marquee,* the moving dashed line that indicates a selection's presence. Choose Selections and examine the button next to Hide Marquee on the menu that appears. If the button has an outline around it, the marquee is hidden. Click Hide Marquee to unhide it.

Another reason you may be unaware of the selection is that your image is larger than the window and the selected area isn't visible. Zoom out (right-click with the Zoom tool, the magnifying glass icon on the tool palette) until you can see the whole image, including the selection marquee.

✔ **You're mistakenly working on an image layer that's empty (transparent) in the area you're trying to work in.** Switch to the background layer and try the tool again. If that doesn't work, pause the mouse cursor over the names of the various layers to see tiny, thumbnail images of the contents of each layer. Click the layer that contains the content you're trying to modify. Refer to Chapter 14 for more help with layers.

✔ **You're painting in exactly the same color as the background you're painting on!** Change the foreground color or background color (refer to Chapter 3).

If you have been trying to use a menu command with no apparent effect, you may have been having an effect within your selection, without knowing it! When you find the area, check it. If it has been altered unintentionally, press Ctrl+Z repeatedly until the change goes away.

"Paint Shop Pro Keeps Asking Me Confusing Questions!"

Many tools have requirements that have to be met before you can use them; for example, you can't use any of the tools from the Retouch toolset on an image that has fewer than 16 million colors, and the Text, Shape, and Pen tools all require the creation of a new vector layer.

Thankfully, Paint Shop Pro is smart enough to automatically take these actions whenever you use the appropriate tool; for example, try to dodge or burn on an image containing fewer than 16 million colors and Paint Shop Pro automatically increases the number of colors for you.

At the time we wrote this book, Paint Shop Pro defaulted to asking you for confirmation on all these minor changes — which is annoying because not only do these questions sound terrifyingly complex, but you also can't do what you want until you click OK anyway. It's sort of like asking, "You can't leave the house until the door is open; is it okay if I open it for you?" If you want to go for a Sunday drive — or *any* drive — chances are that you're going to say yes.

You can stop all these confusing questions by choosing File➪Preferences➪ General Program Preferences and clicking the Auto Action tab. Then click the Always All button and click OK; Paint Shop Pro always takes these actions by default. (If it turns out that you really *didn't* want that door open, pressing Ctrl+Z undoes your last action, complete with any changes that Paint Shop Pro made to accomplish it.)

"The Toolbar or Palette Just Isn't There!"

You can accidentally close or move one of the toolbars or palettes that holds the tool you need, thus stashing the Paint Brush tool where you can't get at it. If you don't see what you need, choose View➪Toolbars or View➪Palettes and look for a likely candidate that would contain the tool you're looking for. (The main offenders are generally one of these three: View➪Toolbars➪Tools, View➪Palettes➪Layers, or View➪Palettes➪Materials.)

If the toolbar or palette is open but has been dragged somewhere that it's not supposed to be, its icon on the menu has a thin gray box around it; choose it twice from the menu to "flash" it, turning it off and then on so that you know where it is. If it doesn't have a box around it, you have accidentally closed it; select it to open it again.

"The Image Is the Wrong Size Inside or Outside Paint Shop Pro"

Paint Shop Pro displays an image in different sizes to fit the Paint Shop Pro window. The program doesn't change the size of the image — it just displays it with a different zoom factor. As a result, an image may look much smaller in Paint Shop Pro than it does in some other program. To see an image in its true size in Paint Shop Pro, press Ctrl+Alt+N.

If you need to change the true size of an image — which is the size it usually appears in other programs (in Web browsers, for example) — refer to Chapter 11. If you need to change its size as it's printed on paper, refer to Chapter 16.

"The Paint Doesn't Come Out Right"

Paint Shop Pro 8 adds a new Materials box, which can make life complicated if you're not sure what's going on. The usual result is that you end up applying paint that isn't what you had in mind. The best solution is to get a good grip on the Material boxes' features, so turn to Chapter 3. In addition, settings on the Tool Options palette can make paint come out in unwanted ways; check Chapter 4 for help with that topic. Here are a few specific things to check:

- ✓ **If the paint is too light and kind of dappled, you may be applying a texture unintentionally.** To paint without a texture, see whether the Texture button (the one in the middle) directly underneath either of the Material boxes is indented. If one of them is, click them to reset them to No Texture.

- ✓ **If the color you're applying doesn't match the color in either of the Foreground or Background Material boxes, you're applying a *gradient* or *pattern*, not plain paint.** Click the Style button (the one on the left) directly underneath the Material boxes, and drag it up to the solid circle to resume using plain paint.

- ✓ **If paint is too thin or too thick, adjust the opacity on the Tool Options palette; higher opacity makes a thicker paint.**

"New Text Appears Whenever I Try to Change Text"

The Text tool, in its normal *vector* mode of operation, lets you click existing text to change it. When you click, the Text dialog box is supposed to appear, displaying the current text so that you can edit it. You have to click right on the text character, not the space between characters — not even within a character's outline, if that character has no fill! Otherwise, you start creating new text. The cursor displays an A in brackets, like this, [A], when it's positioned correctly for editing text.

"The Text or Shape Comes Out the Wrong Color, Texture, or Pattern"

Although you may logically expect your text, drawings, and shapes to appear in foreground color, sometimes they appear in background color! Sometimes, too, the colors can be weak or mottled or otherwise weird. Here's what's going on.

Shapes, drawings, and text are made up of outlines in one color and are filled with another color. The Material box controls those colors. The outlines are done in foreground color (or gradient or pattern) and in foreground texture — but outlines can be very thin or even turned off. In that case, nearly all you can see is the fill color. The fill color is the background color (or gradient or pattern) and background texture (if any). If the background material is turned off (you see a circle with a slash), you may see very little — just the outline.

If patterns or gradients are unintentionally turned on in the Foreground or Background Style swatches, the result can be strangely mottled, or even nearly invisible. Likewise if a texture is turned on for either foreground or background.

To get plain text, choose a background material and click the Transparent button (the one on the right), directly underneath the Foreground Material box.

"The Magic Wand Tool Doesn't Select Well"

The Magic Wand tool, which selects an area based on color (or other pixel qualities), is sometimes not so magic. What looks like a perfectly uniform color to you — one that the wand should be able to select cleanly without gaps or overlaps into unwanted areas — is apparently not so uniform. You may find that when you increase the Tolerance setting, you close the gaps but get more unwanted areas. Here are a couple of things to try besides fiddling with the tolerance:

- Try different match modes on the Tool Options palette, choosing RGB Value, Hue, or Brightness from the menu.
- Don't fuss any more with the Magic Wand tool. Use it to do the basic selection job and then use other selection tools to add or subtract from the selected area. For example, switch to the Freehand tool, set it to

Freehand on the Selection Type menu on the Tool Options palette, and with the Shift key depressed, drag a circle around any gaps in the selection. Likewise, hold down the Ctrl key and drag a circle around any unwanted areas.

✔ Choose Selections⇨Modify to fill in gaps, expand or contract your selection, or exclude specific colors. Refer to Chapter 12 for details.

"The Tool Works, but Not Like I Want"

The key to a tool's behavior is its Tool Options palette. For painting tools, it controls brush size, shape, edge fuzziness, paint thickness, how speckly the paint comes off, and how close together the individual dots are that make up a stroke. For other tools, it may also control how the tool chooses what pixels to operate on (by color, hue, or other attribute) and exactly what effect the tool has. Refer to Chapter 1 for details about the Tool Options palette, which you can enable or disable by pressing F4 on the keyboard.

Sometimes, though, the Tool Options palette hides some options from you because there's not enough room; look for a small vertical row of single gray dots on the palette and hover your mouse over it. If the cursor turns into a double-headed arrow, Paint Shop Pro is hiding some options from you! Click and drag it down to reveal all the options this tool has to offer. (Sometimes, Paint Shop Pro hides things with a small rightward arrow; if that's the case, just click it and *then* look for the vertical dotted row.)

"Paint Shop Pro Doesn't Open Images!"

Have you ever been in line at a grocery store when some rude person shoved his way in front of you, taking your place? Some programs are equally rude, but rather than brusquely take your place in line, they take over responsibility for opening your JPEGs, GIFs, and PNG files without asking you.

You see, when you double-click a file to open it, Windows knows what kind of file it is and assigns one program to open that file type. Certain poorly designed programs assign *themselves* to be that program when you install them, which can be annoying. To put Paint Shop Pro back in charge, choose File⇨Preferences⇨File Format Associations, click Select All, and click OK. Paint Shop Pro is then your default image handler.

If you're using Windows XP, double-clicking an image may bring up the Windows Viewer instead, which gives you a preview of your image; press Ctrl+E to open it in Paint Shop Pro.

Chapter 20

Ten Fast Fixes for Photo Failures

Despite all attempts by camera makers to make photography foolproof, we all still make less-than-perfect pictures. Sometimes, we're the problem — we're too close or too far away or can't figure out how to use the camera's foolproofing features. Sometimes, the problem is that reality stubbornly refuses to comply with our expectations: The sky is overcast, Great-Grandma can't be present for the family photo, or management has decided to cancel a product that appears in the product-line photograph.

Fortunately, Paint Shop Pro has a wide range of solutions, ranging from quick-and-dirty fixes to professional-level retouching. In this chapter, we give you some of the fastest solutions to the most common problems. Refer to Chapter 8 for more details and more ways to fix up photos.

Rotating Right-Side Up

Photos that lie on their side are a pain in the neck. Don't put up with it! Take these simple steps:

1. **Press Ctrl+R — a fast way to pop up the Rotate dialog box.**

2. **In the Direction area of the dialog box, click either the Right (for clockwise rotation) or Left (for counterclockwise rotation) option boxes.**

   If you have added layers to your photo, click the All Layers check box. You probably haven't done so, however, or else your neck would already be stiff from turning your head sideways!

3. **Click OK or press the Enter key on your keyboard.**

 Chances are, all your sideways photos need rotating in the same direction. Fortunately, the Rotate dialog box remembers which rotation you chose in Step 2; for future corrections, all you may need to do is press Ctrl+R and the Enter key!

Getting the Red Out

Suffering from a little too much red-eye? Photo flashes tend to make the normally black pupil of the eye glow red. Here's the fast fix for getting the red out. It works in nine out of ten cases — where only the pupil is red and the iris is unaffected; for tougher cases or more finicky retouching, refer to Chapter 7. Follow these steps:

1. **Choose Adjust⇨Red-eye Removal.**

   The Red-eye Removal dialog box appears.

2. **In the right preview window, drag the image to center the eye.**

3. **Click the Zoom In icon (the magnifier with the + sign) repeatedly until the eye fills the preview windows.**

   Repeat Step 2 as needed to keep the eye centered.

4. **Set Iris Size to zero.**

   This setting should be zero unless the red covers any of the iris (the colored part of the eye). If the red does affect the iris, refer to Chapter 8 for help.

5. **In the left window, click the red area.**

   A circle appears in a square frame in the left window. The circle should be centered on the pupil and cover it to some degree. (If not, refer to Chapter 7.) In the right window, the red area is partly or entirely obliterated. (If that isn't true at first, drag the Refine slider a bit to the left.)

6. **Drag the Refine slider left until a bit of red reappears and then to the right just until that red is gone.**

7. **Click OK.**

Repeat these steps for the other eye.

Photos without Enough Flash

If things are looking a bit dim in a photograph, Paint Shop Pro can often brighten your outlook. Follow these steps for a too-dim photo:

1. **Choose Adjust⇨Brightness and Contrast⇨Automatic Contrast Enhancement.**

   The Automatic Contrast Enhancement dialog box springs into action. The photo may already show sufficient improvement in the sample in the right window. If so, click OK and skip the rest of these steps.

   The preview window on the right shows the result of any changes in this and the following steps.

2. **To make the picture brighter, click Lighter (on the left).**

3. **To improve contrast, click Bold (on the right).**

4. **To get more brightness or contrast, click Normal (in the center).**

   The Mild option gives you less brightness or contrast.

5. **Click OK.**

One problem the preceding steps may not solve is feeble colors (*inadequate saturation,* in geek-speak). If colors appear a bit too gray, see the section "Making Colors Zippier," at the end of this chapter.

If this effect doesn't do the job, check out Chapter 10 for more help with brightness, contrast, and saturation. Nothing can restore image data that just isn't there, however. Things that are way dim will never look natural — unless you do some touch-up brushing.

If you can't see an image well in the right preview window of this dialog box, click the button with the eye icon to see the effect in the main image window. Click the button again whenever you want to see the result of your changes. Refer to Chapter 7 for more help with effect dialog boxes.

Photos with Too Much Flash

If you got a little too close in a flash photo, Paint Shop Pro may be able to help you back off a bit. Try this fast fix:

1. **Choose Adjust⇨Brightness and Contrast⇨Automatic Contrast Enhancement.**

   The Automatic Contrast Enhancement dialog box comes to your aid. The photo may already look better in the sample in the right window. If so, click OK and skip the rest of these steps.

   The preview window on the right shows the result as you make any changes in this dialog box. If you can't see enough of the picture there, click the button with the magnifier and – icon to zoom out.

2. **To make the picture darker, click Darker (on the left).**

3. **To reduce contrast, click Natural (on the right).**

   You can try Flat, too, but it's often too flat.

4. **For the maximum darkening, contrast-reducing effect, click Normal (in the center).**

   For a lesser effect, click Mild.

5. **Click OK.**

 Photos with way too much flash are washed out, which may be harder to fix. If, for example, portions of someone's face are practically white, you need to restore skin tone without affecting the rest of the picture. A little work with the Smudge tool (refer to Chapter 6) can help you push skin color into small white areas. Alternatively, try carefully selecting the entire face area with a feathered edge and then using the Manual Color Correction effect, which we describe in Chapter 7, to change the white area to skin tone. (You may have to disable the Preserve Lightness check box in that effect.)

Revealing Dark Corners

If you need to cast light into the dark corners of your life, Paint Shop Pro can help. Of course, nothing can reveal totally dark details, and — as in life, itself — details that are *very* dark are generally not too attractive anyway, when brought to light. But, given those limitations, here's something you can do to reveal dark corners or other dark areas of your photo.

This approach is the computer equivalent of an old darkroom trick, known as dodging. *Dodging* requires a little eye-hand coordination because you, in effect, brush lightness and contrast onto just the dark portions of your photo. Follow these steps:

1. **Choose the Dodge tool (the white magnifying glass icon) from the Retouch toolset.**

2. **Locate or open the Tool Options palette.**

   Press F4 on your keyboard to toggle the palette on or off.

3. **Make these choices:**

   Size: To lighten broad areas, the best setting for this value is about 25 percent of the width or height of the image, whichever is larger. (Image dimensions appear on the status bar, in the lower-right corner of the Paint Shop Pro window.)

   Hardness: Set this option very low, or at zero, unless the dark area has well-defined edges and you have a steady hand.

   Opacity: A good typical setting is about 10. A higher number gives you a stronger effect per stroke. A lower number gives you a weaker effect.

   Step: A good typical setting is about 25. If you set it too high, you may see a dotty effect.

   Density: Set to 100.

4. **Drag over the dark areas of the image to lighten those areas.**

   Keep the mouse button down and do a first pass over the area. Then release the mouse button and drag again over areas that need more lightening. Return to Step 3 and adjust any settings that you think may be necessary, especially Opacity (strength of effect) or Size. Press Ctrl+Z to undo your most recent pass at the image, if necessary.

As you brush the image, objects in the dark become brighter and the contrast against any black or very dark background is increased. The improvement can be dramatic!

Removing Unwanted Relatives

Removing unwanted relatives is much easier in Paint Shop Pro than in real life. You're not limited to relatives, though. You can use the same Paint Shop Pro tricks to remove other unwanted features, like power lines or passing automobiles.

Like removing unwanted relatives in real life, the task requires some skill. It also requires some sort of continuous or repeated background, like the clapboarded side of a building, a grassy field, a rail fence, water, or shrubbery. If the unwanted relative is blocking more than half of some unique feature (like a fireplace, chair, or china cabinet), the job gets nearly impossible.

The main tool for the job is the Clone Brush tool, which you use to extend the background over the unwanted feature. For example, you can brush out junk on a lawn by brushing lawn, taken from just below or alongside the junk. Refer to Chapter 5 for a full-fledged example (we removed a mat, but the principle is the same). Here's the general idea:

1. **Click the Clone Brush tool (two-brush icon) on the Tools toolbar.**

2. **Right-click the background you want to brush over your object, in an area that has no unique features.**

   For example, if you're removing lawn junk, right-click in the grass, not near other junk. Don't click too near the object you want to remove, either. Because backgrounds tend to have horizontal strips of stuff, like grass at the bottom, trees in the middle, and sky at the top, clicking to the left or right of the object you want to remove usually works best.

3. **Drag carefully across the object you want removed.**

   If, in Step 2, you right-clicked to the left or right of that object, move the cursor only horizontally before you drag. That precaution ensures that you extend the correct strip of background and don't paint grass, for example, where you want trees. As you brush, the Clone Brush tool picks up pixels from under an X that starts where you right-clicked and follows your motion. Keep an eye on the X to make sure that it doesn't pick up pixels you don't want. You may need to reset the X in a new location periodically; return to Step 2 to do so.

You probably need some trial and error to get a feel for the process. Press Ctrl+Z to undo any errors.

One problem with removing relatives and other objects is that if they were initially blocking a unique object, that object now has a hole in it. For example, the relative may well be blocking one arm of a person or half of a piano (if that relative is fairly wide). Fortunately, many objects are symmetrical; if Aunt Katy's left arm is now missing, you may be able to copy her right arm and paste it in place of the left one. (You can even mirror half a face to make a whole one in some instances. Results may be unsatisfactory.)

Use any selection tool (the Freehand tool, for example) to select the object you need to copy (refer to Chapter 12). Press Ctrl+F to float the selection, press Ctrl+M to mirror it, drag it to the correct position, and then press

Ctrl+Shift+F to defloat it. Press Ctrl+D to remove the selection marquee. You may need to do a little painting and retouching because any light striking the object is now coming from the wrong direction.

Adding Absent Relatives

If Great-Grandma just couldn't make the wedding, boost her spirits (or seriously confuse other missing relatives) by creating a picture that includes her with the happy couple. The same trick works for adding anyone or anything. Have a new product to add to your product line? Just add it in to the product family photo. Here are the basic steps, with references to other parts of the book that provide more detail:

1. **Open the original photo (the one *without* Great-Grandma) in a window.**

2. **Press Ctrl+B or choose File⇨Browse to open the image browser.**

   The browser window opens. Arrange the browser and image windows so that you can see both. (For example, choose Window⇨Tile Vertically.)

3. **Drag the thumbnail of the new image (Great-Grandma) from the browser to the main image window.**

   The new image becomes a new layer of the original photo. You can close the browser window now. (Click the X in its upper-right corner.)

4. **With the Eraser tool (refer to Chapter 4), erase everything except the part of the new image that you want (leaving Great-Grandma).**

5. **Click the Deformation tool on the Tools toolbar (second from the top) and drag the new image (Great-Grandma) to the place you want it.**

   Refer to Chapter 13 for help with the Deformation tool.

6. **If the image isn't the correct size or rotation, drag the handles (squares) that appear around the new image to make adjustments.**

   The image may need some repositioning; if so, drag it from any place *except* on one of the handles.

7. **Double-click the image, when you're done sizing and positioning, to apply the deformation.**

Repeat Step 4 to make any additional erasures that you discover are necessary at this point. For example, if Great-Grandma's head and shoulders are to appear behind the wedding couple, erase her from shoulders on down. You're done! Note that you now have an image with layers, so if you save it, Paint Shop Pro asks whether you want to merge layers. Reply Yes.

Zapping Zits

One noticeable difference between professionally done portraits and the ones you (and we) take is that the pros retouch their photos to get rid of unsightly blemishes. Throughout this book, we describe lots of tools useful for retouching and even devote one whole chapter (Chapter 6) to retouching tools. To get rid of a simple blemish, however, is a matter of a few steps. Zoom in on the blemish and then try these steps:

1. **Choose the Smudge tool (the comet streaking to the upper left) from the Retouching toolset on the Tools toolbar.**

   (Refer to Chapter 6 for more information about this tool.)

2. **Open the Tool Options palette, if it's not already open.**

   Press F4 to toggle the window on or off. Refer to Chapter 5 for more information about this palette.

3. **Set the brush size to roughly zit-size on the Tool Options palette.**

   See the discussions of setting tool options in Chapter 5 for help with other options.

4. **Click just to one side of the blemish, on clear skin of similar (but unblemished) color.**

5. **Drag across the blemish.**

   Dragging *along*, rather than *across*, any natural folds or wrinkles is usually a good idea. Also, don't drag from one area of unblemished skin color into a differently colored area.

6. **Repeat Steps 4 and 5 from the opposite direction.**

Making Gray Skies Blue

Don't let an overcast day rain on your parade. You can make the skies blue in a photo, and, even though a snapshot may never look completely natural, it will probably be more attractive. You can't make a gray day look too natural because if it were really taken on a sunny day, the sun would appear to shine on all the subjects in the photo, casting highlights and shadows. Paint Shop Pro has several tools you can use. The following steps, however, outline the simplest approach:

1. **Click the Magic Wand tool from the Selection toolset on the Tools toolbar.**

2. **On the Tool Options palette, set Tolerance to about 20 or 30 for a typical gray sky.**

Press F4 on the keyboard to toggle the Tool Options palette on or off. Refer to Chapters 1 and 4 for more information about this window and its options, like brush size.

3. **Click the overcast area of the image, to select it.**

If the whole sky isn't selected, press Ctrl+D to clear the selection, and then try again with a higher Tolerance value on the Tool Options palette. If more than sky is selected, try again with a lower value. Chapter 12 has more ways to help you select just sky.

4. **Press Shift+U to open the Red/Green/Blue dialog box.**

5. **Increase the number in the Blue value box.**

As you adjust, keep an eye on the right preview window in the Red/Green/Blue dialog box, which is showing you the new sky color. Stop adjusting when you like the color, and click the OK button.

Making Colors Zippier

As we take a photo, we find that our mind's eye makes the colors livelier than they turn out to be in reality, and the photo looks a bit dull. Perhaps it's just that our antidepressant doses need adjusting, but if you have the same problem, try adjusting saturation (of your image, that is). Take these steps and don't call us in the morning:

1. **Choose Adjust➪Hue and Saturation➪Automatic Saturation Adjustment.**

The Automatic Saturation Adjustment dialog box springs into action.

2. **Choose the More Colorful option on the left side of the box.**

3. **If the photo contains a significant amount of skin, click the Skintones Present check box.**

4. **Choose the Weak, Normal, or Strong option on the right side of the box, depending on which choice gives better results in the right preview window.**

Click the button with the eye icon whenever you want to see the effect of your chosen options in the image window.

5. **Click OK.**

If that doesn't brighten up your day, check out Chapter 10 or see your friendly primary care physician.

Index

• *Q* •

• *R* •

Notes

Notes

Notes

Notes

Notes

Notes

Notes

Notes

Notes

Notes

Notes

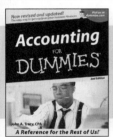

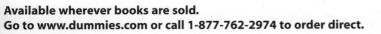

FOR DUMMIES®

A world of resources to help you grow

HOME, GARDEN & HOBBIES

0-7645-5295-3

0-7645-5130-2

0-7645-5106-X

Also available:

Auto Repair For Dummies
(0-7645-5089-6)

Chess For Dummies
(0-7645-5003-9)

Home Maintenance For
Dummies
(0-7645-5215-5)

Organizing For Dummies
(0-7645-5300-3)

Piano For Dummies
(0-7645-5105-1)

Poker For Dummies
(0-7645-5232-5)

Quilting For Dummies
(0-7645-5118-3)

Rock Guitar For Dummies
(0-7645-5356-9)

Roses For Dummies
(0-7645-5202-3)

Sewing For Dummies
(0-7645-5137-X)

FOOD & WINE

0-7645-5250-3

0-7645-5390-9

0-7645-5114-0

Also available:

Bartending For Dummies
(0-7645-5051-9)

Chinese Cooking For
Dummies
(0-7645-5247-3)

Christmas Cooking For
Dummies
(0-7645-5407-7)

Diabetes Cookbook For
Dummies
(0-7645-5230-9)

Grilling For Dummies
(0-7645-5076-4)

Low-Fat Cooking For
Dummies
(0-7645-5035-7)

Slow Cookers For Dummies
(0-7645-5240-6)

TRAVEL

0-7645-5453-0

0-7645-5438-7

0-7645-5448-4

Also available:

America's National Parks For
Dummies
(0-7645-6204-5)

Caribbean For Dummies
(0-7645-5445-X)

Cruise Vacations For
Dummies 2003
(0-7645-5459-X)

Europe For Dummies
(0-7645-5456-5)

Ireland For Dummies
(0-7645-6199-5)

France For Dummies
(0-7645-6292-4)

London For Dummies
(0-7645-5416-6)

Mexico's Beach Resorts For
Dummies
(0-7645-6262-2)

Paris For Dummies
(0-7645-5494-8)

RV Vacations For Dummies
(0-7645-5443-3)

Walt Disney World & Orlando
For Dummies
(0-7645-5444-1)

Available wherever books are sold. Go to www.dummies.com or call 1-877-762-2974 to order direct.

FOR DUMMIES®

Plain-English solutions for everyday challenges

COMPUTER BASICS

0-7645-0838-5

0-7645-1663-9

0-7645-1548-9

Also available:

PCs All-in-One Desk Reference For Dummies (0-7645-0791-5)

Pocket PC For Dummies (0-7645-1640-X)

Treo and Visor For Dummies (0-7645-1673-6)

Troubleshooting Your PC For Dummies (0-7645-1669-8)

Upgrading & Fixing PCs For Dummies (0-7645-1665-5)

Windows XP For Dummies (0-7645-0893-8)

Windows XP For Dummies Quick Reference (0-7645-0897-0)

BUSINESS SOFTWARE

0-7645-0822-9

0-7645-0839-3

0-7645-0819-9

Also available:

Excel Data Analysis For Dummies (0-7645-1661-2)

Excel 2002 All-in-One Desk Reference For Dummies (0-7645-1794-5)

Excel 2002 For Dummies Quick Reference (0-7645-0829-6)

GoldMine "X" For Dummies (0-7645-0845-8)

Microsoft CRM For Dummies (0-7645-1698-1)

Microsoft Project 2002 For Dummies (0-7645-1628-0)

Office XP For Dummies (0-7645-0830-X)

Outlook 2002 For Dummies (0-7645-0828-8)

Get smart! Visit www.dummies.com

- **Find listings of even more *For Dummies* titles**
- **Browse online articles**
- **Sign up for Dummies eTips™**
- **Check out *For Dummies* fitness videos and other products**
- **Order from our online bookstore**

Available wherever books are sold. Go to www.dummies.com or call 1-877-762-2974 to order direct.

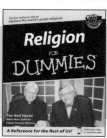
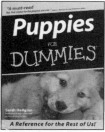

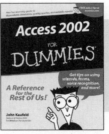